CW01494608

The Politics of Cultural Work

The Politics of Cultural Work

Mark Banks
The Open University, UK

© Mark Banks 2007

All rights reserved. No reproduction, copy or transmission of this publication may be made without written permission.

No portion of this publication may be reproduced, copied or transmitted save with written permission or in accordance with the provisions of the Copyright, Designs and Patents Act 1988, or under the terms of any licence permitting limited copying issued by the Copyright Licensing Agency, Saffron House, 6–10 Kirby Street, London EC1N 8TS.

Any person who does any unauthorised act in relation to this publication may be liable to criminal prosecution and civil claims for damages.

The author has asserted his right to be identified as the author of this work in accordance with the Copyright, Designs and Patents Act 1988.

First published in 2007 by
PALGRAVE MACMILLAN

Palgrave Macmillan in the UK is an imprint of Macmillan Publishers Limited, registered in England, company number 785998, of Houndmills, Basingstoke, Hampshire RG21 6XS.

Palgrave Macmillan in the US is a division of St Martin's Press LLC, 175 Fifth Avenue, New York, NY 10010.

Palgrave Macmillan is the global academic imprint of the above companies and has companies and representatives throughout the world.

Palgrave® and Macmillan® are registered trademarks in the United States, the United Kingdom, Europe and other countries.

ISBN-13: 978–0–230–01921–8 hardback
ISBN-10: 0–230–01921–8 hardback

This book is printed on paper suitable for recycling and made from fully managed and sustained forest sources. Logging, pulping and manufacturing processes are expected to conform to the environmental regulations of the country of origin.

A catalogue record for this book is available from the British Library.

A catalog record for this book is available from the Library of Congress.

Printed and bound in Great Britain by
Antony Rowe Ltd, Chippenham and Eastbourne

For the GeeGees

Contents

Acknowledgements

I am grateful to the following people for their assistance. First, ex-colleagues at Manchester Metropolitan University and the former Manchester Institute for Popular Culture (MIPC), especially Katie Milestone, Justin O'Connor and the late Derek Wynne. It was in the context of the many MIPC discussions and debates on the cultural industries that the idea for this book first emerged. My thanks also to those whom I worked closely with on various research and writing projects at MMU, especially Mike Bull, David Calvey, Julia Owen, Paula Sergeant and David Russell. I am also grateful to Paul Kennedy, Michael MacKian and Shirley Tate who provided helpful information, conversation and advice. Thanks also to Johan Fornäs and Helene Egeland at the Advanced Cultural Studies Institute of Sweden (ACSIS) for providing some valuable writing time and inspiration. I am much obliged to Kathleen Rout for her help in preparing the final manuscript. Particular thanks go to Tim Dant, Gabe Mythen, Balihar Sanghera, Nicole Vitellone and most of all David Hesmondhalgh who kindly read and commented upon earlier drafts of chapters. Finally, thanks to Sara, Ellie and Pip for their unwavering support and love.

1
Introducing Cultural Work

It is commonly said that we live in a 'cultural' age, a 'creative' age, a time of artistic innovators, knowledge entrepreneurs, e-gurus, fashion conceptualists, music-makers and all manner of digital hawkers, traders and image-makers. Certainly, since the 1960s there has been a rapid expansion of activity and employment in advertising, art, television, radio and film, fashion, graphic design, music, software production, gaming and leisure – a group of activities that have now come to be known collectively as the 'cultural industries'. Alongside this, the growth of what Bourdieu (1984) has famously referred to as 'cultural intermediary' occupations – cultural critics, journalists, talent-spotters, promoters and commentators – has helped furnish the markets for cultural industry goods and services. These days, few would doubt that in Western economies the cultural industries have, as Hesmondhalgh puts it, 'moved closer to the centre of the economic action' (2007, p. 1).

Indeed, at a time when all manner of cultural 'assets' are being brought into the realm of economic calculation, Western (and some non-Western) governments have enthusiastically embraced the cultural industries as a solution to systemic crises of deindustrialization, heavily promoting the virtues of cultural production and investing substantial resources in ensuring that individuals and institutions are able to meet the challenges of this new 'creative age' (Seltzer and Bentley, 1999; see also DCITA, 2005; DCMS 2001; Smith, 1998). In turn, cultural industries have also attracted a good deal of academic attention (Banks et al., 2000; Caves, 2000; Davis and Scase, 2000; Florida, 2002; Garnham, 1990; Hartley, 2005; Hesmondhalgh, 1998, 2007; Howkins, 2001; McRobbie, 1998, 2002a, 2002b; O'Connor and Wynne, 1996a; Nixon, 2003; Oakley, 2004; Pratt, 1997, 2000; Scott, 2000; Turok, 2003; Wynne, 1992) illustrating the importance now attached to theorizing how cultural

1

activities have been able to move so rapidly 'from the margins to the centre' of economic life (O'Connor and Wynne, 1996a).

Cultural industries I define as those involved in the production of 'aesthetic' or 'symbolic' goods and services; that is, commodities whose core value is derived from their function as carriers of *meaning* in the form of images, symbols, signs and sounds. Here, the production of meaning is seen to be deliberate and self-conscious, designed to appeal to aesthetic preferences, or related to existing or emergent economies of taste, style and distinction. A list of cultural commodities might include, for example, a television programme, a film, a theatre performance, a music recording, a painting, a publication, a computer game, a website, designer fashion jewellery or furniture, or any other aesthetic object of high-design input; it might also include commodities such as 'cultural' bars, cafes, nightclubs or tourist attractions. While, evidently, all commodities might be argued to have something of a 'meaningful' or 'textual' character (Allen, 2002), it is the *primary* emphasis on aesthetic or symbolic value (rather than use value) that defines a cultural good against a non-cultural good – though identifying to which of these categories a particular good belongs is, as Hesmondhalgh suggests, a fine 'question of balance' (2007, p. 12).

Indeed, it is proving difficult to precisely define the cultural industries. As O'Connor (1999) notes, the definition is constantly changing since more and more commodities and activities appear to be taking on an 'aesthetic' or 'symbolic' meaning. Indeed, whether or not a productive activity can be considered as part of the cultural industries depends very much on the particular social and spatial context in which it is undertaken. For example, activities such as marketing, clothing production and industrial design may or may not be considered as cultural industries; much depends on whether firms are judged as primarily producing utilitarian, formulaic commodities or whether they are seen to be trading on their capacity to produce cultural meanings and lock into local circuits of 'symbolic flow' (O'Connor, 1999, p. 6). In this respect, place is often important as, for example, leather goods from Florence, ceramics from Stoke-on-Trent or fashions from Paris might well be considered high-status and meaningful 'cultural' goods, yet handbags, pots and trousers may be deemed utilitarian (and thus rendered less 'cultural' or 'creative') when produced elsewhere. Further complicating matters is that the term 'cultural industries' also has different meanings in different national contexts – and, as O'Connor (2005) has noted, often the term is not easily reconciled to pre-existing national conceptions of either 'culture' or 'industry'. Thus, we can surmise that deciding what constitutes a cultural industry is a complex and qualitative judgement that is best made within the local context and cannot be reliably imposed from without, using a set of standardized criteria (O'Connor, 1999, 2005; Tepper, 2002).

Despite these difficulties, numerous organizations have now attempted to measure and assess the economic significance of this diffuse industrial sector. In the United Kingdom, evidence provided by the Department of Culture, Media and Sport has estimated that cultural (or, in their term, 'creative') industries account for around 5% of GDP and are currently growing at around three times the rate of the economy as a whole (DCMS, 2001). More recently, figures suggest that UK cultural industries' employment grew by an average of 6% per annum between 1997 and 2003, and by 2004 totalled 1.8 million jobs (DCMS, 2005). In the same year, it was estimated that cultural industries firms accounted for around 7% of all registered companies (DCMS, 2005). In the United States, Americans for the Arts estimated that the number of creative industries firms had grown 5.5% in the year 2004–2005 (compared with 3.8% for other non-creative firms) and that, now, the creative industries represented a 'formidable economic growth sector', 'contributing significantly to the economy of every state in the nation' (Americans for the Arts, 2005, p. 1). While obtaining robust statistics on the size and significance of cultural industries is extremely difficult,[1] most observers now agree that the cultural industries are becoming more important to the competitive offer of post-industrial cities and regions. Buoyed by upbeat assessments from the likes of Florida (2002), Howkins (2001), Leadbeater (1999) and Smith (1998) there is considerable belief amongst governments and economic development agencies that only through attracting a dynamic coterie of creative industries can cities lift themselves from the post-industrial mire. Thus, while the statistics indicate that the cultural sector is still relatively small and underdeveloped, its *profile* is extremely high and shows no sign of diminishing.

This book is about these cultural industries. But it does not seek to assess (as many have expertly done) their size, scope or economic value. Instead, its aim is to reflect on the general character, patterns and processes of *work* that are now unfolding in this nascent economic sector. 'Cultural work' (as I will call it) refers to the act of labour within the industrialized process of cultural production; and it is the *politics* of this work – how it is constructed, managed and performed – that is the specific concern.

Cultural work

We have become used to pronouncements that the economy is now marching to the beat of the 'creatives' – and, principally, it is in the cultural industries that such 'creatives' are perceived to be generating seductive new models for work and industrial organization. The brash disciples of the 'new' economy enthusiastically trumpet the virtues of cultural work – seemingly a dazzling environment of creative autonomy, sensory stimulation and personal fulfilment. Cultural work, it seems, is hardly like work at all. Who would not aspire to work in New York's 'Silicon Alley', London's Soho, in Hollywood or amongst the groups of new bohemians and artistic visionaries that now populate a whole plethora of 'creative' cities, girdling the globe from Melbourne to Manchester, Shanghai to Seattle? New economy enthusiasts insist cultural workers are now free to inhale the evanescent vapour of cre- ativity, having (once and for all) left behind the dull fog of function- ality and bureaucracy – but is this really so? As Löfgren (2003) reveals, various economic gurus, seers and spin-doctors have keenly sought to promote the benefits of the 'new', 'knowledge' or 'creative' economy and a 'culturalized' division of labour based on individual artistry, autonomy and flexibility. Indeed, the future of *all* work is now widely assumed to be adopting a cultural industry model – becoming more creative, autonomous and personally rewarding (Davis and Scase, 2000; Florida, 2002; Howkins, 2001). Such claims make it imperative that we more closely understand what this blueprint for work actually com- prises. Beyond the hyperbole, we still know very little about the work- ing lives of this new army of dot-commers, music-makers, fashionistas, net gurus, brand-builders, cool hunters and image-entrepreneurs – still less about how they might comprise a general model for the future of employment. Indeed, while governments and economic development agencies promote the virtues of the cultural industries in the 'new' economy and actively encourage populations to chase the dream of becoming self-sufficient 'cultural', 'creative' or 'knowledge' workers, what life is like for the thousands of people who have taken this bold step remains something of a mystery.

We should note that, until recently, academics had relatively little to say about cultural work. As Hesmondhalgh has argued, '[m]any books exist on film, recording, broadcasting and publishing (...) yet few make reference to the working conditions and financial recom- pense available to the people working in these industries' (2000, p. 113). Crewe, Gregson and Brooks (2003, p. 75) recently confirmed that 'while the cultural industries have been held up as symbolically significant, little attention has been paid to working practices in which creativity is the enterprise'. However, as interest in the field of 'cultural economy' has expanded (see Amin and Thrift, 2004; du Gay and Pryke, 2002), it is clear that cultural work *has* started to come under closer academic scrutiny, and a body of work is now emerging to provide grounded and empirically rich case studies that detail the conditions and character of cultural work (for example, see Banks et al., 2002; Böse, 2005; Drake, 2003; du Gay, 1996; Gibson, 2003; Gill, 2002; McRobbie, 1998, 2002a,b; Nixon, 2003; Nixon and Crewe, 2004; Pratt, 2000; Richards and Milestone, 2000; Ross, 2003; Slater, 2002; Ursell, 2000; Wittel, 2001). Yet, while this book offers new empirical material to support this venture, providing fresh data is not its principal concern.

Aims of the book

The primary aim of this book is to provide a general introduction to theories of cultural work. This is necessary since, to date, no summary or review articles have been written on this topic, and there are no sociological texts solely devoted to theories of labour in cultural industry organizations. The intention is to provide an overview of the intellectual traditions that appear to be underpinning emergent, empirical studies of cultural work. In particular, I identify three key traditions:

- a set of broadly defined 'critical theory' approaches, derived from 'Frankfurt School' Marxism, that understand cultural work as an alienating and 'desocialized' endeavour, a nefarious product of the industrialized 'culture industry';
- a 'neo-Foucauldian' or 'governmental' approach that identifies cultural work as a vehicle for the application of managerial (and thus capitalistic) authority; a form of control that not only relies on discursively constructed and practically applied 'mechanisms of rule', but is also exercised through workers' own apparent willingness to act as dutiful 'enterprise subjects';
- a (more optimistic) liberal–democratic theory that understands cultural work as a potentially radical enterprise given expanded opportunities for aesthetic critique, (sub)political organizing and the re-moralization of economic practices in the prevailing contexts of 'institutional individualization' and 'reflexive modernity'.

These traditions should not be seen as exhaustive or even wholly comprehensive, but merely as central to the emerging debate on cultural work as undertaken in the context of Westernized critical social science. The aim, however, is not simply to provide a superficial 'checklist' of theories of cultural work, but to reflect on how each approach has more substantively theorized what I consider to be some fundamental features of the political organization and practice of cultural work.

The 'art–commerce relation'

In each of the sociological traditions identified, cultural work is routinely presented as an arena of political struggle, principally in terms of how artistic desires for *creative autonomy* and independence exist in uneasy tension with capitalist imperatives of profit-generation and *controlled accumulation*. This division is deeply entrenched and appears to derive from the apparent incommensurability and relative autonomy of the categories of 'art' and 'commerce' (or more broadly, 'culture' and 'economy') first established in modern societies. As Raymond Williams identified, in the post-Enlightenment period, culture was invoked to provide a 'practical separation of certain moral and intellectual activities from the driven impetus of a new kind of society' (1958, p. 17). Culture offered an aesthetic realm distinct from the vulgar incursions of modernization which threatened to replace 'authentic' values with a calculative economic rationality (see also Slater, 2002; Williams, 1980; Wolff, 1993). Where art and culture promised individual freedom, the economy appeared to provide only collective enslavement to the commercial imperative. Thus, the worlds of art and commerce have long been judged diametrically opposed. But while this distinction remains salient, it also appears increasingly under threat as the economy (as a whole) is now routinely judged to be 'more cultural' in its content and operations, and culture too is said to have become more 'economized', as the logic of rationality has more effectively penetrated the hitherto resolute defences of 'pure' aesthetics and particularized meaning (see du Gay and Pryke, 2002; Lash and Urry, 1994; Negus and Pickering, 2004; Ray and Sayer, 1999). It is in the cultural industries where the apparent coming together of artistic and commercial imperatives is most pronounced and most demanding of our investigation. Yet, while these imperatives appear to be converging, they must also in a crucial sense always remain separate. Indeed, as I will establish, one unique and distinctive feature of cultural work is the necessity (at least for capital) of *maintaining* (rather than eliminating) the tension between autonomous impulses of creative workers and the demands of managers for standardized, predictable production. This is because it a commonly held view of managers that only through allowing creative workers certain 'freedoms' will they be empowered and inspired to produce the new, culturally distinctive commodities that capital requires (Ryan, 1992). The separation of art and commerce is thus a *necessary* feature of cultural industries production and must be at least partially maintained – though, as will become clear, both managers and creative workers may attempt to tip its delicate balance in favour of 'art' or 'commerce' according to their own preferential interests.

As the cultural industries have emerged as a distinctive convergence of the cultural and the economic, various observers have taken to the task of theorizing the ways in which art and culture, as a set of autonomous and critical practices, have come to intersect with the rationality of the accumulation imperative. This book aims to examine how each of the sociological traditions identified understands the 'power of art' (in terms of the relative autonomy of the aesthetic and the creative freedoms available to the autonomous cultural worker) relative to the 'power of commerce' (in terms of the ability of managers and firms to direct and control this creative cultural production). Clearly, as we will see, each tradition variously emphasizes where the balance of power in the art–commerce relation lies, and how its tensions are routinely created, negotiated and resolved.

The creative cultural worker

Throughout, the emphasis of this book is on a particular kind of labourer, namely the *creative cultural worker*.[2] The first explanation for this is relatively straightforward. The creative cultural worker (aka the 'artist', the 'designer', the 'director', the 'writer' and the 'musician') is very much at the centre of the cultural industry labour process; it is they who are primarily responsible for the production of those symbolic commodities judged to be essential components of the transition to a 'post-industrial', 'creative' or 'knowledge' based economy. However, rather surprisingly, accounts of such workers have been largely absent from (or at least significantly under-theorized in) those recent, emergent accounts of cultural industries that I have identified. As Hesmondhalgh confirms, while such workers are 'the primary workers in the making of texts' (2007, p. 5), we still know very little about them as individuals or about the conditions under which they produce. This may derive from the relative academic novelty of the cultural industries *per se* – and observers may not have had time to theorize the cultural worker amidst the clamour to assess the economic impacts of the sector as a whole. Yet, often, it seems, part of the problem is that the notion that cultural work is actually *work* (that is, an economic activity for which one receives payment) appears to have largely escaped the attention of critical social science. Traditionally, labour theorists have tended to focus on those more 'authentic' forms of work that underpinned the formation of industrial societies – such as those 'core' production activities attendant upon primary manufacturing and 'heavy' industry. Arguably, cultural work, with its connotations of 'art' and 'creativity', its idiosyncratic practices, evasive structures and its generation of seemingly trivial, superfluous and luxury goods, may have appeared somewhat distant from the 'essences' of economic life and so failed to ignite the enthusiasm of those more concerned with the 'real' world of manual labour and the formularized production of utilitarian goods. Even students of the service sector, and the now vast range of non-manufacturing-based occupations, have failed to pay much attention to cultural forms of work – buoyed perhaps by a belief that the worlds of art and culture lay outside the remit of economic analysis, or informed by a more widespread prejudice that such frivolous worlds were improper concerns for the serious-minded scholar. Some analysts have indeed emphasized that a reluctance to study cultural workers may stem from some deeply held prejudices towards regarding cultural production as 'real' work – with employment in music, art, fashion, television and so on, often being understood as a 'fun' or pleasurable vocation rather than as structured economic activity. For example, in their discussion of the work undertaken by actors, Dean and Jones stress how labour process theorists have yet to overcome their reluctance to view creative work as a 'profession or career option that involves many of the same [political] issues as other kinds of work' (2003, p. 531).[3] Initially then, it is an empirical necessity that we learn more about the working lives of creative cultural workers, not only to help ground the numerous (positive and negative) claims being made by them, or on their behalf, but also to ensure that the cultural worker is recognized as precisely that – a *worker*.[4]

The second (and more crucial) reason for choosing to focus on the creative cultural worker is related to the particular relevance of this role in the context of the art–commerce relation. The creative cultural worker exists at the very axis point of political struggle between the forces of art and commerce. It is the creative worker, as the *particular focus and embodiment* of the art–commerce relation, who must most evidently balance the desire to indulge in disinterested, creative self-expression against the necessity of accumulation. Ryan summarizes the implications of this positioning:

> Capitalist relations are partly defined by their distinctive form of labour; the labourer is employed by the capitalist as an anonymous production factor, as labour power. As historically constituted however, the artist is a named individual with unboundable creativity and talent. As a social object, therefore artists exist in opposition to capital and present capitalists with major difficulties in incorporating them in the production process as labour power. (Ryan, 1992, p. 28)

The role of the manager is to try and control and temper the capricious creative to corporate accumulation imperatives – this may be easier in some cases than others. Some workers, we might surmise, may choose to prioritize the goals of their paymaster. The requirements of capital for profitability (through saleable commodities) and continued accumulation (guaranteed by incomes from formatted and standardized products) may encourage cultural workers to adopt or endorse production methods that vitiate against free expression, experimentation and creative innovation – in return for wages, royalties, continued employment, or maybe even, in time, wealth and fame. Alternatively, the enduring aspiration amongst workers to invent or create cultural goods may be driven by non-economic, 'irrational' motives such as the simple desire to make *art* that reaches 'beyond' the accumulation imperative and the trappings of material necessity. A compulsion for the production of beauty (or even the production of 'social' goods) may outweigh the necessity of production for profit. Of course, aesthetic and commercial imperatives may not always be polarized, for the necessity of making money may also be entirely compatible with artistic ambitions – the Beatles were both great artists and enormously profitable. It remains the case, however, that artistic desires for creativity and autonomy are not always easily accounted for or controlled by rational economic systems, nor are they always conducive to capitalist requirements for profit and accumulation – and this book seeks to examine this tension, particularly as experienced and personified in the creative cultural worker.

Ordinary workplaces

In seeking to understand the art–commerce relation, and its embodiment in the core activities of the creative cultural worker, it is upon 'ordinary' firms and the mundane and everyday contexts of cultural production that I choose to focus. My concern is largely with those

(UK-based) creative workers predominantly employed in small and medium-sized fashion, graphic design, music-making, television and new media firms, as well as freelancers and sole traders working as artists, musicians, television producers, fashion designers, web designers or as retailers of various kinds. The first reason for this is purely practical – my own research has mostly been undertaken in the context of freelance, small and medium-sized enterprises (see Appendix 1). More substantively, while in social science the focus is often on the 'mega-corporation', it is actually in such small firm contexts that the majority of cultural workers are now currently employed (Americans for the Arts, 2005; DCMS, 2001; O'Connor, 1999); yet we know relatively little about how such enterprises are internally organized. What we *do* know, contrary to industry hype, is that in most firms cultural workers are not 'stars', nor are they rich or even particularly successful – in fact, the majority of cultural workers toil in relatively anonymous enterprises, either living off the erratic incomes from 'projects' or more conventionally on low or subsistence-level wages. Glamour is at a premium, and wealth and fame are uncommon. Further, in spite of their apparent 'freedom' and 'independence' many workers and small firms are involved in relations of dependency with larger, corporate or multinational enterprises that strongly determine conditions of 'independent' production. While some examples I use are derived from studies with cultural workers working in and around large corporations (e.g., Davis and Scase, 2000; Ryan, 1992), this is the exception rather than the rule. The intention is to illuminate on how the art–commerce relation is played out in the lives of ordinary creative workers operating in commonplace contexts of cultural industry production – an often humdrum world inhabited typically by small firms and freelancers struggling only to keep afloat amidst the turbulent waters of the 'new' 'creative' economy.

The structure of the book

Following this introduction, Chapter 2 examines how a diffuse body of Marxian 'critical theorists' has accounted for cultural work. Adorno and Horkheimer's development of the concept of 'cultural industry' is discussed and its uptake and adaptation by more contemporary critical theorists (e.g., Garnham, Miège, and Ryan) analysed. Critical theory approaches have suggested that the consolidation of the 'culture industry' – the industrialized and corporatized form of capitalist cultural production – has led to a thoroughgoing debasement of cultural values and the de-autonomization of cultural work. Condemned to serve as alienated labour, cultural workers are assumed to be devoid of active subjectivity and suppressed 'from above' by managers and owners. Recent observers (such as Bourdieu, McRobbie, Miller and Rifkin) have shown how globalization has further exacerbated the consolidation of the cultural industry, through enhanced take-overs and mergers, intensified labour market competition and the introduction of oppressive and precarious forms of flexibility. I show how the autonomous and creative worker, the inheritor of the traditions of 'craft' cultural production (Ryan, 1992), is now argued by critical theorists to be an endangered species as corporations seek to further rationalize and format creativity in a more competitive economic climate.

While critical theory approaches imagine the cultural worker to be a docile body, amenable to 'top down' management, writers on 'governmentality' (developing the work of Foucault) have now alerted us to the ways in which workers are now more likely to actively manage *themselves* – and so appear complicit in their own subjection. Chapter 3 examines the work of governmentality theorists such as Rose, du Gay, McRobbie (again) and Ursell who argue that the proliferation and normalization of 'enterprise' discourses now encourages workers to not only conform to corporate values but also view the uptake of such values as crucial to their own personal development and self-interest. Evidence is presented from the television and fashion industries to show workers are widely encouraged to view themselves as 'autonomous', 'freelance' or 'creative' – since this serves to insulate their critical faculties against the more damaging impacts of the shift to more flexible, institutionally de-layered and individualized corporate climates. Workers are shown to be highly tolerant of oppressive conditions of work as a result of the efficacy with which enterprise discourses instil in them the belief that *only* through work can freedom be obtained. However, while a sense of autonomy may be obtained in reflexive cultural production, I then reveal, from my own research, the double-edged character of 'self-enterprise' by examining how it can reinforce discourses of 'self-blaming' amongst 'failing' entrepreneurs and workers, and potentially disaggregate collective forms of organizing and representation amongst cultural workers.

Building on both critical theory and governmental approaches, Chapter 4 addresses how 'creativity' is defined in the mundane, ordinary contexts of cultural work. In its idealized form, creativity provides a discursive frame through which to promote non-traditional management, aesthetic modes of working and positive individualization in terms of the 'freeing' of creative staff. However, while recognising the progressive potential of such transformations, the main concern here is to reveal how a commitment to creativity can also provide a convenient cloak disguising the (re)application of traditional bureaucratic management and instrumental rationality (Ryan, 1992). In order to evidence this, it is shown how the demands of a flexible economy for 'creative' organizations has led to a new breed of managers dedicated to 'soft' (or 'creative') management. Soft management adopts a non-traditional, deTaylorized approach to workplace organization, disavowing formality, discipline and hierarchy and promoting 'mutuality' and cooperation as the keys to economic success (Davis and Scase, 2000). It is revealed, however, that the freedoms of soft management may be illusory as cultural work often remains tied to conventional strategies of management, albeit ones now dressed in a more post-modern business idiom (Thrift, 2002). Further, the chapter details how the fashionable disavowal of hierarchy by soft management, rather than freeing creatives, can have the obverse effect of bringing creatives and creativity into line with other workers subject to (camouflaged) disciplinary regimes, and, ironically, lead managers to redefine *themselves* as 'creative'. Drawing on the work of McRobbie (2002a), Nixon (2003) and Ross (2003), the chapter then proceeds to examine the governing of the 'creative self'. It is demonstrated that prescribed codes of dress, personal appearance and personal leisure choices are crucial to the formation and administration of an increasingly homogenized creative worker identity. A discussion of the much-vaunted 'creative workplace' then reveals that – rather than being rooted in progressive radicalization – institutional assumptions made about how to best foster a creative environment tend to rely upon banal aestheticization, the reproduction of traditional categorizations of difference and, finally, in the context of creative 'culture management', a pervasive commodification of personal and social relationships.

Having examined the critical theory and governmentality critiques, Chapter 5 attempts to recover a more positive, 'liberal-democratic' vision of cultural work. This perspective derives explicitly from Beck and Beck-Gernsheim's notion of radical individualization in 'reflexive' or 'second' modernity. Building on this work, but also the writings of Giddens and Lash and Urry, it is argued that a more flexible regime that encourages entrepreneurial diversity and innovation, combined with an individualized social environment that has transferred authority for self-realization to personal and local domains, would appear to offer substantial opportunities for more diverse social formations – including new forms of cultural production. I examine how the same systemic pressures that appear to generate governmentalized, 'regressive' individualization may simultaneously be providing the social conditions for the (re)construction of a diverse range of 'progressive' and socially embedded forms of cultural work. First, the revival of the aesthetic realm amidst the mooted expansion of 'aesthetically reflexive' or artistic tendencies under individualization is discussed (Lash and Urry, 1994). Second, developing the ideas of MacIntyre (1981) and Keat (2000), some illustrative evidence of cultural workers (re)engaging in more 'practice-led' (communitarian) and 'craft' forms of production is offered. Third, the idea that cultural work might yet act as a focus for the renaissance of more social and ethical forms of economizing is explored. Here, then, in contrast to earlier chapters, cultural workers are partially re-cast as autonomous, *moral* actors that remain capable, even in highly corporatized and governmentalized work contexts, of valuing and seeking to uphold (traditional, aesthetic or socially embedded) non-economic values.

In Chapter 6, I examine the relationships between geography and cultural work. Beginning with a rehearsal of conventional Marxian arguments concerning the mooted globalization of 'culture industry' production, I then go on to examine the arguably more 'progressive' and spatially nuanced theory of 'cultural clustering', and scrutinize the social and spatial relations of 'reflexive production' perceived to underwrite local cultural economies (Lash, 1994; Scott, 2000). However, while notions of 'clustering' carry connotations of the 'good', reflecting the traditional positive affirmation given to place in defiance of modernization, it is then argued that an economy based on 'decentralized accumulation' (Wayne, 2003) in core-city clusters and localities can, paradoxically, undermine collective values and diminish the progressive and creative elements of cultural production. Relatedly, the chapter then examines the consolidation of a more instrumentally directed social embeddedness in cultural industry clusters – that is what Wittel (2001) refers to as 'network sociality', a form of social commons that contrasts markedly with those more harmonious social relations widely perceived to underpin clustering activity. The idea that reflexive and agglomerated production is inherently progressive is therefore challenged. Yet, finally, and in contrast, the possibilities for more socially and politically progressive forms of clustering *are* revealed, based once again on a reading of liberal-democratic theories of individualization. Here, the term 'mixed economy of clusters' is employed to indicate the increasingly diffuse and varied nature of cultural industry production, and to underline the renascent possibilities for alternative economies to flourish in discrete, and often marginalized, urban milieux – ones populated by workers committed to a diverse array of aesthetic, communitarian and ethical (non-economic) values.

Finally, Chapter 7 provides a critical review and summary of the freedoms and constraints of individualized cultural work, concluding with some speculations regarding the likelihood of more 'progressive' forms of cultural work emerging in the future. The main arguments of the book are summarized and some tentative conclusions drawn.

Thus, by combining the insights of some prominent social and cultural theorists, a selection of supporting case studies and indicative findings from my own empirical research, the aim of this book is to provide a synthetic and balanced review of different theories of cultural work. It is, therefore, intended as something of an introductory 'primer' for the reader in its attempt to summarize the general tenor of critical debate in this nascent field of enquiry. Given this aim, while I acknowledge that cultural work is an *internally* complex form of labour, where the articulation of the art–commerce relation may be evidenced in an array of apparently unique and distinctive management structures, and create a variety of labour identities and social effects, it will soon become evident that my approach is generalized rather then specific. I do not distinguish in depth between different organized forms of cultural work – say between music, fashion, television or art production – but take it as read that a basic tension between artistic and commercial imperatives exists (to varying degrees) in each of these fields. It is the different ways that the sociologists (and others) have theorized the fundaments of the art–commerce relation (and how the relation is broadly evidenced in acts of cultural work) that is my primary concern. This is not to deny the very real necessity of undertaking work that can identify more closely the specific rules and rhythms of labour *within* different cultural industry sub-sectors (see, for example, Caves, 2000; Hesmondhalgh and Pratt, 2005; Murdock, 2003; Oakley, 2004) – but, for the sake of clarity, it is general synthesis, rather than specific analysis, that is my purpose here. Inevitably, in attempting work of this nature, certain intellectual nuances may be omitted or become lost in translation – though I have tried to remain as faithful as possible to the basic arguments of each theory (and theorist) identified.

This generalized approach is also justified since, in broad terms, previous accounts of cultural work have tended to be somewhat polarized, veering between those who see it as wholly creative and emancipating – as market 'freedom' and individualization provide opportunities for reflexive production, aestheticization and self-reincarnation (e.g. Davis and Scase, 2000; Florida, 2002; Howkins, 2001; Leadbeater 1999) – and those sceptics who condemn cultural work as dystopic and desocialized as the economy becomes more thoroughly commercialized and captured by a neo-liberalized market rationality (e.g. Bourdieu, 1998; McGuigan, 2004; McRobbie, 2002a, b; Miller, 2004). Crewe, Gregson and Brooks confirm that there is indeed 'a tendency within current literature to present the cultural industries in terms of binary oppositions – as being either empowering, flexible, creative and fun, or following the classic small-firm model, as risky, precarious, transitory and economically marginal' (2003, p. 75). No doubt there are accuracies and inaccuracies on both sides. In this book I work to evaluate these opposing perspectives, seeking without prejudice to explore both the 'regressive' and 'progressive' features of cultural work – the intention being to neither condemn nor celebrate cultural work, but to dispassionately examine its organization, its power structures and its range of social and political effects.

2
'Culture Industry' and Cultural Work

The aim of this chapter is to outline various critical theories[1] of cultural work as undertaken within cultural industries. It first provides a review of Adorno and Horkheimer's account of the 'culture industry', before demonstrating how its insights have come to underpin more recent ('post-Adornian') accounts of the industrialization and commodification of culture (e.g., Bourdieu, 1998; Garnham, 1987, 1990, 2005; Hesmondhalgh, 2007; Jameson, 1984; McRobbie, 2002a, b; Miège, 1979, 1987, 1989; Miller et al., 2003; Rifkin, 2000; Ryan, 1992; Scherzinger, 2005; Steinert, 2003 I then discuss how, for 'critical theorists', the social relations of cultural work are closely tied to this dystopian industrial vision. As is shown, while early critical theorists had little to say about labour, an assumption that the relative freedoms of pre-industrial 'craft' forms of cultural work were being displaced by controlled systems of industrial production was tacit. Following Marx, it was generally assumed that workers would become alienated and estranged from some natural human essence (or the 'species-being'), as autonomous labour became shackled by private interests and directed towards standardized production for commercial ends. However, conversely, post-Adornian observers have more strongly suggested that cultural work *is* partly distinctive and non-standardized, in so far as elements of creative craft production continue to persist in industrialized societies, and, indeed, remain *essential* as a source of innovation in the cultural industry production process (Garnham, 2005; Miège, 1979, 1987; Ryan, 1992). However, while craft production implies relative autonomy for workers, there is considerable scepticism amongst these writers that such work will continue in its traditional form, given the efficiency with which cultural industry firms now attempt to restrict creative freedom and reproduce and recycle successful commodity formats. Thus, while cultural industries may vary in terms of their level of standardization and rationality, the basic Marxian assumptions – that labour tends towards objectification and alienation – remain intact. Indeed, critics now suggest that even in more advanced, globalized economies, characterized by various kinds of 'post-industrial' work processes that appear to resuscitate the conditions of craft production, the consolidation of corporate monopolies ensures that cultural workers remain, like their 'industrial' predecessors, largely dehumanized and desocialized – subjects whose lives are controlled by capital, even in their efforts to attain freedom in a more 'open' and 'reflexive' economic climate (Bauman, 2000; Bourdieu, 1998; Hardt and Negri, 2000; McRobbie, 2002a).

In conclusion, I suggest that while critical theorists have raised awareness of the shared fate of cultural labourers as members of a specific and alienated non-capitalist class, they have tended to ignore, first, the micro-level strategies, embedded mechanisms and organizational forms through which workers are dominated, and, second the varied subjective responses of workers to their situation, in terms of the range of personal and shared meanings and actions that are generated as a consequence of being positioned as 'cultural labour'. Put together, this has ensured that, for critical theorists, cultural work is axiomatically understood as a somewhat 'brute' form of oppression rather than (as others might argue) a process that involves an array of complex and contested power relations mediated by individuals located in differentiated social and organizational contexts. In critical theory the cultural worker is abject, since not only do workers appear to 'bow to the command, the direction and the supervision of the capitalist' (Marx, 1990, p. 1010) but also, it is argued, all *potential* for workers' autonomous subjectivity appears suppressed by the pervasive hegemony of capitalist relations of production. I thus suggest that the 'critical theory' approach, while useful in providing a schematic, macro-level account of the relations between capital and labour in industrialized cultural production, is perhaps inadequate for understanding either the specific relations of domination or the varied subjective motivations, experiences and exchanges that actually take place in cultural industry contexts – put another way, while its portrait of cultural work provides some compelling strokes of background colour, it fails to paint in the finer foreground details.

The emergence of 'culture industry'

The term 'culture industry'[2] originated from the so-called 'Frankfurt School' of critical theorists, deriving in particular from Adorno and

Horkheimer's (1944/1992) *Dialectic of Enlightenment*, which contained a powerful critique of cultural production as undertaken within the confines of industrial capitalism. Here, in Adorno's essay *'The Culture Industry: Enlightenment as Mass Deception'*, the term was applied to describe the emergent industrialization of the production of cultural texts, such as films, music, books and so on, *and* to their effective dissemination amongst national populations. As Garnham (2005) notes, 'culture industry' was employed polemically to highlight the emergent linkages between historically separated realms of culture and economy and to reveal the processes of commodification (and subsequent alienation) that underpinned this marriage.

The culture industry critique emerged from intellectuals openly hostile to modernization's capacity for impeding the development of an autonomous, moral individuality. As inheritors of German Idealism, Adorno and Horkheimer understood culture as an autonomous realm of spiritual necessity, a place where real and authentic human needs might be deliberated and striven for in the context of a 'reflective comprehension of the present' (Bernstein, 1991, p. 8). Yet, while (as Habermas later noted) industrial modernization had permitted a new bourgeois public sphere to emerge, one concerned with breaking feudal obligations and implementing a new discursive realm of ideas and creative expression (see Bourdieu, 1993; Garnham, 1990; Habermas, 1989), Adorno identified the emergent consolidation and integration of the economy, and the creeping hegemony of a rationalistic and bureaucratic attitude, one that began to undercut and erode the foundations of an autonomous cultural terrain. In industrial society the logic of accumulation began to overshadow other social concerns, and when culture became more thoroughly subject to commodification (through the enhanced production and reproduction of 'mass' market music, newspapers, fiction, cinema, sports and other cultural entertainments) then, Adorno argued, it became depersonalized and divested of its authentic qualities. Cultural plurality and chaos gave way to uniformity and standardization.

For Adorno (and others), commodification undermined cultural freedom by ensuring that practices, ideas and desires were dislocated from the relatively autonomous public sphere and re-embedded in the rational machinery of industrial production (see also Debord, 1967; Habermas, 1989; Marcuse, 1964). Consequently, cultural workers and consumers become alienated, the former by virtue of de-autonomization and absorption into the system of waged labour, the latter through their inability to exercise choice and autonomy in cultural matters. For an idealist such as Adorno, when placed in the service of capital, culture lost its special status as the discursive and contemplative realm that could nurture free, creative and 'serious' intellectual expression.

As cultural production became rationalized and instrumentally focussed it also became apparent that the *content* of culture industry products was becoming important for enabling dominant groups to lever in administrative forms of social control.[3] While the transcendent joys of popular music, the shared pleasures of the picture palace or the collectivizing energies of the popular press appeared to provide signposts to freedom, for the Frankfurt School, such forms nourished only false consciousness, alienation and despair. The outpourings of the culture industry were designed only to encourage conformity and blithe acceptance of the status quo. Indeed, by specializing in the reproduction of banal and mollifying formulas, ones that impeded the development of 'autonomous, independent individuals who judge and decide consciously for themselves' (Adorno, 1991, p. 92), the culture industry provided only the semblance of freedom, for the promise of individual liberty was actually an elegant mask for the firm *suppression* of creative impulses:

> The sacrifice of individuality, which accommodates itself to the regularity of the successful, the doing of what everybody does, follows from the basic fact that in broad areas the same thing is offered to everybody by the standardized production of consumption goods. But the commercial necessity of connecting this identity leads to the manipulation of taste and the official culture's pretence of individualism which necessarily increases in proportion to the liquidation of the individual. (Adorno, 1991, p. 35)

Thus, the 'hostile sisters' of 'vulgarization and enchantment' (Adorno, 1991, p. 36) had proved especially effective in convincing populations of the merits of the culture industry and encouraging meek acceptance of their (apparently) debased cultural offerings. It was argued that in their repetitive, formulaic address and pervasive encroachment into all arenas of everyday life, the products of the industrialized culture industry forced individuals into a state of muted compliance and diminished the possibilities of any serious and challenging 'aesthetic protest' (Adorno, 1967, p. 132).

The work of the Frankfurt School (and Adorno's in particular) has attracted substantial criticism. This has largely centred on the structural bias perceived to underpin the work. Critics have tended to object to the notion of an all-powerful industry foisting its products on compliant bodies with 'empty' minds (see, for example, discussions in Dant, 2003; Elliott and Lemert, 2006; Held, 1980; Kellner, 1989; McGuigan, 2004; Swingewood, 1998). Certainly, Adorno has relatively little to say about the possibilities of actors creatively or independently evading the strictures of commodification and alienation. The logic of accumulation dominates to the extent of foreclosing any possibility of 'resistance' in the ways that (say) 'active audience' theorists would pre-scribe today[4] Second, Adorno's assumptive belief in the essential power of culture, in its ability to light the path to transcendence and 'truth' in a world otherwise beclouded by utilitarian logic, when considered through contemporary eyes, appears both idealistic and, as many have suggested, perhaps somewhat 'elitist'. Certainly, his defence of artistic modernism and condemnation of popular forms appear eccentric in the contemporary context of a (postmodernized) social science. Nonetheless, Adorno's ideas continue to influence those contemporary writers critical of the commodification of the cultural realm, and a number of them have sought recently to resuscitate and further develop his ideas (see Abbinnett, 2003; Gunster, 2004; Jarvis, 1998; Lash, 1994; Scherzinger, 2005; Steinert 2003; Witkin, 2000).[5]

Contemporary critique of 'culture industry'

Since Adorno's essay, the Left's understanding of the 'culture industry' has slowly evolved, first into a more empirically informed Marxian pol-itical economy approach that attempts to describe and account for the consolidation of the cultural industry through interrogating the on-going activities of various state and private monopolies and commercial organizations, and, second, into a more culturally focussed 'aesthetici-zation' critique that emphasizes how the culture industry has been able to develop through the further commodification of non-economic (personal, social, emotional, religious, artistic) realms. Both approaches, while often critical of Frankfurt School thinking, exhibit clear sympathies and continuities with their intellectual concerns.

In the first instance, observers have sought to develop a critical line of inquiry that retains something of the spirit of Adorno and Horkheimer's original formulations, but takes issue with what Garnham calls 'the super-ficiality of its economic analysis' (2005, p. 18). Efforts have been made to more accurately and decisively account for the economic significance and structure of the 'cultural industries' (Hesmondhalgh 2007; Miège 1979, 1987, 1989; Ryan, 1992) while examining their interrelationships with prevailing modes of social, political and cultural regulation and governance. Garnham's own work in attempting to assess theoretically and empirically the significance of industrialized cultural production has been leading in this regard (1987, 1990, 2000, 2005). His eloquent analyses of the historical emergence of the media (and the cultural industries more generally) have been consistently underpinned by a belief in the 'demonstrable reality that symbolic forms are in general produced, distributed and consumed in the form of commodities and under conditions of capitalist market exchange' (2000, p. 39). While Garnham's position has been refined to more adequately account for the possibilities of actors evading or negotiating the closures of the market, he remains committed to the idea that economy remains structurally determining, acting beyond the 'plans and desires' of the individual, setting the field conditions under which cultural producers, consumers (and workers) are routinely compelled to act.

Miège's (1979, 1987, 1989) investigations into the cultural commodity and the varied logics of cultural production and Golding and Murdock's (1991) work have also been important in presenting refined understandings of the ways in which cultural production is strongly shaped by the dynamics of economic systems. Indeed, moving away from Adorno, Miège (1979, 1989) was one of the first to pluralize the term 'culture industry' into 'culture industries', in order to emphasize the complex and varied nature of production activities. While retaining a focus on the determinations of economic structures, he is concerned to demonstrate that the power of cultural industry corporations is inconsistent and uneven, and so alerts us to the necessity of analysing cultural production as a diffuse, rather than coherent, set of activities (see also the review in Hesmondhalgh, 2007). Miège's work is amongst the first to suggest that the degree to which managers exert control, or to which workers possess autonomy, will vary across cultural industries subsectors, depending on the specific systems employed to enable production, distribution and the allocation of rewards, as he comments:

> It does not take much research to discover that every type of capital from small family capital to large-scale multinational capital is present in the culture industries. But one can also see that between one branch and another there are notable differences, in particular a very different rate of penetration of monopoly capital. (Miège, 1979, p. 306)

To assume the existence of a totalizing, coherent and all-powerful 'culture industry' makes little sense in the context of Miège's identification of what is a diffuse and uncertain field of cultural production and consumption. Similarly dispensing with rigidity of Adorno's model, Golding and Murdock purport to provide a critique of cultural production that argues against the notion that the economy provides the force of 'determination in the last instance' and favours instead the idea that the economy chiefly operates in the *first* instance (see also Hesmondhalgh, 2007). That is, the economy is a force that determines 'the key features of the general environment' in which cultural production take place, but cannot provide 'a complete explanation of the nature of that activity' (Golding and Murdock, 1991, p. 19). While the emphasis remains on how 'micro contexts are shaped by general economic dynamics' (ibid., 1991, p. 18) and on the ways in which the culture industry monopolizes production, manipulates public discourse and alienates consumers, there is some openness to the idea that the production, use and meaning of cultural goods may not be as standardized and predictable as Frankfurt School theorists would appear to suggest. Ryan's (1992) work is also sympathetic to a Frankfurt School approach in that it elaborates the structural conditions which impel cultural production, yet it also departs from Adorno's formalism in its efforts to examine the embedded institutional contexts in which particular worker–subjects operate (see below). Notwithstanding these specific refinements, we can argue (as Ryan suggests in relation to his own work) that these varied approaches are 'more or less Marxist' in that they take 'the basic social structures Marx identified as "capitalist" for granted' (1992, p. 2) and focus their energies on explaining how the economic consolidation of industrial firms and organizations is what broadly determines the conditions of cultural production and consumption.

A further (but related) development of Adorno's ideas is to be found amongst those critics who have chosen to emphasize how the cultural industries have developed and expanded on the basis of further colonizing the aesthetic, emotional and spiritual realms. Since Adorno's work, the commodification of art, culture, emotional and personal relationships, human experiences, beliefs systems and forms of spirituality has proceeded apace. This has led a range of critics (e.g., Baudrillard, 1981; Debord, 1967; Harvey, 1989, 2001; Jameson, 1984; Rifkin, 2000; Steinert, 2003) to criticise capitalism's enthusiastic search for new cultural and aesthetic realms to commodify as merely indicative of its invasive and totalising nature:

> The cultural industries – including the recording industry, the arts, television and radio – commodify, package, and market experiences

as opposed to physical products or services. Their stock and trade is selling short-term access to simulated worlds and altered states of consciousness. The fact is, they are an ideal organizational model for a global economy that is metamorphosing from commodifying goods and services to commodifying cultural experience itself. (Rifkin, 2000, p. 365)

Not only are all forms of cultural or aesthetic experience vulnerable to commodification, but, for the likes of Jameson, art itself has lost its autonomous purpose, for now aesthetic production cannot stand alone and instead must subordinate itself to market imperatives in order to prosper:

> What has happened is that aesthetic production today has become integrated into commodity production generally: the frantic economic urgency of producing fresh waves of ever more novel-seeming goods (from clothing to airplanes), at ever greater rates of turnover, now assigns an increasingly essential structural function and position to aesthetic innovation and experimentation. (Jameson, 1984, p. 56)

For such critics, the accelerated commercialization of art, culture and the 'realm of the senses' is linked to capitalist efforts to insulate against future crises by investing in new areas of commodity production. The explosion in the range and volume of cultural goods is driven by a capitalist logic that seeks constantly to bring new commodity forms into the market arena. While these innovations might herald potential benefits in terms of enhanced 'consumer choice', it is now widely argued that aesthetic production has led to a debasement or cheapening of the cultural realm in so far as motivations for appropriation tend to be instrumental and profit-seeking, rather than related to cultural edification or 'human flourishing'. In short, market rationality tends to dictate the range and quality of cultural products as well as override any moral dilemmas of aestheticization (Jameson, 1984; Sayer, 1999).

'Aestheticization' is also now more firmly embedded in the material qualities of cultural commodities. For Adorno, the development of cultural industry led to the creation of goods that were differentiated only by their emphases on 'the effect, the obvious touch, and the technical detail' (1991, p. 125) – surface variations that served only to obscure commodities' underlying standardized character. In the decades that have elapsed since the development of the 'culture industry' thesis, the process of creating product differentiation through *design* has come to assume a more central importance in the dynamics of cultural production. While design has a practical purpose in that it may enhance product utility (use-value), more commonly, the differentiated design of clothes, electronic goods, music, TV shows, home furnishings and so on is driven by the desire to generate 'sign-value'; that is to provide consumers with an opportunity to pursue a constantly renewable range of 'specialist', 'designer' and 'labelled' goods that befit their real or imagined social status (Bell, 1976; Bourdieu, 1984; Featherstone, 1991). Indeed, the 'branding' of goods, the coupling of goods to particular images and styles of life, is now a common strategy for generating sign-value and, more prosaically, ensuring that major corporations can command market share and renew their seemingly inexorable 'assault on choice' (Klein, 2000, p. 130; see also Heath and Potter, 2004).

The prevalence of design aesthetics and the wider currency of symbolic value has led observers such as Lash and Urry (1994) to suggest that the consumption of 'signs' (that is aesthetic, informational and image-based rather than functional or utilitarian goods) is the defining feature of contemporary economies. Such an epochal claim echoes Baudrillard's (1981) more pessimistic (postmodern) ruminations on the ubiquity of the sign in the formation of a deterritorialized and desocialized consumer society. For Baudrillard, sign-value operates independent of both use and exchange values in so far as the value and meaning of a commodity is now reliant upon its positioning relative to other similarly signified goods in the broader circulation of signs – rather than being contained within functional or utilitarian purpose, or even within its potential for exchangeability with other commodities. The image of a commodity and the meaning it generates has no real referent other than to the range of other signs in circulation. As Lury (1996, p. 71) avers, 'for Baudrillard people have become merely the vehicles for expressing the differences between objects', and the possibilities of escaping the immanent logic of a wholly signified society increasingly fade as we ever more enthusiastically consume for desire rather than need, and attempt to cultivate distinctive consumption habits in order to differentiate ourselves in the vigorous hustle for social position. Baudrillard's view may seem overstated and leave little room for manoeuvre on the part of consumers or producers; nonetheless, in its evocation of a fluid system of 'signs' it communicates an important message for observers of contemporary capitalism and cultural industries – that the aesthetic domain has come to exert a more profound influence on the materiality of commodities, their conditions of circulation and their given social meaning.

Thus, in developing Adorno's ideas (either explicitly or indirectly), these various critics have emphasized how the continued industrialization of cultural production and the enhanced commodification of the aesthetic realm have ensured that the cultural industries have been able to reinforce a powerful position in Westernized societies. Yet, even now, ongoing transformations in the structure of capitalism appear to provide cultural industries with the opportunity to obtain even greater shares of wealth, power and control. As a range of critics have suggested, including Bourdieu, Harvey, Jameson and Rifkin, the social and economic impacts of *globalization* now appear to have had exacerbated the scale and scope of the cultural 'standardization, commercialization and rigidification' that Adorno (1967, p. 122) first identified in the high-modern period (see also Miller et al., 2003; Wayne, 2003) – this point I will return to in Chapter 6.

Cultural work and workers

Having outlined a critical theory of cultural industries, how might we understand cultural work in its context? Initially, it must be acknowledged that while much has been written about the industrialization of culture and the expanded commodification of the aesthetic realm, critical theorists have had relatively little to say about the cultural industry labour process. As Dant (2003, p. 42) has argued, '[i]n general, critical theories neither focus on work as a distinct sphere of life, nor provide a detailed empirical account of the organisation of work'. Why should this be so?

It is clear that members of the Frankfurt School rarely studied work in any depth – indeed they appeared to take its organization and meaning somewhat for granted. For example, while Marcuse often wrote about the alienating effects of labour, his observations that work 'cripples all human faculties and enjoins satisfaction' (1955, p. 276) and that industrial production instils a 'drugging rhythm' (1964/1991, p. 26) were not backed by substantive empirical observations. Adorno himself had little to say about work other than provide general comment on its mechanical and repetitive nature, characteristically suggesting, for example, that 'the more the process of self-preservation is effected by the bourgeois division of labor, the more it requires the self-alienation of individuals who must model their body and soul according to the technical apparatus' (Adorno, 2000, p. 170). By and large, with their focus directed elsewhere (mainly towards a more general and abstract critique of the *total culture* of modern life rather than its empirical manifestations) the Frankfurt School seemed content to uphold Marx's idea that the commodification of labour power tends towards alienation and estrangement – without making much effort to verify empirically this claim.

Similarly, echoing their intellectual forbears, more recent critical accounts of the cultural industries tend to acknowledge the importance of work, but, in general terms, leave its organization and meaning somewhat unexplored. To give two prominent instances, Garnham's (1990) otherwise comprehensive account of the emergence and consolidation of media and cultural industries does not seek to address the specific character of cultural industries work, despite recognizing the necessity of doing so. Similarly, in an influential study, Mosco (1996) enthusiastically endorses the work of theorists who have attempted to investigate the embedded contexts of media production (for example, Fishman, 1980; Gans, 1979; Tuchman, 1978; in similar vein see also Tunstall, 1993; Davis and Scase, 2000), yet his own wide-ranging and insightful analyses of the political economy of the media and communication industries (he does not specifically use the term 'cultural industries') do not extend into a consideration of the media workplace or offer an analysis of labour processes. Mosco's work is a salutary reminder that it is mainstream of academic Media Studies that has taken the lead in analysing the contexts of cultural production (often from an empirical perspective largely unconcerned with class analysis), while students in the Marxian 'culture industry' tradition have mostly failed to analyse cultural work in any depth. As an aside, it is also worth noting that writers in what Hesmondhalgh (2007) refers to as the 'Schiller-McChesney' school of North American media and cultural studies, a tradition strongly influenced by Marxian political economy (if not directly by culturally focussed Marxism of Adorno and the Frankfurt School), while providing many detailed and valuable analyses of power, ownership and control of the media and cultural industries (for example, McChesney, 1993, 1998; Schiller, 1969, 1989), have also tended to overlook the embedded social relations of cultural commodity production.

Thus, in general terms, cultural workplace studies remain rare, and the charges levelled by Held (1980, p. 373), that in the work of Adorno, Horkheimer and Marcuse 'the importance of analysing particular patterns of social relations, the labour process (the experiences people have of it as well as its structure) and political organizations, is downgraded' also rings true in the range of recent critical theory writings on the cultural industries. Dean and Jones (2003, p. 529) similarly criticize the lack of attention paid to social relations of production in post-Adornian cultural and media studies, bemoaning the 'persistent privileging of representation, distribution and ownership, and a concomitant lack of attention to relations of production, the labour process and labour and trade union struggle'.

The 'missing subject' in cultural work

Correspondent with the general neglect of the labour process has been a lack of attention paid to the issue of individual *subjectivity* in the cultural workplace. Once again, much of this neglect stems from the Frankfurt School and Adorno, for whom the worker–subject could only be understood in relation to the 'huge economic machinery' (Adorno and Horkheimer, 1992, p. 127) which constituted its practices and values – the idea of a transcendental, free-thinking subject was anti-thetical to Adorno's view of subjectivity as a 'social effect' (ibid., p. 126) of the efficient administration of capitalist production and, in particular, the depersonalizing effects of the culture industry. The subsequent neglect of the worker–subject in critical theories of cultural industries stems from this concern to emphasise only the objective and systemic ways in which capitalist cultural production impacts on the social realm.

However, the disregard of the worker-as-subject has perhaps not been particular to critical theorists of the cultural industries, for as Blair (2003, p. 678) suggests, a reluctance to explore social subjectivity at the point of production perhaps stems from some general 'long standing difficulties in [Marxian] industrial sociology of adequately theorizing a contextual agent'. Put simply, given the structuralist inclinations of Marxist theory, there has been a tendency to conceptualize all work-places in schematic fashion, as 'general sites of exploitation', and to understand workers in similarly one-dimensional terms, either as (as Marx himself argued) mere 'personifications of labour' or alternatively as simple 'bearers of class relations' (see du Gay, 1996; Knights, 1990; Marx, 1990; Thompson, 1990; Willmott, 1990;), rather than as active or critical human subjects. As Willmott comments in relation to Marx's own writings there is an assumption that 'the experience of wage la-bour can only deny, and never confirm, the subjectivity of human beings' (1990, p. 354), and, as such, we might surmise that efforts from the Marxian Left to understand the cultural labour process as a com-plex field of interactions forged in the context of both systemic-objective *and* subjective, personal and experiential motivations would either appear unnecessary or politically suspect. Similarly, du Gay (1996, p. 13) confirms that (for Marx) 'because complete human persons could never exist under conditions of alienation, subjectivity could have no force of effect'. With the labouring class, rather than the individual, understood as both the victim and agent of social change, any efforts to study the personal, subjective experience of work could be seen as a dangerous indulgence, deflecting attention from the more vital task of theorizing and overcoming structurally embedded class inequalities. In analyses of the cultural industries we can thus observe evidence of what Thompson (1990, p. 114) more widely refers to as the 'missing subject' in political economy studies of the labour process.

A lack of sociological focus on cultural workers is also understandable given that such workers have been long promoted as 'creative subjects', that is, as singular and unique talents, 'mavericks' or 'innovators' and it is, of course, 'something of a sociological commonplace to de-emphasise the individual creator and seek to emphasise, if not valorise, the social and collective' (Negus and Pickering, 2004, p. 51). In some quarters, a focus on cultural workers, as 'creative' agents or subjects, is viewed with acute suspicion because of sociological inclinations to view creativity as a phenomenon that ought not to be theorized at the romantic level of the 'individual genius', but must be more adequately theorized as an outcome of social structure – and, indeed, largely rejected as a bourgeois myth (see Bilton, 2006; Bourdieu, 1993; Negus and Pickering, 2004; Rampley, 1998). Thus, a focus on workplace creativity *in itself,* and the 'creative' worker, runs the risk of appearing to idealize, naturalize or label as voluntary that which is substantially generated in the context of social and political structures.

Given these varied objections, it is not altogether surprising that critical theorists of the cultural industries workplace have been broadly inattentive to the enigmas of experiential variation, personal subjectivity and human agency in everyday work contexts. Outside of a general theory of the 'alienated worker', one whose quests for autonomy are increasingly undermined by the economic imperatives of (now globalized and post-industrial) capitalist firms, we learn very little about the cultural worker as an individual or active subject, one whose working life might be composed of myriad conflicts, struggles or negotiations, or whose practical efforts to turn work into a meaningful vocation may lead him or her into areas of social action that confound their casting as alienated labour. The potential for radical critique implied in the shift towards 'flexible' and 'individualized' forms of production (Beck, 1992; Lash and Urry, 1994), with its emphasis on a recovery of the self-reflexive and active worker, are unexplored in a framework that emphasises the ongoing systemic reproduction of the institutions of capitalism, cultural industry monopolies and the corresponding suppression of cultural labour, *en masse.*

Craft production – and its decline

Despite a general reluctance to address subjectivity and theories of workplace action, one area where post-Adornian critics *have* contributed to an understanding of cultural workers has come in accounts of the enduring and necessary role of traditional creative 'craft'[6] production in cultural industry contexts (Miège, 1979; Ryan, 1992; Williams, 1980). In craft production, control over the conception, design, and manufacture of a cultural good is possessed by individual or small groups of workers, operating at close quarters in 'workshop' conditions. In cultural industries, this is both prevalent and necessary because, as Ryan argues, artistic production requires the 'imagination and talent of gifted and named individuals who require space to work, free from expectation especially of commercial kinds' (1992, p. 104). Indeed, despite the widespread modernization of capitalist production, it remains widely held that original artistic production cannot proceed by any other means than embedded, humanized forms of 'workshop' production – for artistic labour cannot be standardized or mechanized without compromising its effectivity. This fact has encouraged some post-Adornian critics of cultural industries to now acknowledge the importance of individual subjectivity in the workplace, for as the likes of Garnham, Miège and Ryan have recognized, capitalism must offer creative workers some degree of 'space' and autonomy in order to spark ideas; otherwise there can be no new cultural production of any real value – merely standard reproductions of the same generic formats, openly subject to diminishing returns. Paradoxically then, in the context of cultural production, ordinarily rational capitalism has a vested interest in ensuring that capricious and irrational workers are nurtured and rewarded. While as Garnham (1990) notes, workers may still be alienated by virtue of their lack of control of all of the conditions of production (not to mention distribution and profits), it is fair to say that he (like Miège and Ryan) now assume that to some degree, cultural workers cannot be *wholly* alienated – for craft production allows them to maintain a spiritual, emotional or artistic connection with their work, even as it is harnessed by capitalists to generate new, innovative and meaning-laden commodities that can be turned into profit. Thus, the distinctive feature of cultural industry work is that which must combine 'the structures of both capital and art' (Ryan, 1992, pp. 13–14), that is, it must satisfy both commercial and artistic standards of excellence to obtain value – and it is this double necessity (the 'art–commerce relation') which has enabled traditional forms of creative craft production to endure even within highly specialized and rationalized cultural industries:

> Since artists cannot be reduced to simple labour-power, the creative stage of production in the corporations of culture is unlike industrialised Fordist production systems, but organised along similar lines to a capitalist workshop. Within this structure, some of the traditional freedoms accorded artists are preserved whereby executants can countermand the organisational power of creative management. (Ibid., p. 29)

Such comments remind us that maintaining a balance between standardized, controlled accumulation and preserving the unruly creativity, art and autonomy that makes creation of new commodities possible is *the* distinctive feature of cultural production, one that must be considered in any analysis of the cultural labour process – a view Hesmondhalgh endorses:

> [O]ne of the defining features of the complex professional era of cultural production is [cultural workers'] unusual degree of autonomy, which is carried over from preceding eras where artists, authors and composers worked independently of businesses...It shows that the metaphor of the traditional factory production line, often used in critiques of industrial cultural production, entirely misses the point. Because of the history of attitudes towards symbolic creativity... factory-style production is widely felt to be inimical to the kinds of creativity necessary to make profits. (2002, pp. 55–56)

Ideally, craft production permits the free expression of innovation and creativity required to generate new and distinctive products – the task of capital being to try and exploit creativity without suffocating it. As many have argued, even in cultural industries that have largely adopted standardized systems of assembly, reproduction and distribution (mass printing of newspapers, reproduction of art prints, manufacture of CDs, videos, DVDs, computer games and so on), the *genesis* of commodities, their original production, has always been tightly bound by workshop systems and social relations which privilege ideas-generation amongst small networks of creative specialists, located either within or exterior to the firm[7] Indeed, for some, in post-industrial or 'post-Fordist'[8] regimes, the shift towards more flexible, specialized and 'self-reflexive' manufacture is argued to be *expanding* traditional, community or craft-based production systems in the cultural industries, as firms emphasize close co-operation and the importance of originality and design in the 'vertically disintegrated' production process (Lash, 1994; Lash and Urry, 1994; Scott, 2000 – see Chapter 6).

Ryan (1992) provides a comprehensive and empirically rich account of the persistence of craft production in the contexts of the television and newspaper industries. Here, close-knit and embedded relations of production (in 'project teams') remain important for enabling the production of new, creative programmes and texts, and managers recognize the necessity of allowing creatives the scope and autonomy to part-determine their own working practices – lest they kill the geese that lay the golden eggs. Ryan comments that '[a]ny attempt by employers to reduce the necessary component by demanding less time and devotion by the artist, runs the risk of a shoddy or mediocre and hence unsaleable artwork' (1992, p. 114). Thus, to reiterate, it is the unusual qualities of the cultural commodity, its *double articulation* not only as a utilitarian but also as an aesthetic good, which has ensured its continued generation within craft-relations of production.

The study of workshop relations of production marks a distinctive break from the Frankfurt School since it stresses the endurance (and indeed necessity) of creatively led, craft systems of production even in advanced industrialized contexts.[9] The Frankfurt School's tendency to assume universal processes of rationalization and alienation in the workplace are thus tempered by this more nuanced consideration of the ways in which certain groups have been able to secure degrees of relative autonomy as a consequence of their privileged status as 'creative' workers.

Post-Adornian theorists thus appear to paint a more positive picture of cultural work, one where the durability and necessity of craft production seems to guarantee that creative cultural work will persist as a relatively autonomous and meaningful endeavour – the artists have survived. However (as this is *critical* theory), such studies do also tend to emphasize how the continued rationalization of production is now placing creative autonomy under serious threat. As Ryan and others have acknowledged, the encroachment of market rationality is now, more than ever, threatening to overwhelm innovative and independent craft production, primarily as firms look to produce more standardized and formatted goods, in established styles and genres, which minimize risk and guarantee profits. Music companies, television companies, film studios, book publishers, the clothing and fashion industries all appear to be focussed on producing generic and formularized goods, distinguishable in minor detail, but indistinguishable in essence. In a globally competitive environment, it seems firms are now much less likely to take risks speculating on new and untried styles, genres and products. In this way, while managers recognize the necessity of creative craft production, they are forever seeking ways through which they can rationalize and control it in order to generate more stable, reliable profits:

> The historical problem facing capitalists engaged in the production and circulation of cultural commodities has been how to devise a system of employment which enables artists to create genuine original and marketable works of art which are stamped with signs of genius, but which also disciplines the creative process and brings it under the control of the firm, such that management may set the standards, rate and timing of creation and keep labour costs to a minimum. (Ryan, 1992, p. 104)

But while firms constantly seek the blueprints for commercial success through establishing reliable standardized formats, it is, of course, also important to ensure that consumers *appear* to be offered new cultural commodities in order to satisfy cultural demands for newness, stylistic renewal and change. It is no surprise then that promotion and marketing, advertising and public relations industries have grown significantly in advanced capitalism, helping to ensure cultural firms can differentiate their products and services in a more competitive market – and hide the 'eternal sameness' that underpins their apparently differentiated goods. For critical theorists, a constant media circulation of trends, styles, listings, commentaries, critiques, images, symbols and forms of cultural life now ensures that consumers are fully informed about those vital commodities that, according to Debord, are only useful for 'producing habitual submission' (1967, p. 33) – but are nonetheless skilfully promoted to stimulate our desires and provide immaculate models for self-formation and the development of subjective purpose. The capacity of advertising to finesse the similarities between goods, to promote as different that which is the same, indeed to urge us to buy over and over again similar goods that may have no intrinsic meaning other than those provided by advertisers and promoters themselves, is what helps camouflage standardization and formatting and, by implication, eviscerate genuinely creative and autonomous craft production. Yet, as I have averred, some degree of creativity in production remains necessary, for while advertising can make even identical goods appear radically different, there are limits to its effectiveness – consumers are not necessarily fools. Craft elements of production have survived because ensuring that a pool of new commodities is available, ones that exhibit some apparent distinctiveness, newness or originality compared with their predecessors is entirely necessary and requires the ideas, innovations and sparks of ingenuity that can only be provided by (relatively) autonomous and unfettered creative workers. As Witkin (2000, p. 165) remarks in relation to advertising and formatting, '[s]ooner or later ... the possibilities of invention are exhausted and the culture industry must return to the sources of authentic aesthetic creation that lie beyond the compass of its design initiative'. Yet, while craft-based cultural production remains necessary, we should recognize (as Garnham, Hesmondhalgh, Miège and Ryan argue) that firms are constantly seeking ways in which production can be further standardized and rationalized in order to extract the maximum profitability, and minimize the waste, both from the creative worker and creative work process. Craft creativity remains crucial, but as Ryan puts it, is becoming increasingly controlled and bureaucratized by 'crystalliz[ed] canons of practice and their supervised application as formats' (1992, p. 123; see also Williams, 1980).

More recently, given the avidity with which large corporations are now seeking to establish globally integrated systems of production that can generate internationally marketable products, it is perhaps no surprise that for some theorists (e.g. Bourdieu, 1998; McRobbie, 2002a, b; Miller, 2004) traditional craft-based cultural work now appears entirely denuded of its creative potential. This is somewhat ironic given the pervasive promotion of 'creativity' as a cornerstone of the new cultural industries-led economy (DCMS, 2001; Florida, 2002; Howkins, 2001). Yet, McRobbie argues that since the mid-1990s cultural industry firms (of all sizes and across all sectors) have become increasingly driven by globalized 'neo-liberal'[10] market imperatives and so the opportunity for genuinely creative, independent cultural work has now been seriously diminished. She further suggests that we are now witnessing a 'decline in creativity' (2002a, p. 524) in cultural work and – just as Adorno argued in the 1940s, that 'rugged individualists have been outlawed' (1990, p. 306) – McRobbie now surmises that '[t]here is nothing like the vibrancy and collective (and competitive) spirit which characterized the earlier period' (McRobbie, 2002a, p. 524). She offers that

> cultural production is increasingly driven by the imperatives of market and consumer culture, and the banality of pop promos, TV and cinema advertising is concealed by the technological euphoria, the association of newness and youthfulness, and of course by the parties, the celebrity culture and the cheque in the post. (Ibid., p. 525)

Bourdieu reflects on the creative and intellectual poverty of television work undertaken in an industry that 'offers an increasingly depoliticized, aseptic, bland view of the world, and [is] increasingly dragging the newspapers into its slide into demagogy and subordination to commercial interests' (1998, p. 74). Scherzinger (2005, p. 29) complains that innovation by workers in the music industry is 'rigidly subordinated to the same logical management of facts, figures and statistics. Unorthodox and oppositional music forms give way to niche-based formularism'. It indeed appears that in cultural work, as in cultural production as a whole, we have reached the apogee of the 'standardization, commercialization and rigidification' that Adorno first identified over 60 years ago – for these critical theorists, craft production, even under more 'flexible' post-Fordist conditions, has finally been stripped of autonomy and divested of radical creativity.

Recognition of the decline of creative autonomy in cultural labour also underpins Lazzarato's (1996) and Hardt and Negri's (2000) assessments of the rise of 'immaterial labour' in ostensibly 'postmodernized' or information-led economies. The rapid growth of various kinds of globally integrated corporations, producing cultural, informational, semiotic or knowledge-based goods, has led these (more postmodern) Marxist critics to surmise that substantial numbers of workers are now primarily engaged in acts of 'immaterial production'; that is where labour 'produces an immaterial good, such as a service, a cultural product, knowledge or communication' (Hardt and Negri, 2000, p. 290), as opposed to the (arguably) simpler and less ambiguous commodities of industrial society. In terms of the culture industry, immaterial production is realised in the now expanded array of meaning-laden goods, texts, signs, symbols and cultural communications, appearing to effortlessly circulate in globally integrated networks of what Hardt and Negri call the 'informational economy' (ibid., p. 289). Crucially, while industrial production (including cultural production) largely relied upon standardized and repetitive forms of factory labour, with relatively distinct and durable divisions between 'skilled' and 'unskilled', 'manual' and 'non-manual' inputs, the production of informational goods is now based substantially on ensuring that factory 'hands' become more fully embodied as highly skilled, technically adept, intellectualized and creative 'knowledge workers'. At first glance, this would appear to provide opportunities for the *revival* of autonomous and non-alienated forms of cultural work (including forms of craft production), since workers are now more evidently required to become involved in advanced creative and technical manipulation in order to meet insatiable demands for ever more novel and sophisticated ranges of cultural goods (see Lash, 1994; Lash and Urry, 1994). Yet, for Hardt and Negri, the plans and desires of the worker are subordinated by the stringent mechanical regime of immaterial production. With more than a hint of technological-determinism, they argue that the informational economy is not only highly instrumentalized and market-led, but is also fundamentally driven by a strongly mechanized, technically specialized and *computerized* tendency:

> Today we increasingly think like computers, while communication technologies and their model of interaction are becoming more and more central to labouring activities... Interactive and cybernetic machines become a new prosthesis integrated into our bodies and minds and a lens through which to redefine our bodies and minds themselves... We should note that one consequence of the informatization of production and the emergence of immaterial labour has been a real homogenization of labouring processes... With the computerization of production today... the heterogeneity of concrete labor has tended to be reduced, and the worker is increasingly further removed from the object of his or her labor. (Hardt and Negri, 2000, pp. 291–292)

The subjectivity of the immaterial worker is thus subsumed, not simply by local managerial interests, but by the systemic, all-pervasive notion of technically driven 'informatized' and networked production. Within this, despite the necessity of developing pools of skilled and self-directed *intelligent* labour – the cultural worker (as a recognized member of what Lazzarato and Hardt and Negri understand as a new 'intellectual proletariat') is actively prevented from becoming subversive or dissident by highly efficient and 'panoptical management structures' (ibid., p. 297) which serve to ensure that workers are readily acculturated into fluid (but highly monitored) networks of production (a theme I will explore further in Chapter 3). In such a scheme, while workers appear equipped with some degree of agency, they tend only to be conceptualized and represented as expendable 'nodes' in the broader network of transactions and flows that make up the vertiginous terrain of the informational economy – not as critical or active subjects in their own right.

The global picture

For cultural workers, deprived of the traditional autonomy of craft production, the lack of creative control is but one corollary of the shift towards a more globalized and market-dominated regime. While cultural work is presented as a panacea for the ills of economic restructuring and the path to creative personal growth (DCMS, 2001; Florida, 2002; Leadbeater, 1999), if critical theorists are to be believed, it seems that far from offering emancipation and gratifying combinations of personal and financial rewards, cultural work is exploitative, alienating and often poorly rewarded[11]. Workers must learn to navigate the precarious terrain of a more flexible economy that requires employees thrive on low or no pay, juggle multiple jobs and 'projects', relentlessly self-promote and subsist as expendable labour often in contractual hock to large firms and multinationals – while always remaining alert to the possibility of being undercut or 'let go'. As the state pulls away the safety nets of welfare and other social solidarities appear to fade, cultural workers must learn to survive in a flexible and globally integrated economy where social relations are characterized by transience and superficiality rather than permanence and depth (McRobbie, 2002a; Wittel, 2001). It appears that there is little to be done in defiance of this process, for, seemingly by definition, the 'individualization' of work precludes a collective political response (McRobbie, 2002a). Indeed, as Gibson (2003) now observes, rather than resist, cultural workers appear increasingly *resigned* to competitive individualization.

It is also important to mention that while, in Western contexts, independent firms and cultural workers struggle to make themselves amenable to the demands of the flexible and global market, their efforts are being pervasively undermined by the ways in which large cultural firms and conglomerations search the globe for new production locations where deregulated institutional climates, advantageous tax breaks and cheap and compliant labour forces might be accessed and exploited. This is what Miller et al. (2003) refer to as the *new international division of cultural labour*. In the West, the increased range and rapid turnover of cultural goods now rely upon firms finding places where shoes can be stitched more cheaply, where film crews can be hired at fractional cost, where hardware and software can be more economically produced and where unions, health and safety regulations and employment rights exert minimal drag on the production process. The cultural industry labour process has become substantially globalized and arguably it is the freedom of firms to exploit low-cost labour locations that has largely underwritten the rapid growth of cultural industry revenues – and the denudation of craft production – in Western economic contexts. As governments so proudly promote the efficiency and effectiveness with which their music, software, film and fashion industries have been able to tap into and exploit the 'global market', it is worth noting the consequences for non-Western workers subjected to increasingly internationalized relations of domination and exploitation. From the film industry, Miller and Yúdice (2002, pp. 103–104) provide a telling example:

> The success of Titanic in the late 1990s saw Mexico again a key site for offshore production. Restoring Mexico to the Hollywood map gained James Cameron [the director of Titanic] the Order of the Aztec Eagle from a grateful government, which offers Hollywood docile labor, minimal bureaucracy, a weak peso, many US-trained technicians and a new film commission that provides liaison services. Local workers on Titanic in Rosarito, a maquildora sixty miles south of the border, reported horrific levels of exploitation and mistreatment when the state forced out a leftist union in favour of management stooges. Mexico's new film 'union' even maintains an office in LA to reassure anxious industry mavens of its cooperativeness and to remain up-to-date on US pay rates – in order to undercut them.

Additionally, we have become familiar with reports that it is the low paid, poorly protected and, in many cases, systematically abused workers in varied locations (including Indonesia, Turkey, Taiwan, Bangladesh, China, Bulgaria, Romania and India) that now produce the latest designer trainers, T-shirts and trousers, manufacture DVDs and CDs, help make the movies and assemble the consoles for the benefits of Western firms and consumers (Hale and Wills, 2005; Klein, 2000). The culture industry has now expanded to the stage where it is able to exploit, alienate and expropriate labour on an unprecedented global scale. This has the effect of strengthening the hold of capital over labour – in both Western and non-Western contexts.

Summary

In this chapter I have sketched out the Frankfurt School's understanding of the 'culture industry' and identified how its central assumptions have come to underpin a more varied and contemporary critique of the industrialization, aestheticization and (now) globalization of cultural industries and cultural production. For certain critics, Adorno's fears of the impacts of a consolidated 'culture industry' have now become writ large on the global stage.

I then examined cultural work. While Frankfurt School theorists largely ignored work, or assumed its generally alienating effect, more recent studies in the cultural industries tradition have overcome the problem of the 'missing subject' and identified the durability of elements of creative craft production, but within a broader pessimistic scenario that continues to emphasize the socially damaging effects of the commodification and industrialization of culture (Garnham, 1990; Ryan, 1992). More recently, critics have argued that globalization and more 'flexible' economic conditions have further undermined (rather than enhanced) the autonomous and creative foundations of cultural work – either through the widespread imposition of neo-liberal systems of work which prioritize the production of marketable formats over craft-production values (Bourdieu, 1998; McRobbie, 2002a; Ryan, 1992; Williams, 1980) or through the development of standardized forms of technologically driven and closely managed 'immaterial' production (Lazzarato, 1996; Hardt and Negri, 2000).

Overall, these accounts do not present a positive reading of cultural work. While some critics offer that the necessity of producing innovative goods of distinctive aesthetic content has ensured that artists and creative workers have been part protected from some of the more stringent features of economic rationality, this essential contradiction of cultural work, that unruly creativity is necessary in order to generate new goods for standardized production and consumption, appears to be overcome by the skill and veracity with which corporations can now market and advertise recycled, formulaic and standardized goods as brand new innovations. For critical theory approaches, the possibility of genuine and original creativity is slowly being eroded by the increasingly rational process of cultural production – as Ryan, Garnham, Hesmondhalgh and others have argued. For more radical critics such as Scherzinger (2005), the process of cultural commodification, and the attendant alienation of cultural labour, now appears complete.

Overall, then, the 'critical theory' approach provides a comprehensive and compelling critique. Indeed, without wishing to gloss over its internal variations, its basic premises – that capitalist cultural production is inauthentic and corrosive and cultural work alienating and dehumanized – now provides the basis of the orthodox social science understanding of the cultural industries. There are, however, some shortcomings of this perspective. First, there is a somewhat schematic focus on the macro-level of analysis, on the broad trends of production, and a concomitant tendency to spotlight only the larger national and global corporations of the cultural industry landscape. Critical theorists downplay the diverse range of cultural production that takes place at the micro or local level, amongst a differentiated range of producers, and so consequently underestimate how small and 'independent' production of this nature remain both quantitatively and qualitatively significant. Furthermore, there is a general tendency to downplay the importance of *non*-market oriented forms of cultural production – a point we will return to in Chapter 5. Second, as I have shown, a major problem with the critical theory approach is that it tends to operate with a somewhat blunt, binary notion of power, one that sees corporations imposing their will from the 'top' upon fragile, subjugated workers situated at the 'bottom' of the hierarchy. Even post-Adornian discussion of 'autonomous' craft production, with its notion of a more active subject, still tends to emphasize the fragile and uncertain freedoms of work and the constant threats posed by the rationalizing tendencies of the more powerful corporation 'above'. We might question how far this represents an adequate representation of the way power actually operates in workplace environments. For example, while the cultural industries might increasingly impose some kind of assembly line logic on creative craft production, as other social scientists have begun to suggest, the possibilities within firms for worker subordination, resistance and counter-rational practice are underemphasized in critical theory accounts. As Negus avers, reflecting on his observations regarding the 'failures' of corporations such as Sony to fully implement managerial strategy and meet accumulation targets, cultural work is a 'messy' affair where the victory of corporations and management is rarely guaranteed:

> The general point I am making … is about the 'lack of fit' between the rational, macro structures of ownership which are put in place by the corporation through formal acquisitions, and the more messy informal world of human actions, working relationships and cultural

meanings through which companies goals have to be realized on a day-to-day basis. Proponents of the 'corporate control' model such as Adorno and Horkheimer certainly have a point about the way in which large corporations own the technical means of producing and distributing products and reap the economic rewards of the products created by staff. But what they neglect is the way in which cultural production is not simply a technical and economic activity. (Negus, 1997, p. 94–95)

Indeed, Negus's insights suggest that cultural production is a process part-filtered through the *actions of subjects*, ones embedded in particular communities, occupational cultures and motivated by a whole plethora of non-economic social values and political attitudes – ones that can moderate or even usurp corporate intentions. Implied here is a positive re-evaluation of the individual and individualization in cultural work– an argument explored by the likes of Beck (1992), Giddens (1991), Keat (2000) and Lash and Urry (1994) and one I will return to more fully in Chapter 5.

However, for the time being, my concern is with further exploring the more pessimistic critiques of cultural work. In the next chapter, I do this by considering the mooted *governmentalization* of cultural work. Here, critics have sought to examine how power operates 'on the ground', and in doing so, have moved the critical discourse away from a macro-level analysis with its dualistic notion of power to a somewhat more nuanced and micro-level reading of how capital and labour inter-relate in embedded contexts of cultural production – one where, it seems, the manager's role is to facilitate rather than dominate, and where workers themselves appear more actively complicit in their own subjugation.

3
Governmentality and Cultural Work

The previous chapter depicted the 'culture industry' as an asymmetrical field of power, where workers appear to meekly accept their fate, powerless to resist, while the dictates and drives of corporations appear fully formed, coherent and uniformly applied. While useful, this binary theory of power has its limits for helping us to develop a full critique of cultural work, not least for its propensity to treat power only as a given property of the powerful and ignore the power that may reside 'below', so to speak, in varied or diffuse forms. Such an approach also fails to analyse the mechanisms by which power is applied in terms of the specific practices, circumstances and effects that are required in order to ensure that workers behave in the way that managers require. Furthermore, it provides only a schematic account of individual subjectivity and appears to disclaim the possibility of worker autonomy and free action. However, some consideration of these absent issues *can* be found within what we might refer to as a 'governmental' theory of cultural work, one that theorizes the immanence of power in all social contexts and seeks to evaluate the everyday discourses and procedures that help social structures (and, crucially, subjects themselves) to reproduce relations of power. In this chapter I examine how such an approach has helped extend the scope of the conventional critical theory of cultural work, by directing attention towards what Read (2003) has elsewhere referred to as the situated 'micro politics of capital'.

Here, then, the aim is to more fully examine the ways in which cultural workers might be understood as 'governed' subjects, that is, as individuals whose fate and fortunes are, in substantial ways, prescribed by authorities that seek to 'apply economy' (Foucault, 1991, p. 92) to the management and administration of populations. Governmentality approaches suggest that societies are no longer dominated by a centralized, core authority but tend to be administered by a diverse array of agencies and authorities that employ a variety of 'technical' means in an attempt to shape the conduct of social and economic life. Central to this 'conduct of conduct' is the manipulation of individuals' 'desires, aspirations, interests and beliefs' (Dean, 1999, p. 11), not through overt domination, but, first, through *discourses* that provide the communicative 'means through which regimes of power are enunciated' (Rojek, 2001, p. 36), and, second, through ensuring that subjects are embedded in institutional contexts that enable the *self-exercise* of power. This marks a distinctive break with post-Adornian critique and the Marxism of the 'missing subject', since it posits that power is not the preserve of capitalists or the dominant class, a simple force to be impressed on docile labour, but a phenomenon that is immanent to all social formations, and one that works *only through* its specific exercise by individuals in embedded social and institutional contexts. Put simply, we might say that while critical theory approaches have suggested that cultural workers are *forced* to accept capitalist relations of production as a consequence of their powerlessness in the face of corporate power, 'neo-Foucauldian' or 'governmental' approaches suggest that workers are trained to accept and reproduce *for themselves* the precise conditions of their subordination.

After a brief discussion outlining the governmental approach, the first part of the chapter concentrates on analysing some of the specific discourses that have arisen in order to 'govern' the activities of cultural firms and the cultural worker. Primarily (following the work of Rose, du Gay and others) I examine how a discourse of 'enterprise' has arisen as a dominant rationality in Western societies – one that now appears to underpin all social and economic policy interventions, including the promotion of cultural industries. In order to demonstrate this, I then examine the particular construction of UK cultural (or now, rather, 'creative') industry policy as a strategy for the promulgation of enterprise discourse and the appropriate disciplinary management of a potentially recalcitrant and unpredictable cultural labour force. Here it is shown that government operates, not through simple domination, but through discourses that attempt to convince subjects of the necessity and benefits of upholding enterprise values in order to expedite successful cultural production. This, for governmentalists, is an example of how cultural policy acts as a 'mechanism of rule'.

The second part of the chapter examines how 'government operates through subjects' (du Gay, 1996, p. 54) by identifying how cultural workers *themselves* are actively implicated in the reproduction of enterprise values. Here I evidence how workers are not reluctantly subjected to forced domination[1] but provided with a certain freedom to self-determine their conduct in relation to an overarching set of norms and values that provide the signposts and guides for enterprise action (Barnett, 1999). By appealing to workers' self-interest and investing them with responsibilities for self-government, workers are offered 'freedom' – but within the limits of the discursively reproduced 'regime of truth' that sets the parameters of acceptable conduct. To evidence this I draw on Ursell's (2000) and (briefly) Tunstall's (1993) examination of how workers in the television industries 'voluntarily' abet the reproduction of power relations through their own ongoing and responsive efforts to uphold, transform or negotiate enterprise values in workplace life. While enterprise values appear inimical to the interests of the cultural worker, it is shown that, paradoxically, workers view the enterprise culture that subjugates them as the only means through which meaningful and autonomous work can be obtained. In this way, as Knights and Willmott (1989, p. 554) argue, technologies of power are accepted precisely because they appear to offer the freedom, security and stability that, in fact, their 'very presence serves to problematise'.

Finally, while the exercise of power may engender in subjects a sense of 'autonomy', and shore up belief in the necessity of upholding enterprise values, in assessing the personal consequences of governmentality I suggest that becoming 'entrepreneurial' may well generate for cultural workers some unintended negative outcomes. In particular, I argue that the pressure to conform and compete in a more market-led and *individualized* economy may bring with it the corollary of social atomization, and a more pronounced need for self-coping as a consequence of disembedding from collectivized environments and structures of support. It is suggested that strong incitements to become more self-directed, self-resourcing and entrepreneurial may enhance possibilities for worker *self-exploitation* and, relatedly, *self-blaming*. As Beck has demonstrated elsewhere, when individuals are forced to become their own enterprise, not only 'success' but 'failure' also become individualized problems demanding biographical solutions (Beck, 1992). I show how incitements to accept self-responsibility in cultural work can result in an enhanced sense of self-abjection and failure. I suggest this problem is particularly evidenced in cultural work since the image of the autonomous 'artist' or self-resourcing 'creative' is widely promoted as the standard and necessary mode of being. The fetishization of creativity, and industry emphases on reproducing personalized, performative and self-directing modes of work ensures that self-exploitation has become more pronounced in this most 'talent'-driven and individualistic of sectors.

The art of governmentality

In recent years, critical social scientists have sought once again to problematize the historically contested notion of 'government'. Without wishing to traduce its complexity, the debate has perhaps been most notable for its revision of two key ideas. First, the long-standing commonsense that 'government' is largely synonymous with 'state' has been challenged; it is no longer satisfactory to simply understand government as *the* Government, that is, a formal body with an established authority to rule over subjects in a given territory. Government is now seen to appear in a multiplicity of formats and locations, under a variety of mechanisms, authorities and auspices (du Gay, 1996). Hence, the term 'government' has come to be more widely used to refer to the range and 'diversity of ways of managing social reality' (du Gay, 1997, p. 296). Second, and relatedly, the notion that the application of power remains a *special privilege* of the state has also been challenged. While the state often appears to be the primary 'source' of power, it has more recently been argued that power itself is a socially diffuse entity, one that is always present and circulating *within* the system rather than being simply imposed from 'on high'. For Foucault, power is ever present and takes on dispersed, multi-variant forms. Power operates in the quotidian spaces of the home and street, school and hospital, as well as the workplace and is embedded in all institutions and agencies of social regulation and control, as well as being embodied in the practices, demands and desires of ordinary actors (Foucault, 1982).

The term 'governmentality' has emerged as part of a new vocabulary and set of concepts geared to understanding the essence of this dynamic of power. The definition of governmentality that Foucault proposes has three dimensions, the first of which is

> The ensemble formed by the institutions, procedures, analyses and reflections, the calculations and tactics that allow the exercise of this very specific albeit complex form of power, which has as its target population, as its principal form of knowledge political economy, and as its essential technical means apparatuses of security. (Foucault, 1991, p. 102)

Foucault also uses the term to refer to the general 'pre-eminence' of government over others forms of power and organizing (such as feudalism or monarchy), and to the manner in which early modern states sought to 'governmentalize' in contradistinction to pre-modern administrative forms; it is, however, this first definition that is of most interest here, for in it lies the essence of what I wish to elaborate regarding the ways in which cultural work is subject to processes of 'governing' and 'rule'.

In this first definition we are alerted to the relationships between social power and discipline of individuals, and the ways in which the political–economic framework of societies are not simply dependent upon the formal government of abstract systems but on the management and control of individual practices and the self. This means that (as Foucault argues), primarily in the interests of capitalism, the micro-processes of social reproduction, right down to the fine detail of, for example, individuals' work, health, family and sexual conduct have become the focus of discipline through calculated mechanisms of administrative control. What is the origin of this imperative?

For Foucault (1977, 1991), the art of government arises as a special concern of post-Enlightenment societies endeavouring to cope with the demands and complexities of administering modernization. In order to ensure appropriate commitments to new kinds of economic production, and to guarantee obeisance to what Foucault (1977, p. 219) refers to as other 'apparatuses of production' (family, law, schooling, military force, health and so on), newly modern populations became the target of an array of discourses designed to demonstrate the *social and personal gains* to be obtained through dutiful compliance. As Miller and Yúdice (2002, p. 5) comment, through discursive and disciplinary regimes, 'the entire social body was assayed and treated for its insufficiencies'. In this process, self-development and the means to self 'autonomy' are presented as only achievable through commitment to certain prescribed standards of behaviour that revolve around compliance with a set of apparently 'natural' norms, values and bodily practices. Socialized into an acceptance of the virtues of rationally managed systems of work, education, punishment, health and so on, and alerted to the psychological and material penalties of non-compliance, populations quickly learnt to reproduce systems 'by themselves' – avoiding a need for the more costly and counter-productive measures employed by more coercive systems of rule. Discipline provided a solution to the problems of order by creating assurances that complex multitudes would be appropriately managed; not through violence or force but through the efficient distribution of stabilizing norms and values and the active encouragement of self-monitoring and self-regulating behaviours. As Rose suggests, 'each individual was to become an active agent in the maintenance of a healthy and efficient polity, exercising a reflexive scrutiny over personal, domestic and familial conduct' (1999, p. 228).

Thus, in this schema, not only does the individual becomes the focus and target of disciplinary discourses and practices that require reflexive self-monitoring but also as an *active subject* must learn to 'make their own life' in the institutional contexts laid down by governmental authorities. Actors are encouraged to believe that they (and not social structures) are the authors of fate; capable beings that script their own actions, and indeed, must actively do so in order to achieve the promise of a meaningful and rewarding life. Foucault's gift is to reveal how techniques of active *individualization* are central to the exercise of power relations, and to expose how individuals are complicit in the execution of power through their own situated practices.

Thus, under governmental rule, agency does not 'entail an escape from power but a specific exercise of it' (Edwards and Nicoll, 2004, p. 162); that is, individuals are trained to become 'self-determining' active subjects, ones who appear to control their own destiny through their own capacities for (say) workfulness, studying, cleanliness, diligence, moral rectitude, modesty, punctuality and so on. Given the ubiquity of power, and the impossibility of evading its effects, individuals become active subjects only in the ways they present and orient themselves towards disciplinary discourses and practices.

Thus, the idea that individuals are somehow deeply implicated in the reproduction of regimes of power is far more pronounced in governmentality perspectives than in conventional 'theories of state', and indeed (here) the critical theorists' notion of cultural work, where populations (and workers) have tended to be theorised as constituencies who have power exercised over them rather than subjects that play an active and immanent role in power's exercise. As Rose (1992, p. 142) suggests, for Foucault, power is understood 'not as a negation of the vitality and capacities of individuals, but as the creation, shaping and utilization of human beings as subjects'. To understand power fully we must take account of the 'ways in which subjectivity has become an essential object and target for certain strategies, tactics and procedures of regulation' (ibid., p. 143). Accordingly, in the next section I examine how cultural workers (as 'active subjects') appear to have become the 'object and target' of disciplinary discourses that surround cultural work.

Governmentality and cultural policy

As we saw in the previous chapter, for critical theorists of cultural work systematic processes of industrialization, including the globalization of capitalist relations of production, are the primary forces that subjugate and alienate workers. But such 'macro' economistic explanations are perhaps insufficient to explain thoroughly the means by which workers are oppressed. Governmentality critics have now alluded to a range of socially embedded 'mechanisms of rule' through which capitalism is reproduced, and its characteristic forms of oppression articulated. Primary are the raft of regulatory discourses and 'calls to action' that permeate the social fabric and help define core norms, values, attitudes and beliefs, particularly regarding how to conduct oneself as a social (and economic) actor. It is arguable that in neo-liberal societies the central discourse that appears to underpin formation of the cultural worker-self is the discourse of *enterprise* (du Gay, 1996; Heelas and Morris, 1992; Rose, 1992, 1999). In the West, the rise of 'enterprise culture' is most closely associated with the radicalized reforms initiated under Thatcherism and 'Reaganomics' during the 1980s; a period when a new policy and public language based on the primacy of individual needs, choice and market competition and a refusal of the necessity of state intervention became dominant. The language of enterprise has since been imported into all policy contexts and, as I now show, the particular register of (what has become known as) 'creative industry' policy captures this imperative fundamentally.

The 'creative industries' as cultural policy

As Dean (1999) suggests, the 'art of government' is characterized by distinctive assemblage of ways of seeing, thinking and perceiving, which we can take to include the institutional generation of theories and plans that outline strategies for more advanced, efficient forms of governing. This has led Miller and Rose (1990) to observe that governmentality has a distinctly programmatic character, in that it not only constantly sets out specific 'programmes' for social improvements (in the form of policies, research, reports etc.) but it is also underpinned by the utopian belief that social reality is innately 'programmable' in terms of it being always amenable to further improvement. Government is characterized by the constant creation, evaluation and repudiation of programmes for reform, not only to secure legitimacy for governmental authority but also to shore up belief in progress and convince populations that the promised land of the good society remains somehow in sight.

The formation of *policy* can thus be viewed as a means for government to create the conditions of its own legitimacy, for, in order to govern, an authority must work to ensure that there are specific and recognizable terrains that require governing, ones that are amenable to the tools and solutions proposed by that authority:

> All government depends on...the elaboration of a language for depicting the domain in question that claims both to grasp the nature of that reality represented, and literally to represent it in a form amenable to political deliberation, argument and scheming... [Government] becomes possible only through discursive mechanisms that represent the domain to be governed as an intelligible field with...limits [and] characteristics whose component parts are linked together in some more or less systematic manner. (Miller and Rose, 1990, cited in du Gay, 1996, p. 325)

I suggest that cultural work and cultural enterprises constitute one such domain. Understood by national and local governments as an emergent sector of 'cultural' or, more usually, 'creative'[2] industries, and thus comprising an 'intelligible field' amenable to the formulations of market and enterprise discourses, national and local governments have attempted to establish the 'reality' of the sector, through such established technical and disciplinary devices as describing, measuring and evaluating and identifying key actors, relationships and processes (Barnett, 1999; Garnham, 2005). In this way, 'creative industries' have been constructed as a coherent and actionable field of activity. Additionally, cultural/creative industry policies are not benign in so far as they are composed, like all policy, of 'purposive attempts to organize and reorganize institutional spaces, their routines, rituals and procedures, and the conduct of actors in specific ways' (Dean, 1999, p. 32). Put more simply, policy utilizes linguistic and representational devices that seek to define the 'problems' of the industry in order to offer demonstrable (and politically desirable) 'solutions'.

To illustrate, I examine one localized, state-specific intervention into the cultural/creative industry policy field. The *Creative Industries Mapping Document* (CIMD) (first published by the UK Government's Department of Culture, Media and Sport (DCMS) in 1998 and updated in 2001) attempts to estimate the size and economic value of United Kingdom 'creative industries' and detail the policy approach necessary to stimulate growth in the sector. In the CIMD, traditional and/or non-economic motivations and incentives to cultural industry activity – such as a desire to engage in self-determining 'craft' production, effect cultural representation, mobilize political critique or simply pursue *ars gratia artis* – are replaced by a relentless emphasis placed on the application of creativity for profit. Alternative rationalities are absent from a document that sees no virtue in idle (i.e. non-economically productive) creativity nor, indeed, recognises the socially progressive possibilities that might be contained within cultural activities that, either intentionally or unintentionally, fail to become fully realised as market commodities. This might be surprising given that the DCMS is ostensibly tasked with a cultural rather than economic remit, yet as the then UK Minister for Creative Industries, James Purnell (2005, no pagination), recently argued in a speech to the Institute for Public Policy Research, the priority now is to 'give the Department a genuine economic edge' and, most blatantly, concern itself with 'how we can turn talent into hits and hits into profit'.

In the CIMD, the discourse of enterprise pervades descriptions of the desirable qualities envisaged to underpin useful creative industry. As Chris Smith, the then Secretary of State for Culture, suggested in the document foreword: 'I want our creative industries to continue to seize the opportunities of a fast-changing world, to think "out of the box," to innovate, to be flexible and swift, and to strive to realise their full potential (DCMS, 2001, p. 3).'

Throughout, the document's emphasis is on the need for businesses to 'pursue flexible strategies' (ibid., p. 13), ensure that their 'potential contribution...is maximised' (ibid., p. 18), and, of course, 'think creatively' (ibid., p. 3) – examples of what Miller and Yúdice (2002, p. 1) refer to as cultural policy's 'systematic, regulatory guides to action'. Discussion of issues of traditional import to cultural policy – such as overcoming inequalities, tackling issues of access, building citizenship, (re)generating community and so on – are absent. Indeed, there is an implicit assumption that such concerns might be tackled in one of two ways: first through economic 'trickledown', that is, because creative industries are seen to be good for economic development and generating 'wealth and employment' (p. 18) then this will automatically translate into wider social benefits, or, second, through the ways Smith implies that the business-led model of applying creativity to strategies for economic growth might usefully serve as a role model for 'societies looking for new ways to tackle [other] issues and improve the quality of life' (ibid., p. 3) – the implication being that other failing social realms are potentially rectifiable providing they adopt an enterprise model.

The CIMD describes the creative industries in distinctive terms. First and foremost, they are construed as the leading edge of the 'knowledge economy' (p. 3) and vital to the competitiveness of the United Kingdom in a global marketplace. Around 13 distinct sectors[3] are identified, separated and methodically ranked in order of their contributions to revenues, employment and exports – the principal means through which their value is ascribed. The distinctive value of each sector is analysed, statistics are provided to indicate the performances of the sectors against international competitors. Firms are presented in wholly objectified terms, they are portrayed as vital nodes or 'hubs' in an emergent network of global producers, as fundamentally rational organizations, engaged in mechanistic pursuit of profitability and growth, always pro-active and tactically astute and, as we have seen, inherently 'flexible and swift'. The message is clear; properly creative industries are based on enterprise rather than artistic values.

Yet, of course, despite its accomplishments, the creative industries sector is presented as a sector with 'special needs' (p. 3), ones requiring government interventions in order to effectively mobilize greater success. These needs are articulated in terms that make them appear obviously amenable to current programmes of neo-liberal government. Thus we are told that creative industries are variously deficient in their ability to 'respond to global opportunities' (p. 13), attract 'private support' (p. 15), 'find skilled and creative people' (p. 14) and so on – those needs that belong to alternative value spheres (such as demands for subsidies and state financial support, support for creative freedoms or non-market activities, recognition for forms of minority or oppositional cultural production) are wholly absent; indeed this blindness to non-commercial culture arguably reflects broader transformations in society at large, where the very idea of a non-commercial or non-instrumental cultural public sphere is being made to appear politically suspect (see McGuigan, 2004).

Further, the CIMD states there is a need for industry and government to 'continue to work in partnership' (p. 13). The government's half of this partnership is concerned with applying economy through the encouragement of the latest tools of enterprise management, in order to appear to service the 'special needs' identified before. Thus, government of the creative industries is revealed to be a mechanism for promulgating enterprise initiatives (there are numerous references to the enabling efforts of 'task forces', 'Cultural Consortiums', export advisory groups, Small Business Service, venture capitalists and so on) for facilitating future growth. Indeed, promoting growth and profit and tackling 'issues which impact on [industry] growth potential' (p. 13) is the *raison d'etre* of the document. Further, the traditional role of government, to collect and generate statistics regarding its populations, is evidenced by the insistence of the necessity of obtaining robust data and undertaking 'further research' (passim) in order to ensure 'effective targeting of effort' (p. 17) for fulsome future growth.

As an example of what governmentalists would refer to as a 'mechanism of rule' the *Creative Industry Mapping Document* could be argued to successfully inculcate new economy values into the field of cultural work. It strives to install a prescriptive, default model of 'active entrepreneurship' into the heart of cultural production. Its efficacy in doing so is perhaps indexed by its widespread translation and reiteration in the guise of the plethora of regional and city-based creative industry programmes and initiatives that are now ubiquitous features of the United Kingdom and international policy landscape (DCITA, 2005; Garnham, 2005; Hartley, 2005; Hesmondhalgh, 2005). Of course, the particular effectiveness of the CIMD in promoting entrepreneurial activity is difficult to specify empirically – nonetheless, its uptake and influence on other local, regional and international policy makers suggest that its values have become part of the mainstream doctrines of global 'creative industries' policy – and its claims and principles have come to underpin concrete economic interventions that provide (or deny) resources for cultural industries activity.

The CIMD and its ilk have moved some way from the earlier efforts of local authorities (such as the 1980s Greater London Council) to promote cultural industries as a solution to problems of integrating economic *and* social development; where provision through the market was judged to necessarily coexist with initiatives to promote craft endeavour and activities of community and grass-roots organizations. Today non-commercial creative production in the United Kingdom is becoming increasingly reliant on the dwindling base of local authority arts and culture budgets or the capricious hand of National Lottery funding. It is certainly not recognized as important in terms of 'creative' industry policy thinking and initiative.

'Creative industries' policy, then, is a primary mechanism for inculcating enterprise values into the cultural industries – but it is effectively supported by other governmentalizing 'calls to action'. To take one prominent example, it might be argued that the attraction of cultural work has been further enhanced by the emergence of a more vivid and intensified discourse of 'stardom' and the current widespread fascination with creative celebrities (Rojek, 2001). Related to this, the elevated extension of what McRobbie calls the 'auteur relation' into hitherto mundane arenas of cultural work has proved similarly enticing to prospective workers, as she describes:

> Through the profusion of profiles and interviews with hairdressers, cooks, artists and fashion designers, the public (especially young

people) are presented with endless accounts of the seemingly inherent rewards of creative labour. The flamboyantly *auteur* relation to creative work... is now being extended to a much wider section of a highly 'individuated' workforce. (2002a, p. 517)

Creative or cultural industry 'celebrities' are symbolic testaments to the meritocratic principle idealized to underpin neo-liberal democracies – namely, that anyone can 'make it' providing they possess both talent and individual application.[4] The proliferation of media formats now promoting cultural work, and their increasingly upbeat and uncritical tone, suggests to populations that creative work is both highly prestigious and more easily attainable; yet, for some critics, this is merely one further example of how governmentalizing discourses serve to buttress capitalist values. Rose (1999, p. 261) for example, avers that it is through the 'promotion of "lifestyle" by the mass media, by advertising and by experts, through the obligation to shape a life through choices in a world of self-referenced objects and images, that the modern subject is governed'.

To summarize, cultural policy (in the form of 'creative industries' promotion) increasingly acts to prescribe and 'govern' the character of cultural production and, in turn, cultural work. Such policy is predicated less on domination or coercion and more on convincing populations that creative industry jobs are both good for the economy and good for the *self* in that they offer enhanced opportunities for workers to obtain meaning, self-fulfilment and personal autonomy in their work. In the context of wider discourses of enterprise, such as the positive affirmation now given to the individual pursuit of wealth, celebrity and fame, such incitements may lead people into forms of cultural work that are widely promoted as being autonomous, 'creative' and lucrative, yet, for the majority, will offer no such rewards. It is these (and other supporting) discourses that now act to provide the intellectual resources for helping populations define the 'reality' of the cultural work domain.

Governing cultural workers

While enterprise discourses may incite people to take up cultural industry occupations, how are people actually governed once they arrive at work? Here, government comes into its own in the context of discrete practices of *management*. As du Gay (1996) and Thrift (2002) have argued, the rise of new managerial discourses of 'total quality management', 'corporate excellence', 'creativity', 'team-building' and so on have become more prominent in recent years, buoyed by the new prestige afforded to enterprise, and the necessity of ensuring effective competitiveness in high-stakes market economies. For theorists of government, the power of managerial discourse lies in its abilities to set the ground rules for individual and collective workplace action, helping to construct 'mechanisms of rule' that reproduce hierarchies and set the frameworks of responsibility and reward allocation in firms, as well as helping to embed workers within the productive life of society at large. Discourses help socialize workers into an acceptance of the necessity of a culture of enterprise and help map their own role within it – as du Gay (1996, p. 53) offers, the efficacy of discourses derives from their capacity to ensure that 'people come to identify themselves and conceive of their interests in terms of those new words and images and formulate their objectives in relation to them'. Self-identification is crucial, for, as du Gay further details in his studies of retail management in the fashion and beauty sector, while managers efforts to control the workplace are thoroughgoing and pervasive, it is vital that workers recognize the corporate culture as not simply authoritarian but as individually 'empowering':

[T]he internal world of the retail enterprise is being re-imagined through the discourse of enterprise as one in which customers' needs and desires are to be satisfied, productivity is to be enhanced, quality service guaranteed, flexibility increased and innovation fostered through the active engagement of the self-fulfilling impulses of all the organizations' members... Within retailing organizations, store managers and shopfloor employees are increasingly represented as enterprising subjects: that is, individuals who calculate about themselves and work upon themselves in order to better themselves; in other words, as people who live their lives as an 'enterprise of the self'. (du Gay, 1996, p. 145; see also Rose, 1990)

Here du Gay further reiterates a crucial claim of governmentality theories, namely, that workers are not 'dominated' into passivity but are themselves active and part responsible for ensuring the efficacy of mechanisms of rule. Foucault's understanding of power as multiple and strategic, unconfined to one overarching source or authority, is realized in the ways in which cultural workers in apparently disempowered contexts might themselves be identified as active agents of power.

Indeed, this recognition of the importance of the desires, plans and actions of cultural workers is partly what distinguishes the governmentality critique from the critical theory approaches previously discussed. For example, Ursell's (2000) work on the UK television industry provides an illuminating example of the ways in which freelance workers, precariously positioned in a highly flexibilized, deregulated industry, both choose to accept and reinforce patterns of governmental rule, not only through accepting the ignoble constraints of enterprise culture but also in actively seeking to form their own structures of enterprise in order to indemnify personal rewards. As she identifies, freelance producers, writers, directors and so on now make-up the majority of the workforce in heavily commercialized and vertically disintegrated economy of television production (see also Tunstall, 1993; Willis and Dex, 2003). Following some stringent measures of deregulation in the 1990s, a marked intensification of industry competition has seen television and, indeed, other media sectors, seek to reduce costs and offload risks by shedding expensive tied-labour, thus forcing the bulk of television industry workers to become independent or self-employed freelancers. Required to be actively entrepreneurial and self-promoting, television industry workers must work hard to ensure that they, and not one of the many thousands of other similarly qualified competitors, secure the all important short-term contract. In the context of freelance production, Ursell argues that, crucially, it is freelancers *themselves* who have largely taken on the task of constructing and regulating their own labour markets. It is they who must identify and recruit labour for the commissioned project, they who are charged with responsibilities for constructing and delivering projects to the executive producer in the commissioning company, and it is they who are in control of the regulation and disciplining of co-workers. The strategies employed to do this, as Ursell notes, are devised by the freelance producers themselves and tend to involve entrepreneurial forms of recruitment, such as recruiting through networks or informal economies of favours, and often involve seeking to reduce downstream costs by haggling over the costs of labour and various inputs required to realize any given project. Tunstall (1993) in his account of television production work also captures the scenario well:

> The producer of a series run often has one, two or three million pounds to spend; and there are several possible strategic paths which could be followed. Do you do all the location filming first? Do you work alternate weekends? Do you start in the studio when the days

are shorter in March? In the past all such decisions were heavily influenced by union rules. Now it is the producer who sits down, maybe for quite a long time, worrying away at the cheapest and most efficient use of the available time, resources and people. The producer makes a management plan, carries it out and is held responsible for it. (Tunstall, 1993, p. 206)

Thus, precariously positioned freelancers are themselves actively implicated in reproducing enterprise values through their own strategies of economizing, giving credence to the claim that workers may voluntarily seek to uphold systems of power that – while ostensibly appearing to undermine and diminish personal security and interests – also appear to provide the only means for establishing the precarious rewards that are being offered. Why do they do this? Knights and McCabe volunteer an explanation: 'Employees welcome a sense of self-organization; for when individuals organize their (our) own work it becomes more meaningful and therefore its intensification may be ignored or even denied' (Knights and McCabe, 2003, p. 1588).

To be (or to appear to be) in control of ones' destiny is what encourages workers to endorse the systems put in place to expedite flexible production. In television, the 'seduction of autonomy' (Knights and McCabe, 2003, p. 1613) is sufficiently powerful to override any misgivings, constraints or disadvantages that might emerge in the everyday reproduction of this highly competitive and uncertain domain. The pay-off for enhanced uncertainty and employment risk, television workers are told, is the freedom to work more flexibly, informally and in accordance with ones' own biographical preferences and ambitions. An example of how, as Foucault (1982) argued, the application of power can proceed only through the provision of freedom.

In other sectors critics have now alerted us to the prevalence of enterprise discourses and the pervasive individualization of cultural industries employment (see for example Bourdieu, 1998 on television; Crewe, Gregson and Brooks, 2003 on independent fashion retailing; Gibson, 2003 on popular music; McRobbie 2002a, b for a more general overview). While individualization, as Beck (1992) argues, can imply the progressive breaking of social bonds, in the case of newly 'flexible' cultural work, it appears for others to involve a more regressive shifting of collective, social responsibilities onto the shoulders of individuals, and the absolving of corporate responsibility to uphold traditional social obligations, forms of worker support and protection and collective systems of reward. McRobbie (2002a, b) argues that 'being flexible' essentially means that one must do whatever is required to support commercial interests. It increasingly requires working longer or unsocial hours, taking on-board additional responsibilities, relocating according to company demands and certainly committing oneself to the commercial imperatives of the firm over and above non-work commitments (Blair, 2003; Gill, 2002; Richards and Milestone, 2000; Ursell, 2000). Currently valued are those 'flexible', 'creative' workers with the ability to 'go the extra mile', 'think outside the box', 'live for the project' and show dedication by working long hours or under oppressive circumstances. To be described as a regular '9–5' worker is no longer a commendation of diligence but a term of disapprobation. While flexible working is found in other industrial sectors, its virtues are more vigorously promoted in the *cultural* industries, where positive connotations of creativity, independence and nonconformity are used to underwrite the promotion of these non-traditional styles of work that appear to offer choice and flexibility for workers, but are more likely designed to ensure that firms extract greater surplus values from labour. Correspondent with the celebration of the flexible, self-directed, 'creative' worker, comes a heightened focus on assessing individual 'performance' and the pervasive individualization of systems of reward (Bourdieu, 1998; Gibson, 2003; McRobbie 2002a; Nixon, 2003; Ursell, 2000). Today, individuals are perpetually required to demonstrate their co-operation with enterprise ideals, in work and beyond, and are ever reminded of their responsibilities by programmes of government that promote working as the primary social obligation. Yet, the discourse of enterprise and the informal cultures of production that permeate cultural work endow workers with the belief that they are somehow freer than 'wage slaves' or those unfortunates working in mundane occupations elsewhere – so helping to guarantee their ongoing co-operation.

But are workers simply fooling themselves here? As Ursell (2000) notes, there is strong evidence of collectively generated systems of status and hierarchy and self-determined patterns of governmental rule in freelance production contexts that can lead not only to exploitation of co-workers but also to reductive forms of *self*-exploitation. That is, just as freelancers might on occasion gain from these flexible systems of rule (down pressing wages, calling in favours) so they might also end up becoming their victim; being underpaid or having to work for nothing on a 'prestige' project, exhaustively covering multiple roles to save costs, or exploited by the commissioner due to an absence or insufficiency of legal protection in increasingly informalized or casualized employment contexts. In breaking the bonds of tradition, the governmentalized, individualized cultural workplace can inveigle workers into a precarious and high-risk game of economic survival – one that may have damaging consequences for the self. Indeed, as I now explore, for that growing body of cultural workers who are the targets of mechanisms of rule, the provision of 'freedom' may prove to be partial or even entirely illusory.

The consequences for the self

The governmental critique emphasises the ways in which the operation of power is dependent upon 'freedom of choice', but what are the real consequences of these choices? Workers may appear to accept the necessity of self-management and promotion, but how do such workers negotiate the demands of production? And what are the emotional consequences of making oneself into an enterprise subject?

Self-exploitation

As Bourdieu starkly reminds us, serious stresses stem from the intensity of pressures now endured by reflexive workers:

> Thus the absolute reign of flexibility is established ... [and] competition is extended to individuals themselves, through the individualisation of the wage relationship: establishment of individual performance objectives, individual performance evaluations, permanent evaluation, individual salary increases or granting of bonuses as a function of competence and of individual merit; individualised career paths; strategies of "delegating responsibility" tending to ensure the self-exploitation of staff who, simple wage labourers in relations of strong hierarchical dependence, are at the same time held responsible for their sales, their products, their branch, their store, etc., as though they were independent contractors. (Bourdieu, 1998, p. 1)

For Bourdieu, a systemic transferral of responsibility from collective to individual domains is acknowledged as a root cause of increased levels of workplace anxiety, stress and other forms of debilitation – indeed, it is not too fanciful to suggest that Bourdieu blames flexible, individualized work for turning self-reliance into a modern pathology.

While firms and institutions continue to individualize, in the manner Bourdieu suggests, it is arguable that it is in the context of *self-*employment where the stresses and strains of individualization are most keenly felt; for in such situations entrepreneurs are often wholly self-reliant and unable to rely on *any* kind of institutional support (Douglas, 1992). Single entrepreneurs or contracted freelancers, typically working in solitary, 'virtual' or 'network' environments, may have little recourse to the plexus of support offered by managers, colleagues, the union or the occupational therapist – indeed, in such environments, these structures may simply not exist.

In addition to the absolute primacy of discourses of creative self-application, it is highly likely that the particular *allure and glamour* of the cultural industries further leads workers (particularly those self-employed in small/micro enterprises) to self-exploit. In the particular case of cultural industries, workers carry the burden of creative aspiration and dreams of artistic 'consecration' (Bourdieu, 1993) into the highly competitive market arena and the popular idea that cultural workers need to suffer to make great(er) art may further encourage individuals to self-exploit to a level beyond that which would be imposed by the most fervent of capitalist employers (McRobbie, 1998). In short, we might say that the love of art can lead workers to neglect the care of the self. As Gibson (2003) reveals, dreams of future fame are often sufficient to sustain music industry workers even under the most oppressive and burdensome of workplace circumstances. Gill (2002), McRobbie (1998, 2002a) and Ursell (2006) similarly argue that it is not uncommon to find self-employed fashion designers, web designers, television workers, artists and so on working long hours, often through the night or over weekends, taking no holidays, drawing a minimal (if any) salary, skipping meals and rest, forever pushing themselves to the limit in order to not only satisfy their own passion for creative self-realisation but also (and perhaps more often) to meet deadlines and contractual obligations imposed by others.

In order to evidence more specific instances of self-exploitation, I turn to McRobbie's (1998, 2002a) in-depth study of a group of young fashion designers in London. While initially optimistic regarding the capacity of designers to evade the problem, she has since suggested (McRobbie, 2002a) that self-exploitation has become an inevitable function of an industry that tends to treat its workers as little more than expendable chattels. For independent designers, the tight control exerted by the majors over the conditions of collaboration was usually the precondition for self-exploitation. Collaborations with majors meant heavy workloads, specialized production demands and unique contractual specifications that independents needed to fulfil or risk being replaced by someone more malleable and compliant. Further, the relative lack of financial, institutional or infrastructural support in independent fashion (in the way of creative finance experts, specialist business advice agencies, investors, mentors, workspaces) often led

McRobbie's designers to take on a surplus of roles in their own (or others) firm (and sometimes second jobs), so further increasing the burden of self-responsibility. Arguably, under such intense conditions, self-exploitation becomes inevitable.[5]

As in McRobbie's study, a number of designers I have interviewed found that collaboration with major retailers led to the imposition of oppressive production demands and encouraged the propensity to overwork in order to ensure that the required quantity and quality of production was maintained. Designers reported on the perceived injustices and unreasonable demands imposed by such collaborations and reflected on the resultant negative impacts on their own working conditions (Banks, 2000). Yet, it was the more mundane, day to day strains of cultural entrepreneurship that most readily incited self-exploitative tendencies.

To take an illustrative example, amongst those interviewed was 'Sonia', an independent fashion designer, running her own retail unit in Manchester city centre. Her self-professed desires for a 'creative' career and her enthusiasm for design, manufacturing and selling her own clothes had made her typical of many young designers emerging from local universities. What she also shared with many of her peers was a profound lack of business skills, few opportunities for training and great difficulty in managing manufacturing, retailing and financial aspects of her business. To offset this, at first, Sonia went into business with another similarly positioned designer, and while this generated benefits, it is fair to say that the overall experience for both of them proved to be extremely demanding:

> If I'd been on my own I just couldn't have done it. But the girl I was with it made it easier, it was brilliant, she virtually moved into my house, one of us would be working here the other would be sewing at home. We'd come home, have tea, watch TV until about eight o clock and then we'd start work again and we'd work until about three in the morning and one of us would go to bed, whoever was going into the shop, the other person would stay up. And we did that solidly for six months and we looked dreadful. Nobody could believe how hard we worked.

While this kept the business alive, it had impacts in other areas, not least in affecting Sonia's ability to learn and develop necessary new skills:

> But if you're successful and things are going [well], then you're on that circle where you don't find out anything about the business,

you don't learn anything because you don't have the time to think hang on how can I make this easier? How can I offload some of this? Because you're just in a panic you know?

The rhetoric of enterprise culture places great emphasis on entrepreneurial 'war stories' particularly regarding rites of passage and 'hard knocks' to be endured while building a business. Sonia's story might be dismissed by neo-liberals as part of the evolutionary struggles of economic life, a necessary phase to be endured in the short-term before failure or success is eventually decided. However, Sonia revealed in an interview that she had actually worked under those intense conditions for almost three years – and in the subsequent six years in business had seen only minor improvements in income and working conditions – indeed the future appeared to offer only the further prospect of meagre rewards and indefinite self-exploitation.

We might ask of Sonia, 'Why does she go on'? Why not seek out a plausible escape route from the precarious grind of fashion design and retail? The answer was revealed when Sonia was prompted to talk about her *feelings* for her work, her motivations, energies and ambitions; this was when, miraculously, the dark clouds were suddenly dispelled:

Sometimes it's really really awful because like your friends are all in fabulous jobs and it's really really secure, and they've finished their PhD's and just managed to find the job of their dreams and you just think...then you remind yourself that you actually like what you're doing and I have a fabulous lifestyle....It's not really about money long term because you wouldn't be doing this, no way. It's just about satisfying something.

Sonia is not an isolated case. The charms and allure of cultural work, the desire to be artistic, autonomous, creative and self-directed was further revealed in interviews with other fashion designers, as first 'Sally', and then 'Louise', here typify

The business was totally secondary. It was nothing to do with anything, I mean I was just...making things that I liked. Money was good but it was I kind of would have done it regardless I think. I would imagine I would have carried on, I can't imagine *not* doing it.

Usually I work every day of the week, three days last week I did over 12 hours...But I do it not for money but for love.[6]

In exasperation, McRobbie (2002a, p. 521) asks, what are to make of the 'young woman fashion designer working 18 hour days and doing her own sewing to complete an order, 'loving' her work but self-exploiting herself'? The appeal of symbolic production lies precisely in its possibilities for providing creative fulfilment – yet such desires can lead to enhanced self-exploitation. In all forms of creative cultural work, the 'seduction of autonomy' is strong enough for workers to deny the hardships of individualized work and to eclipse the feelings of exhaustion and despair. As Ursell similarly identifies in relation to the television industry, cultural workers occupy a contradictory space where self-application leads to the enhancement of both personal freedom and constraint:

> The willingness of individuals to work in television production is partly to be explained by the tantalizing possibilities thereby for securing social recognition and acclaim, that is self-affirmation and public esteem, and partly by the possibilities for self-actualization and creativity (be it aesthetic or commercially entrepreneurial). For the workers, television production is simultaneously a source of potential rewards, both material and existential, and a source of definite exploitation. At its heart are processes of commodification, in large part activated and realized by workers themselves. (2000, p. 819)

This provides a further example of the 'intimate connection between subjectification and subjection' (Ursell, 2000, p. 821), where the pursuit of individual freedoms provides a strong incentive to work, yet takes place within conditions set down by capitalist production and its associated mechanisms of governmental rule. In fashion, as in television, and in other cultural sectors, the price of 'creative freedom' may be unduly high.

Self-blaming

The corollary of being responsible for one's own personal development and success comes, naturally, in an enhanced sense of responsibility for one's personal failure. We might therefore suggest that a further consequence of governmentalized work comes in the form of an enhanced culture of *self-blaming*. Self-blaming arises as traditional explanations of business failure – such as recession and economic downturns, lack of governmental support, bureaucratic inefficiency or institutional uncompetitiveness – lose their legitimacy in a more individualized economic climate. In the enterprise-led economy the entrepreneur/worker has 'only themselves to blame' for the shortcomings of their business or occupational disaffection – it is the individual who is not creative, pushy or talented enough, rather than an economic system that can only ever provide a limited number of winners (and substantially more losers). Economic failure is increasingly presented as failure of the self. In cultural work, self-remonstrations take on the form of 'I'm not creative enough' or 'I just don't have the talent' or 'my designs were no good'. As Beck and Beck-Gernsheim suggest, such forms of self-blaming are not isolated instances of individual perception; rather they now reflect what has become a 'culturally binding mode of attribution' one founded on the principle of 'your own life-your own failure' (2002, p. 24).

So, while self-reflexivity is widely promoted as a positive outcome of the move towards new flexible and enterprise-led regimes of work – enabling workers to plan, reflect on and re-evaluate their endeavours, and anticipate the consequences of future actions – it is also the case that self-reflexivity can engender a turn 'against' the self, as perceptions of failure generate pathological tendencies in the form of self-criticism and blame; for, as McRobbie suggests, self-reflexivity not only carries an emancipatory potential but is also, simultaneously,

> a form of self-disciplining where subjects of the new enterprise culture are increasingly called upon to inspect themselves and their prac-tices, in the absence of structures of social support (other than indi-vidualized counseling services), then reflexivity marks the space of social responsibility, self blame. In this sense, it is a de-politicizing, de-socializing mechanism: 'Where have I gone wrong?' (McRobbie 2002a, p. 522)

As the likes of Bauman, Giddens and Beck have long argued, the com-pulsive self-management of risk has come to characterize the contem-porary workplace; decisions historically negotiated in the context of institutional, collective or community contexts have been devolved to the individual level. Thus, to return to Sonia, an enforced and unsatis-factory engagement with networks of 'expert systems' (business and enterprise support agencies, training and education organizations, banks, accountants, suppliers and collaborators) had unleashed various psychological stresses, leading to feelings of disenchantment, low self-esteem and lack of self-confidence – she often referred to her own feel-ings of ineptitude when dealing with the 'experts'. When asked how she coped with the problems in the business, she revealed a tendency to turn inwards on herself:'It is awful you know, because you bring it all back on yourself all the time, you just think it's me, it's me because you *are* [the business] and you can't get away from it.'

As Douglas writes, failure in individualized situations 'meets none of the kindly exonerations that failure meets in a hierarchy' (1992, p. 231) – self-blame and the search for 'biographical solutions' now represent significant stresses to be endured by the modern worker, alone. Once again, (as in Ursell's sample of television workers) only Sonia's deep-seated love of work and her powerful sense of autonomy and creative freedom were able to offset these feelings of failure. Here then we see a further fundamental contradiction of the art–commerce relation; for while art and craft production can progressively challenge or moderate the pursuit of market values (embodied in the actions of autonomous workers), commercial concerns are also prone to exploit the worker's characteristic love of their art by making more excessive demands on workers' time and efforts, safe in the knowledge that they will feel sufficiently 'aesthetically motivated' to tolerate even the most oppressive of working conditions.

It is clear that self-blaming further intensifies as institutional authorities and mechanisms are absolved of responsibility for entrepreneurial failure. Faced with a multiplicity of discourses that reinforce the autonomy, and thus potential culpability, of the 'enterprising self', success and failure are understood as a triumphs and tragedies of individual design. In this way, it is easy to see how 'social problems can be turned directly into psychological dispositions: into guilt feelings, anxieties, conflicts and neuroses' (Beck and Beck-Gernsheim 2002, p. 24). As Bauman offers, 'risks and contradictions go on being socially produced; it is just the duty and the necessity to cope with them that are being individualized' (2001, p. 34), and, as McRobbie (2002a) further reminds us, it is of course highly *convenient* for capitalism to have an individualized workforce of self-governing self-exploiters driven to succeed (or fail) through their own talent and effort – for this can only help further the retreat of systemic obligations to provide those costly social safety nets that would offset the more deleterious social impacts of entrepreneurial failure. What remains unclear is how far the sense of creative 'freedom' articulated by Sonia (and so many others) can offset the risks, constraints and problems imposed by neo-liberalized market systems.

Summary

In this chapter, the passive 'alienated worker' of critical theory has been recast as an 'active-but-governed subject'. In contrast to the 'top down' notion of power outlined in Chapter 2, I have sought to demonstrate how the cultural worker has come to be governed, not by force or coercion but by subjectivizing discourses of enterprise; ones that take on multiple forms as they underpin policy interventions, pervade institutions of social reproduction and stimulate self-regulating practices in work and everyday life. In the context of cultural work, techniques of governmentality have been doubly evidenced, first, in the construction of cultural policy (and other supporting) enterprise discourses and second, in the situated practice of constructing the entrepreneurial, creative self. The argument that has been made is that the relationship between 'subject and subjection' is more pronounced in the cultural sector given the emphasis placed on entrepreneurial self-application *and* on promoting the self-absorbed pursuit of creative fulfilment, consecration and/or stardom above other competing interests.

The binary model of power that underpins critical theory approaches has been shown to be a blunt instrument compared with the ability of governmental analysis to highlight micro-political conflicts in embedded workplace settings, where subjects and subjection are intimately entwined. As Barratt has noted, neo-Foucauldians 'have challenged forms of analysis which privilege a single (economic) form of oppression [and] begun to highlight the dominant 'logics' or regimes of truth which underpin the organisation of the workplace, the processes of shaping and enacting identities which occur in that context' (2004, p. 193).

Workers have been shown to work, not necessarily because they are forced to, but because they *choose* to – albeit within a prescribed discursive and practical framework that part determines and mediates that choice.

The governmentality critique has also been most revealing in its dissection of the ways in which power is continually being recast and internalised into routine, self-directed behaviour. It is arguable that the pervasiveness and power of an ethic of self-determination and the tendency amongst cultural workers to occupy (what can appear) a state of self-exploitative delusion can be partially attributed to the success of neo-liberal cultural and economic policy, and to discourses of self-management and enterprise in promoting their own virtue at the expense of alternative realms of identification based on competing forms of value. The notion of state and systemic power being embodied in the constitution of the active self appears all too evident in the ways in which workers appear willing to subjugate themselves to the 'desocializing' demands of markets. The capacity for self-exploitation in cultural work is evidenced in the willingness of workers to accept oppressive conditions as the necessary price for 'creative freedom' and, as such, tends to reflect a broader movement towards voluntary self-monitoring and abasement in the interests of accumulation and ostensible self-development. Workers are being conditioned to adopt a self-exploitative, self-blaming mode.

Is there a way out? Certainly, if workers do feel alienated or oppressed, one obvious (traditional) course of action is to collectivize and strive for improved terms and conditions. Indeed, the fact that government is not irresistible and routinely fails (Foucault, 1991) should provide at least some opportunities for self-organized cultural workers to establish more equitable or just working conditions. Yet, as critics now tell us, this is perhaps less likely to happen than in cultural industries than in other, more traditional sectors since governmental incitements to adhere to 'creative' enterprise values appear particularly strong. As McRobbie (2002a) surmises, the thoroughgoing individualization of cultural work, with its intrinsic preference for newness and novelty, its fetishization of individual, 'creative' talent and its preference for personalized, performative modes of work, increasingly appears, perhaps more than other industries, to render collective identities extraneous or redundant. Perhaps it is now futile to expect any forms of organizing that might displace the ideological primacy now afforded creative autonomy in the flexible cultural workplace. Indeed, as critics have revealed, the 'charismatic ideology' (Bourdieu, 1993) and 'creative' status of autonomous cultural work has all but corroded efforts to unionize and collectivize in order to offset inequalities and exploitation. Amongst cultural workers, it appears a general antagonism has calcified towards collective forms of action which remain symbolically linked to the tired and pedestrian climate of the 'old' economy. Dazzled by the promise of future fame and locked into discourses that promote the virtues of 'making it', primarily through individual effort and creative talent alone, alternative forms of (self) government appear unlikely to emerge (Gibson, 2003; Löfgren, 2003).

Of course, we should acknowledge that governmentality theory has its critics. For McGuigan, such theory can provide, at best, only a crude summary of the politics of the cultural field, for he argues it is an approach that 'obscures historical distinctions between state and market, politics and economics' and one where 'government and capitalism are treated as undifferentiated elements of disciplinary power' (2004, pp. 15–16). Indeed, there is some truth in McGuigan's observation that government appears as a 'naïve object', that is an under theorized and undifferentiated system that imposes its will on equally undifferentiated and somewhat docile, rather than active, population. For Ursell (2006, p. 163), such an unqualified and broad-brush theory of governmentality tends also to 'detract attention form the elites whose economic and political decision-making continues demonstrably to shape the life experiences and possibilities of the many', for when (as Foucault claimed) power is seen to be everywhere it is simultaneously nowhere – and so it can easily be made to appear that all become 'equally responsible for everything' (ibid., p. 163). Greater effort, therefore, needs to be made to discern the 'actual differences of government' (McGuigan, 2004, p. 16), particularly in terms of how different disciplinary regimes and regulatory practices operate and how, in different social contexts government and resistances to government are able to operate. Barnett (1999) and Sayer (2004a) are similarly critical of those who overemphasize the power of governmental discipline and neglect its capacities to fail, as well as its socially and spatially differential effects.

Indeed, writers often overlook the fact that, as Knights and McCabe (2003) suggest (and as Foucault himself argued), in being provided with the capacity to become self-governing, the opportunity for workers to resist or challenge power becomes enhanced:'Power and knowledge are embedded within social relations such that those whom power is targeted are themselves active participants in its production and reproduction but also in its potential demise through acts of transgression, dissent and resistance' (Knights and McCabe, 2003, p. 1593).

Given that subjectivity is understood by Foucault as the power to act, there should always be possibilities to 'resist the grip' (Foucault, 1977, p. 27) of power even as one is being 'disciplined' by it. Yet it is instructive that while neo-Foucauldian theorists of government often press the claim that power is diffuse and generative, an enabling as well as constraining force, accounts of cultural work (and cultural policy, see Barnett, 1999) have thus far failed to provide compelling evidence that the active subjects of cultural work might be able to significantly offset some of the more totalizing and invasive impacts of market culture.[7] For example, while (drawing on de Certeau, 1984) du Gay details some of the disruptive 'tactics' employed by fashion retail workers in response to the 'strategies' of management – undermining training initiatives, contravening staff-uniform policies, misleading senior managers and the like – he appears to suggest that since these actions tend to be low-key (often hidden) and conducted not 'autonomously of official norms but always in relation to them' (1996, p. 171) they can have only limited transformative potential. That is, tactics merely represent an insubordinate response to, rather than a repudiation of, managerial power – the basic relations of production and control remain intact since more radical challenges to managerial prescriptions would most likely ensure, in practical terms, a failure to progress or outright job loss (see also Bogard, 1996 on the limits to tactical subordination in cultural work).

Thus, for du Gay, workers may have the capacity to 'resist' – but it does not necessarily add up to much. As an alternative, Ursell's (2000) tantalizing but rather underdeveloped claim that workers may undertake cultural work not only as a means of securing pleasure and self-respect but also as a route to new kinds of social networks, affirmations and affiliations offers the prospect that governmentalized economies might offer the potential to develop alternative modes of work with more socially progressive aims and intentions. But how this radical appropriation of government might actually translate into an effective programme of progressive social action remains (in the governmentality literature), as yet, unclear. Similarly, while (breaking out of their techno-pessimism) Hardt and Negri (2000) recognize something of the opportunities opened up by the failure of governmental regimes to control the 'multitudes' of immaterial labourers and newly 'informatized' workers, their analysis stops some way short of outlining practical instances of how governmental rule might be adequately resisted. Outside of the cultural industries literature, in their neo-Foucauldian study of call centres, Knights and McCabe identified insubordinate workers that could 'draw on what is often the subjugated knowledge of their non-work lives to display scepticism and some resistance to the ever-encroaching demands of modern production' (2003, p. 1616), illustrating the potential reversibility of power relations, providing hope that in the cultural industries, governmental rule might be resisted and transformed – yet even here resistance appears somewhat limited and 'tactical' in nature. Thus, for the most part, while government is recognized as a 'congenitally failing operation' (Rose and Miller, 1992, p. 190), critics of cultural work have tended to view challenges to power as minor perturbations that pose little threat to the overarching rationalities of government (Bogard, 1996; du Gay, 1996; McRobbie, 2002a; Miller and Yúdice 2002; Nixon, 2003; Pritchard, 2002; Ursell, 2000) or, as in the case of Hardt and Negri, significant – but yet to be mobilized – potentials. Clearly, the practical capacities of individualized cultural workers to counter corporate instrumentality ought to be more central to Foucauldian/governmental analyses – otherwise, critics run the risk of overemphasizing the controlling and constraining aspects of power, so mirroring the somewhat one-sided notion of power contained within the more conventionally Marxist critical theory approaches.

The possibilities for cultural workers to resist or subvert capitalist 'rule' will be further considered in later chapters. For now, I want to continue the investigation into how the self-steering, enterprising subject is being construed in cultural work, by analysing how the specific phenomenon that is the *creative self* is now being constructed in the routine, everyday contexts of cultural work. In amongst the widespread exhortations for workers to become more 'creative', we find a mode of social control that is preoccupied with promoting through discursive and practical means the social 'duty' of becoming an enterprising subject, but particularly emphasizes the individual personal and social rewards to be gained through voluntarily becoming a member of the what more optimistic observers have identified as a new 'creative class' (Florida, 2002).

4
The Construction of Creativity

Two theories of cultural work have been identified. The broadly defined 'critical theory' tradition has identified the likely alienation of cultural workers as firms and managers seek to manipulate and control the conditions of cultural production 'from above'. In contrast, a theory of 'governmentality' has revealed how cultural workers are now subjected to a range of discourses and practices designed to promote the virtues of *self*-application to capitalistic imperatives. Drawing on both theories, this chapter examines how the idea of 'creativity' – that most valued of assets in the new enterprise-led, cultural industries – has itself become the focus for both 'top-down' *and* self-administered forms of management.

I first comment on the ways in which managers in cultural industry firms seek to define and control the parameters of creativity 'from above'. Drawing on Ryan (1992), I show how firms' efforts to manipulate creativity in craft production stems from a need to ensure that their potentially wayward and undisciplined workforces commit themselves to corporate business imperatives. The imposition of 'top-down' managerial prescriptions for enhancing creativity (notably creative 'project teams') is discussed. Developing Ryan's ideas I then reveal from my own research how managers are increasingly seeking to present *themselves* as creative economic actors, which serves the dual purpose of promoting their own 'special' talents while also undermining the autonomy and unique status historically afforded creative workers in cultural industries craft production. The corporate capacity to prioritise standardized, formatted production, controlled by capable managers, is thus enhanced as creative cultural workers are further deprived of autonomy over their work. The second half of the chapter deals more fully with the ways in which governmental discourses of creativity and enterprise become embodied in actors' 'creative selves' and articulated through the specific management of the creative work environment. Here, I demonstrate how corporate-friendly forms of creativity are discursively constructed and practically reproduced in different workplace contexts, through manipulation of the self and its aspirations and the 'informal' control of the workplace environment. Thus, the aim of this chapter is take a holistic and critical view of the 'creativity issue', drawing on both critical theory and governmental approaches, in order to move toward some general conclusions regarding the meaning and application of creativity in cultural industry management contexts.

The creative fetish

Alongside the rise of cultural or 'creative' industries, Western societies have witnessed an explosion of conferences, commentaries, training tools, policy reports, books and articles devoted to 'creativity' and its effective utilization for competitive economic advantage (see Seltzer and Bentley, 1999; Bilton, 2006; Hartley, 2005; Howkins, 2001; Florida, 2002; Rickards, 1999). Where once creativity in business was deemed extraneous, 'flaky' or irrational it has now been recast as a most desirable corporate asset (Jeffcut and Pratt, 2002; Osborne, 2003). Much business and management literature has attested to the positive benefits of a more creative workplace culture and argued that creativity has become a crucial element for ensuring successful management and effective corporate growth (Bilton, 2006; Stacey, 1996).

Indeed, for some, the pre-eminence of creativity has led to its full institutionalization in the social structure. One prominent intervention has come from Florida (2002) who examines the growing dominance of a diverse cohort of workers whose occupations and social attitudes reflect an economic climate where, in his terms, creativity has become the 'decisive source of competitive advantage' (ibid., p. 5), as he avers:

> The economic need for creativity has registered itself in the rise of a new class, which I call the Creative Class. Some 38 million Americans, 30 percent of all employed people, belong to this new class. I define the core of the Creative Class to include people in science and engineering, architecture and design, education, arts, music and entertainment, whose economic function is to create new ideas, new technology and /or new creative content. (Ibid., p. 8)

For Florida, creativity is not only widespread but the 'new ethos' that 'powers our age' (ibid., p. 5). Howkins (2001) makes a similarly ostentatious claim, suggesting that the so-called creative economy is now becoming the 'dominant economic form' (2001, p. xiv) and people who can generate ideas its most valued assets. In more measured terms, Davis and Scase (2000, p. 2) have offered that creativity is now 'at the foreground of management theory and practice' and likely to become more crucial to production as advanced economies evolve. These observers share a belief that a more creative economy, or an economy where human capacities for creativity are turned towards progressive ends, can overcome social and economic inequalities and effect future economic growth. For example, while Florida suggests creativity is not an 'unmitigated good' he nonetheless sees it as an 'economic force that increases the resources with which we may do good in the world' (2002, p. 325). Howkins and Davis and Scase also tend to see creativity as an abstract, progressive force, and are inclined to underplay its political dimensions, particularly its potential for misapplication in the interests of power.

Recognising these problems, others have taken a more critical line on this prevailing creative fetish. As Osborne has noted, creativity is routinely and uncritically idealized as some transcendental, emancipatory force:

> We live it seems in a veritable age of creativity. Those engaged in the creativity industries – experts of various kinds, managers, media workers, designers, futurologists, public relations practitioners, psychologists, consultants, marketing gurus, educationalists, 'thinkers of the unthinkable', doyens of 'promotional culture', sensationalist artists and postmodern philosophers – all variously signal that to be creative is the highest achievable good. An age in which creativity is actually a kind of moral imperative, then. For who could imaginably be against creativity? (Osborne, 2003, p. 508)

Indeed, creativity is now presented by policy makers and firms as a kind of holistic therapy, an all conquering remedy to soothe the more injurious aspects of modern economic life. Yet, as Pratt has observed, it is perhaps creativity's elusive definition (rather than its calculable impacts) that allows it to serve as managers' and policy-makers' universal remedy:

> The notion of creativity as a unique individual quality that may animate individuals and networks is an attractive yet illusory idea. The notion does not seem held down by mundane issues of application and

implementation and it is perhaps for this reason that politicians like to invoke it as a general 'fix it'. (Pratt, 2004, p. 119)

In sympathy with these more sceptical observers, this chapter seeks to develop a critical analysis of this most magical prescription. It builds on an emerging critical social science perspective that primarily understands creativity as a contested *political and social process*, one where conflicts of interest and struggles for recognition are intrinsic and where the management of creativity is judged inseparable from the wider politics of labour and the structural contexts within which firms now operate (Banks, 2005; Bourdieu, 1993; du Gay, 1996; Jeffcut and Pratt, 2002; Negus and Pickering 2004; Nixon, 2003; Prichard, 2002). Thus, continuing the initial theme of exploring the regressive features of cultural work, this chapter examines the politics of creativity and some of its more dubious impacts on the lives of workers. It challenges more popular, upbeat notions of creativity as only a 'positive input' by showing how the corporate mobilization of apparently 'liberating' discourses and practices of creativity may instead act as camouflage for the pervasive (re)application of some somewhat traditional and instrumentally focussed management practices and business strategies.

Initially, drawing on the work of Ryan (1992), I develop a discussion of managers by elaborating how post-industrial imperatives to develop flexible, responsive and creative cultural industry organizations have led to the emergence of a new kind of 'soft' (Thrift, 1997) or 'creative' manager of craft production. It is offered that through introducing such 'emancipatory' mechanisms as the 'project team', managers are increasingly adopting the seductive veil of 'facilitator' or 'friend of creativity', in order to mask the pervasive reapplication of traditional and formulaic management in the interests of capital accumulation. Further, I show how some managers' increasing efforts to redefine *themselves* as creative, and identify creativity as a general corporate attribute, leads to an undermining (rather than the promotion) of the autonomy and special status traditionally afforded creative workers in cultural industry production. Developing on the governmentality approach of the previous chapter, it is then suggested the promotion of individualized (and highly aestheticized) values in the cultural workplace has led to the emergence of managerially prescribed 'creative selves' and, relatedly, 'creative workplaces'. It is proposed that while these discrete embodiments and environments might offer the appearance of freedom, in reality, their principal effect is to ensure that worker conformity and adherence to corporate goals and accumulation imperatives. In this way we might judge them as broadly 'governmental' forms of control since managers are shown to have a vested interest in ensuring that workers exercise their 'freedom' to forge a creative persona and embed themselves into a corporate-led 'creative culture'.

The new creative manager

As I have intimated, in cultural work managers play an important role in defining, managing and controlling creativity. Indeed, for creativity theorists such as Bilton (2006) it is managers who are judged the crucial brokers of ideas and creativity in the post-industrial 'knowledge' economy. Bilton and Leary (2002) similarly argue that for managers the crucial task is ensuring that creative elements and non-creative elements (what they call the 'suits') can work together to ensure that mutual needs are served and commercial goals obtained. The idea that managers – rather than artists, designers, people more traditionally understood as creative – must now manipulate and control creativity has also become a routine part of new economy rhetoric. Indeed, this reflects a broader shift whereby business itself is now seen to be like an 'art' and, rather than the creative cultural worker, it is those best able to execute *business* that are now seen to be the real 'creatives' – as one manager quoted in Ray and Myers (1989) illustrates:

> The highest art form is really business. It is an extremely creative form, and can be more creative than all the things we classically think of as creative. In business, the tools with which you're working are dynamic: capital and people and markets and ideas. (These tools) all have lives of their own. So take those things and to work with them and reorganize in new and different ways turns out to be a very creative process. (manager from Ray and Myers' study cited in Bacas, 1987/2006, no pagination)[1]

Increasingly then, it is the managerial arena that is perceived to be the crucible of creativity, and the effective manager one who can encourage and stimulate this most precious attribute – but, of course, not for its own sake. The role of the manager is to ensure that creativity is disciplined to the instrumental purposes of the firm – making money remains the overarching objective that structures how creativity is defined, developed and employed.

To further elaborate this process it is worth reflecting again on the work of Ryan (1992) who provides a highly effective Marxian critique of the ways in which creative managers work to uphold accumulation imperatives in cultural industry organisations and firms. Like Davis and Scase (2000), who see creative management as a process of 'mutual adjustment' (drawing on Mintzberg, 1983), Ryan begins by asserting that creative management is a 'remarkably benign' (1992, p. 111) form of control, acting as an enabling rather than constraining force over craft production. Indeed, from his experience in (mostly Australian) publishing, music production, television and the newspaper industry he first avers that creative cultural workers (writers, actors, directors, announcers etc.) are largely able to 'complete their work with minimal supervision' (ibid., p. 111) as their status as 'artists' ensures their protection from some of the more rationalizing strictures and bureaucratic excesses of organizations. Creatives have been further protected as managers have traditionally found it more expedient to extract surplus value from improved distribution, promotion and reproduction than they have from rationalizing creative practice. Nixon (2003) similarly shows how London advertising agencies in the 1990s institutionalized the separation of creative and non-creative functions by establishing creative departments, teams and systems to act as a canopy for the protection of individual creatives. Indeed, such a move was designed to allow the creatives the opportunity to assert their independence and set up a tension between 'creatives' and 'suits' that was seen as conducive to ideas generation. In similar vein, Ryan first sees cultural production as a kind of protected and residually embedded 'craft creativity', where the social relations of production echo those of the 'capitalist workshop' of small scale, independent manufacture that prevailed prior to the advent of a more integrated capitalism characterised by mechanisation, a specialised division of labour and bureaucratic management.

However as his study develops, Ryan begins to observe (in more Weberian fashion) the encroachment of a set of more modern – that is , economically 'rational' and 'bureaucratic' – values into the practice of managing creative craft production. This begins to transform his perception of the nature and extent of the freedom now available to creatives in cultural firms. As firms come under increased pressure to compete in market situations, managers are handed the task of ensuring that creatives temper their muse to meet intensified demands for productivity and efficiency. As Ryan observes, this not only 'diminishes any separation of art and the market' (1992, p. 127), but recasts the relationship between creative cultural worker and creative manager. As the imperatives of accumulation begin to more thoroughly dictate the terms and conditions of work, managers assume a more direct, executive authority, ensuring co-ordinated production of commodities through the use of techniques that rely on traditional bureaucratic distinctions (lines of authority and systems of discipline) as well as implementing functional distinctions between tasks, roles and the permissible actions of individuals. However, in order to mask what are, in effect, re-established relations of domination, and to ensure that some degree of artistic and creative autonomy is retained, Ryan observes how organizations increasingly turn to the 'project team' as a compromise solution to the problem of ensuring controllable, predictable accumulation while avoiding artistic disaffection and creative stasis.

The creative project team circumscribes the dangers of unfettered creativity by imposing a grid of 'authority relations and patterns of consent' (Ryan 1992, p. 133), whilst ostensibly providing a loosely integrated framework for the cultivation of creative autonomy and artistic endeavour. The creative worker is sold the idea of the team on the basis that it provides 'freedom within limits', and retains some semblance of an autonomous role for the creative – alternatively, the project team may well prove attractive to creatives for the ways it can provide legitimation and formal recognition for what may have previously been amorphous and imprecise creative roles. Yet Ryan sees the project team as a device for ensuring that managers have the power to determine the conditions and shape the outcomes of commodity production; and one that prescribes workers must always subjugate themselves to the authority of the team in order to be seen to be performing their roles adequately.

Now, it is not just Ryan's larger cultural corporations and bureaucracies that are subject to the strictures of the 'team'. The concept of the manager as 'team leader' has also become established amongst small and micro cultural industry firms and organizations, as evidence from previous collaborative work has suggested (Banks et al., 2002). Here, in a number of the marketing/advertising and graphic design firms interviewed, managers often talked of the need to regulate or 'reign in' the creative. The following manager, a keen exponent of the 'project team', typified the emergent ethos: 'The creative mind is a very interesting thing to try and control, that's my job in a way.'

Managers routinely defined creative workers as capricious and unpredictable, and often felt unable to trust them to deliver projects in line with the firm's business objectives or client's requirements. This unpredictability was evidenced by what one manager referred to as a tendency for designers to 'design for themselves' and that is why managers had to ensure that they were able to control and adequately stage-manage creative performance – as this manager of a small advertising and graphic design firms articulated: 'The secret of dealing with people like this is to manage the environments so the problems don't arise ... its like herding cats, if they all want to go in different directions they will.'

In these small firms, just as in Ryan's larger organizations, once the 'teams' were established, managers attempts to co-ordinate and discipline the creative process was most clearly evidenced in the pursuit of *formats* (see also Davis and Scase, 2000; Hesmondhalgh, 2007). For cultural firms and organizations, the production of 'more of the same', or at least very similar, represents a commercial strategy for overcoming the indeterminacy and inconsistencies of the cultural marketplace. The mass reproduction and replication of formats and genres in film, television, photography, music, and literature and so on is based on the assumption that stylistic variations on established successful themes are more likely to succeed commercially than untried, speculative products.

Ryan gives an example of the production planning undertaken by Australia's Grundy Television for a new police drama series, *'Bellamy'.* Here, based on rational audience research and utilizing knowledge of previously successful formats, Ryan shows how the corporation management meticulously planned the characterization, narrative structures and plot themes of the show prior to any actual writing (i.e. the creative work) being undertaken. As Ryan states, the aim was to ensure that 'each script materialise[d] the background strategic and operational assumptions of the format' (1992, p. 171), with 'creative' writers being permitted only to add a little stylistic spice to the already well-established recipe. Ryan's point is that creativity and art are increasingly shaped by organizational imperatives to guarantee profitability, with managers playing a central role in determining the ambit and scope of creative practice.

Formatting is also now becoming increasingly evident at the level of small and micro-firms, particularly amongst those acting as sub-contractors for larger corporations, increasingly inveigled into relations of 'alliance capitalism' (Hesmondhalgh, 2007; see Chapter 6). From my own research (Banks, 2005), this manager of a small multimedia company articulated the importance of ensuring that his creatives worked to the imposed demands of their paymaster's format:

> Occasionally they get stroppy [upset] because they don't want to give something up. We've had that on colour in the past particularly, and they will say they're doing it for themselves ... but [I say] no they're doing it [for the client] .... They were designing for themselves and designers can do that occasionally.

Increasingly, a primary role of the creative manager is to ensure that industry conventions and style are adhered to in order to generate a commercial product. Formatting of tried and tested formulae, ensuring subscription to commercial 'standards', minimising supposition, conjecture and contingency all become part of the province of professional management of cultural work – a process with outcomes that Ryan describes thus:

> By transforming the production of originality into a process governed by company-advocated rules, formatting serves to rationalise the otherwise arbitrary and idiosyncratic play of imaginative creativity and routinely steers artists towards repetition of the particular cultural forms in which companies have invested. To the degree that the corporations have been successful in this production strategy, it drives the creative stage of production further towards its structural subordination to the imperatives of accumulation. (1992, p. 178)

While, as Hesmondhalgh (2007) notes, formatting may not necessarily inhibit creativity (for focus, creativity often requires parameters and limits) a move towards standardization will tend to undermine artistic autonomy and place creativity firmly in the service of accumulation.[2] The arguable consequence of this is the downgrading of autonomous creativity and alternative production, and the diminution of critical potential inherent in creative activity.

Thus, the weight of evidence forces Ryan to reconsider his earlier (more optimistic) view, and he eventually concludes that through a system of more rationally directed, commercially sensitive management, creative cultural workers are increasingly being recast as mere (and potentially expendable) units in the broader calculus of cultural production:[T]he corporations of culture have transformed the nature of artistic labour; it turns artists into a generalised capacity to perform creative work – it positions them in the labour process as creative labour-power (1992, pp. 138–139).

Such concerns are now being more widely echoed in the cultural sector. This is evidenced in the growing band of artists, producers, presenters, writers and so on who complain of being turned into 'cogs in the machine' by the 'suits', 'bureaucrats' and 'money men' who they suggest routinely hamper creativity and traduce the traditions of craft production through their tendencies for rationalization and standardization (Murdock, 2003). While Ryan recognizes the necessity of craft production (see Chapter 2) and thus retains some faith in the artist's ability to evade rationalization, he concedes that the balance of power in the art–commerce relation has now been further tipped in capital's favour and that the consolidation of creative management within the project team context represents the thoroughgoing corporate appropriation of the creative process, and a corresponding diminution of the possibility of critical, creative dissent. What is of particular concern is that this now increasingly occurs at the level of small 'independent' firms, amongst the 'autonomous' capitalists, as well as in the larger, more staid and conventional, commercial corporations and bureaucracies. Indeed, it appears that in all capitalist production contexts, as Adorno once envisaged, creativity is becoming relentlessly standardized and pervasively formatted.

Managers as creatives

While Ryan argues there has been something of a retrenchment around hierarchical management as managers re-establish relations of domination (albeit under the seductive veneer of the project team), we can see in other contexts that the traditional distinction between the 'management' and the 'creatives' has comes under challenge in the cultural economy. Indeed, such is the value and prestige given to creativity, it is perhaps no surprise that some managers themselves now show an increasing tendency to define their *own* operations as creative, in order to signal their personal dynamism and originality in what has become a more individualized economic landscape. Indeed, this move is seemingly endorsed by commentators such as Bilton and Leary who see the role of the manager and the creative as almost synonymous:

> In fact, if they are doing their jobs properly, the artist and the manager are not so far removed as they first appear. Both are manipulating and exploiting ideas; the process through which value is added is no longer by way of the linear 'value chain' but by creating a space within which individual talents, experiences and perceptions can collide in interesting ways. (2002, p. 61)

This blending of manager and creative is perhaps most common in micro and small enterprises and organizations. Large corporate bureaucracies such as national newspapers, television companies, publishing houses, major advertising agencies, record companies and so on insist on retaining at least some departmental and job distinction between 'creator' and 'manager' (Davis and Scase, 2000; Nixon, 2003; Ryan, 1992); yet such a distinction is brought into question in small and micro cultural businesses where employees are fewer, job roles are less distinct and multitasking is more common. Here, creatives may lose the 'exceptional status' (Nixon 2003, p. 42) they have been (at least historically) afforded in larger creative organizations.

Amongst small cultural firms the idea of 'manager as creative' is now widespread. In one sense this is obvious – many small and micro firms may only be composed of one or two people who must clearly combine managerial and creative roles. However, particularly amongst intermediate small and medium sized enterprises (SMEs), with more staff and specified job roles, this can often take the form of managers imposing a fundamental redefinition of creativity in favour of themselves and at the expense of the traditional 'creative'. Indeed, this manager I encountered in a medium-sized advertising and graphic design company constructed a quite fanciful scenario to describe his executive authority in the creative production process:

> The way I liken it in my own mind is the way in which grand master painters worked... he only did bits of it, he had specialists who sorted other bits because they were damned good at doing it and that's how they turned out so many portraits. If he did everything himself it just wouldn't have flown. I think its very similar to that – there are many people who can actually make the decision... no that's the wrong way to describe it... in many cases my colleagues will have rejected many solutions before they come to me and say this is the one we want to fly with and nine times out of ten I just say 'yes', because its purely a sense check.

Many managers interviewed tended to downplay traditional notions of creativity (drawing, composing, designing and so on) in favour of describing creativity as being about 'problem-solving', 'meeting clients expectations', 'managing staff', 'negotiating solutions', 'selling the client the product' and so on – all managerial, rather than creative, tasks and responsibilities. Creativity was most often defined as the (managerial) ability to negotiate the deal, manage the client and deliver the 'whole package' – rather than a quality inherent in the design or drafting of the product itself. The account of this manager of a new media SME captures the subtleties of this redefinition:

> One guy is in his own estimation not very creative, but if the problem is defined to him he is actually very creative in coming up with a solution, but you've got to define the problem very tightly otherwise he's totally confused. This guy.... a solution he's come up with

is very creative because I don't believe that anybody has ever done it this way before. Fine. But is that creativity? Or was the creativity in defining him the problem?

Implicit in this recasting of the 'manager as creative' is a disavowal of the special status historically afforded those designers, artists, writers and so on who have hitherto carried the banner of creativity in corporate life and established a certain degree of autonomy and privilege in the undertaking of creative craft production. While, on the one hand, this has democratic potential in that it redefines creativity as a more generally held social attribute, it must bear the inverse that if creativity is now held by managers, then the traditional creatives may not only lose their privileged status but become subject to same systems of control and discipline imposed on other employees. Interviews suggested that in situations where managers assume the mantle of creativity or where everyone is (at least notionally) deemed creative, it does not follow that creative freedoms are routinized into practice – it is rather more likely to ensure that creative work is divested of its privileged status as it is relocated to the nub of the manager/client relationship, and creative cultural workers themselves (recast as ordinary labour) become subject to the same conventional forms of rational, bureaucratic management as other employees. As creativity is 'democratized', made to appear a quality possessed by or available to all, then the rationale for ensuring that those traditionally identified as creative workers are provided with privileged autonomy is undermined.

To summarize; the rise of the 'creative manager' can be seen as an organizational response to the demands of a more flexible economy where the need for 'softer', more intuitive and innovative forms of leadership are routinely cited as crucial to success. The disavowal of traditional 'hard' management and its replacement by a 'softer' variant would appear to be predicated on an openness to the social and economic potential of creative, co-operative, 'mutually adjusted' social relations in workplace environments. While there is some evidence to support this (see Davis and Scase, 2000), the fact that tools of creative management such as the 'project team' and the 'democratic' effacement of 'old fashioned' hierarchies and norms can also help enforce traditional relations of domination has largely gone unnoticed. I would suggest that while control has become superficially 'softer', accumulation imperatives continue to ensure that managers find ways to exert a powerful grip on creative practice and cultural production. Indeed, at the level of the small firm, the redefinition of creativity as an attribute of management, rather than a discrete capacity of the gifted 'creative', marks an interesting shift in the discourse on corporate creativity, in that it promotes the virtues of management, and disavows the speciality of creative craft production – a further blow to the autonomy of the artist.

Managing the 'Creative Self'

In the bourgeois myth of aesthetic creation the autonomous subject is the wellspring of creativity. As Bilton and Leary (2002) and Rampley (1998) remind us, such prestigious and civilized thinkers as Plato, Kant and Freud have helped buttress the idea of the creative as the capricious and gifted loner prone to divergent modes of thought and anarchic action. Additionally, given creativity's mysterious form and uncertain origins, it is no surprise that, for some, geniuses are born rather than made. In Galton's (1869) principle of 'hereditary genius', creativity was a genetically transmitted gift, a rare quality found amongst the 'best sort' of people who had 'naturally' emerged as judges, commanders, statesmen and the like – politics and historical privilege didn't much come into it (see Negus and Pickering, 2004). Today, the popular belief in 'talent' as an innate quality, and the enduring fascination with the origins of the 'creative mind' suggest we have not strayed as far from Galton's formulation as we might at first think. As McFadzean (2000) identifies, numerous writers have enthusiastically attempted to pin down the creative 'essences' of great scientists, artists and writers, such as Michael Faraday (Gooding, 1996); Vincent Van Gogh (Brower, 1996), George Bernard Shaw (Tahir, 1996); Sigmund Freud (Bruchez-Hall, 1996) and Karl Popper (Kurz, 1996). The management literature increasingly seeks inspiration from industry role models such as Apple's Steve Jobs or Microsoft's Bill Gates, or management and creativity gurus like Tom Peters. Indeed in business and management discourse the idea that the creativity is a product of individual 'inner conditions' is pervasive, and continues to stimulate a whole range of behaviouristic interventions designed to make employees harness their creative potential for productive ends (de Bono, 1971; Buzan, 1995; Groth and Peters, 1999). The use of organizational learning techniques to produce creative individuals and firms is widespread. Thrift (2002) reports on the various strategies and techniques of creativity manipulation open to the contemporary firm, which even extend into employing artists, dancers, actors and so on in order to teach firms how to mobilize their latent creative 'potential'.

In the following section I focus on the ways in which 'creative selves' are not – as managers would tell us – wholly natural, spontaneous and autonomous, but are tightly prescribed and strongly (if somewhat tacitly) governed by discourses and management systems within which creativity is defined and valued. It is suggested that creative selves rely upon inherited and approved forms of expression that 'set the tone' for acceptable self-performances and in doing so compromise individual capacities for forging independent identities. In this I follow the work of Prichard (2002) who argues that what counts as creativity in work is part constituted through discursive practices that set parameters and codes of conduct regarding how to be creative and how to adequately embody the appearance and style of a creative person. His work, in turn, draws on Foucault in order to emphasize that the creative workplace is replete with devices that can 'identify, classify and regulate' (Prichard 2002, p. 266) the creative self in order to guide more effective production. Similarly, du Gay has suggested the useful notion that creative identities at work are not natural, but somehow 'made-up' by managers, that is, they are elaborate fictions created by managers seeking to prescribe acceptable forms of worker conduct and monitoring of the worker self: 'the idea of being 'made-up' suggests a material/cultural process of formation or transformation ('fashioning') whereby the adoption of certain habits or dispositions allows an individual to become – and to be become recognised as – a particular sort of person' (du Gay 1997, p. 314).

In what follows I assess how this 'making-up' of the creative self in cultural work occurs through the regulation, by managerial discourses and practices, of the body, the self and the cultural workplace environment.

Creative clothes and appearances

The construction of creativity in cultural work is evidenced in the performances and impression-management strategies of employees who must constantly appear to be creative, independent-minded, innovative and 'thinking the unthinkable' (Osborne, 2003, p. 508). In media, music, design and art (and to a lesser extent across other non-cultural sectors) we are witnessing the new centrality of creative style and dress and the manipulation of the body in business interaction and exchange – all key elements of what Löfgren (2003, p. 247) now refers to as the 'catwalk economy'. Thus, as well as creativity becoming objectified as a calculable unit of production, it is increasingly presented as an innately desirable, and indeed necessary, *mode of being* that actors must cultivate in order to empower themselves and their firms in a precarious market situation.

Critics such as Nixon (2003), Nixon and Crewe (2004) and Ross (2003) have made much of the importance of personal appearance in reproducing (inherently masculine) cultures of creativity in cultural work. The self-conscious development of a distinctive, though seemingly 'casual', creative style is evidenced in the widespread rejection of the formal suit and business wear in favour of informal attire of (branded and expensive) trainers, jeans, T-shirts, topped off with fashionable haircuts and the latest accessories. Nixon and Crewe relish in detailing the appearance of some the critical movers and shakers they interviewed in London's advertising industry:

> Chris Bradshaw, an established art director, wore a navy-blue crew necked t-shirt under a navy, pale-blue and white zip-up top, dark blue jeans and trainers. He was shaven-headed and sported a closely-cropped moustache and short beard restricted to his chin. Paul Cantelo, a young creative director at Serendipity, wore a Ben Sherman short sleeved check shirt, jeans and reef surf wear sandals. (2004, p. 136)

As they suggest, styles of self-presentation go some way to establishing the security and belonging of the budding creative; McRobbie also notes how informal cultures of work, based on 'club culture sociality' are composed of a whole 'symbolic panoply of jargon, clothes, music and identity' (2002a, p. 520) that provide crucial props for the construction of creative identities. In meetings, negotiations and networking events, looking the part helps convince others that you are, in fact, creative.

While, for men, the approved 'uniform' tends to be clear-cut, there is a good deal of ambivalence that surrounds dress codes for female creatives. The uncertain choice to subscribe to the masculine norm of casual wear, albeit with feminized touches, or to adopt a more 'serious' business-like style of dress was one that was played out amongst Nixon's (2003) sample of advertising workers. From my own research, the account of this female manager of a new media marketing company captures this dilemma:

> I'm becoming this other person ... because you've got to, its the only way you survive, its the only way you can survive in business, it's to put the smart gear on, wear the Chanel suit, put a bit of make up and

a bit of lipstick on because women who wear subtle make up and nice clothes get further you know what I mean? This is all stuff I hate, you've got to trust me, I hate it, but if it means the net result is I get my own way I realise I've got to do that. I wouldn't push it on anybody else to do it, but I've personally got to do it.

Such an account appears to support the notion that processes of governmentality are strongly gendered. In image-conscious industries such as advertising and marketing (and as Richards and Milestone (2000) have also noted in the context of the music industry) women are constantly made aware that to achieve 'autonomy' they must tolerate a work climate where managing their personal appearance to meet the expectations of watching others is paramount. In his study Nixon concludes that, generally, there is 'a fundamental problem for women creatives concerning how they should behave in the strongly masculine worlds they were forced to inhabit' (2003, p. 210), one we see articulated here through the self-conscious and anxious negotiations surrounding dress and personal appearance.

Creative leisure

Informal dress codes are just part of the wider effacement of the now unfashionable distinction between production and play. As work and leisure combine, creative selves are seen to be drawn to activities that help bolster their status as dynamic, cutting-edge workers, operating at the limits of conformity and convention. Extreme, physically demanding or unusual sports, exotic or unconventional travel destinations, counter-rationalistic belief systems, alternative therapies, hedonistic play and distinctive and/or excessive consumption are all part of the contemporary creative self (see Giddens, 1991). We might question however, how original and unorthodox these leisure choices turn out to be. For Bourdieu (1984), leisure choices made reflect the shaping powers of the 'habitus', and yet while the choices and dispositions of the creative cultural workers appear to extol the virtues of autonomy and creative self-expression, in their regularity and predictability they may produce only conformity and a reproduction of historically ascribed social roles. Bourdieu describes the ways in which attempts by intellectuals of the 'new petit bourgeoisie' (of which creative cultural workers are a part) to cultivate 'alternative' practices that 'defy the gravity of the social field' (1984/2003, p. 370) can all too quickly become sterile and standardized, and thus mirror the petit bourgeois conventionality they were initially designed to evade.

This unconscious conformity is inadvertently evidenced in Florida's (2002) descriptions of the seemingly distinctive lifestyle and leisure choices made by the 'creative class', of which cultural workers make up a significant part. Florida argues that creative class workers are driven by an omnivorous desire for cultural goods and are more likely to achieve fulfilment through seeking out 'active, authentic and participatory' (ibid., p. 167) leisure experiences. As Florida has it; 'In practical everyday terms, this means running rock climbing or cycling rather than watching a game on TV' (ibid., p. 167). While this would appear to mark them out as eclectic and experimental consumers of the unconventional, it seems that the leisure preferences of the creative class are first predictable in so far as they tend to reflect a conventional individualistic and bourgeois ethos of 'self-improvement' in the context of 'communing' with or 'conquering' nature. Considered in the context of Barthes' blunt appraisal of the 'Blue Guide' travelogue in *Mythologies,* where the 'cult of nature and of puritanism' is to be found within in the 'bourgeois promoting of the mountains' and where 'clean air' and the conquest of landscape represents 'civic and moral virtue' (1973, p. 81), Florida's identification of cultural workers 'alternative' preferences for biking, rock-climbing, snowboarding and so on begin to appear somewhat more conventional. Second, we might re-evaluate the progressive nature of the creatives' penchant for what Florida calls 'indigenous street-level culture', identified as a preference for 'a teeming blend of cafes, sidewalk musicians, and small galleries and bistros' (2002, p. 166). While this may represent a welcome alternative to the kind of commodified and sanitized 'street' culture that has now emerged as a dominant trope of post-industrial urban renewal, it is hard to see how – given Florida's identification of the self-satisfying and hedonistic nature of the creative class (2002, pp. 316–317) – such 'participation' can translate into anything but conspicuous consumption, where being 'active' may not extend much beyond the enjoyment of the 'diverse' cultural or multicultural spectacle (Harvey, 1989; Peck, 2005). Overall, the impression gained is that Florida's creative class are self-interested, pseudo-cosmopolitan consumers rather than critical or active producers of 'alternative' forms of social and economic space. They are, as others have described, 'neo' or 'bourgeois bohemians' (Brooks, 2000; Lloyd, 2006) or 'blue jean conservatives', ostensibly radical but, underneath, conformist and status seeking.[3]

While creative class leisure preferences may exhibit a tendency to reproduce conventional, bourgeois values of the 'active citizen', also worthy of attention is the way in which the leisure habits of the creative class tends to reflect and uphold traditional (gendered) social roles. For example, Florida suggests that it is the intellectual and largely desk (or studio) bound basis of creative work that encourages the creative class to seek out physically demanding and life-affirming pursuits for their leisure time, a reversal of a tradition that once saw work as the site of hard, physical labour and the home as the site of intellectual and sedentary leisure. There is a kind of missionary zeal in Florida's own ruminations on the benefits of bicycling and in his assertions regarding how 'fit regions are also creative regions' (2002, p. 178), and, indeed, it is hard not to pick up his prescriptive, utopian thread. Nonetheless, his account does rest on some masculinist assumptions regarding the universal availability of leisure time amongst creative workers (see Adkins (1999) and Richards and Milestone (2000) for an alternative view) as well as the range of pursuits deemed sufficiently challenging to satisfy the physical and mental demands of the creative. While Florida (without much evidence) argues that creative workers eschew traditionally masculine competitive team sports, there remains much conquering and domination of nature in his chosen pursuits of rock-climbing, mountain biking, kayaking and trail running (amongst others). It is not difficult to identify which culturally valued aspects of masculinity are being reproduced here – individual resourcefulness, toughness and ruggedness (Messner and Sabo, 1990). We are left wondering whether corresponding accounts from female (or even ethnic minority or more traditionally working-class) creatives would reveal both alternative leisure interests and differently defined 'creative selves' more generally.

Creative workplaces and environments

> Offices look and feel different now. At some small high-tech or design firms, the ambience can seem downright raucous: bold wall-sized artwork and posters, broken surfaces with exposed pipes and beams, lounge areas and play areas, blaring rock music. (Florida 2002, p. 122)

> Naturally the founders had made it their business to 'satisfy the internal client', and [provided] perks that were common to the industry – in-house masseur, video-gaming room, gym membership discounts, regular social excursions and some very famous parties. (Ross 2003, p. 73)

If the creative self is socially prescribed, and embodied in characteristic bodily performances and modes of self-presentation, so too the creative workplace can be seen as a product of socially established conventions and norms regarding the environmental attributes best able to foster creative practice. Primarily, as a context for the production of the creative self, the working environments of creative firms tend to reflect the desire to portray a corporate image of 'autonomous', 'unforced' and unregulated creativity – this takes on a number of regularized forms.

The explicit rejection of a Taylorized system of cells, units or rows of workers, efficiently time-managed, clocking in and out, overtly disciplined and monitored represents an attempt to 'free up' workspace in line with the ethos of the new economy. A disavowal of bureaucratic management is most evidently signalled by the emphasis on informality and 'fun' in the workplace. Indeed, in his study of new media firms in New York's 'Silicon Alley', Ross (2003) suggests workplaces to be liminal zones between work and leisure, where managers must accept the provision of on-site distractions and entertainments as the necessary price for ensuring that firms attract top creatives at the peak of their productive powers. Some firms, he observed, went one step further and saw the deliberate cultivation of a play ethic as instrumental to competitive advantage:

> in new media companies, neo-leisure was not simply tolerated as an unavoidable cost of doing business in the information age; it was actively encouraged as a way of adding value to an employee's output. Play was viewed as an activity that could catalyze ideas and serve as a battery source for recharging flagging energies at the workstation. The permissive workplace could take a playful turn at any moment, and however spontaneous the result, it was all part of the business plan. (Ross 2003, p. 88)

The relaxed informality, sense of 'fun' and a commitment to play would often carry over into parties and social events. In playful environments where creativity might be encouraged by people 'strumming guitars in the afternoon' (Ross, 2003, p. 134), Nixon and Crewe also found workers eager to embody the image of the 'creative' and freely participate in the more exuberant aspects of industry 'cultures of hedonism' (2004, p. 140) – often involving late-night drinking and partying as well as workplace fooling around:

> Certainly within advertising agencies, the informality of office life allowed strident forms of masculinity and homosociability to flourish. In its more benign form this might include male practitioners

playing football down the office corridors, while more problematic manifestations included horseplay such as decorating the office Christmas tree with condoms and sanitary towels, having Barbie dolls in bondage pinned to office doors and deploying derogatory and highly sexualised epithets for female colleagues. (2004, p. 135)

Such tales of homosociability (not to mention debauchery and excess) are common to both Nixon and Crewe's and Ross's accounts and broadly illustrate the particular version of masculinity that tends to dominate in advertising and new media sectors.

Similarly, during my own ethnographic fieldwork with one particular advertising firm, it was specified by managers that employees were explicitly chosen for their perceived ability to fit into the long hours and social culture of the 'team', rather than for their academic or industry credentials – with long 'bonding sessions' down the pub being the ritual means of ensuring assimilation. As Nixon (2003) illustrates, in the creative world, individuals who take offence, don't 'fit in' or express non-conformist lifestyle or leisure interests may be marginalized or ridiculed. In his study, women, older men, any kind of 'shrinking violet' (not to mention the negligible numbers of ethnic minority employees) all appeared as inimical to the culture of aggressive homosociability exhibited by London's advertising industry.

The construction of creativity is thus heavily entwined with (often strongly gendered) performative codes that not only involve transforming and indeed surrendering the body to prescribed sartorial and leisure conventions, but also involve creating the 'right' environment and participating in certain kinds of informal and 'playful' activities deemed appropriate for the nurturance of a creative culture. In advertising and publishing these appear to be substantially based on hegemonic versions of masculinity, and while Nixon and Crewe's examples may appear extreme, as others have found, the music, media, leisure, fashion and design industries also tend to allow men the freedom to indulge themselves through some highly 'clubbable' and male-dominated social relations (Adkins, 1999; Gill, 2002; McRobbie, 2002a; Perrons, 2003; Richards and Milestone, 2000). As we saw in the previous chapter, the governance of workplace cultures is not simply enforced through domination but relies on workers own willingness to recognise and accept the virtues of the prevailing arrangements – and, as Nixon has shown, any criticism of the masculinist cultures of cultural work tend to be rebuffed through managerial and policy discourse that stresses the necessity of informal, creative, networked and clubbable social relations, but is also blunted by the apparent willingness of workers to routinely accept such cultures as an inalienable 'fact of life' in cultural work.[4]

Creative environments and 'culture managers'

While playful work environments might appear 'free', the necessity of turning a profit encourages managers to try and rationalize playfulness and discipline fun. Managers may ostensibly appear to endorse play in work and encourage eccentric or erratic performance but, in actuality, increasingly seek to govern the form and content of fun through their own 'loose' but highly structured interventions. More broadly, efforts to stimulate creativity often rest on the governmental manipulation of workforce sociability under the banner of improving workplace 'culture'. While workers may voluntarily attempt to make themselves more creative, often the need to ensure that workers uphold the performance and ethos of the organization can only be met through interventions which institutionalize what Ross (2003) identifies as organized or 'enforced' fun.

Grugulis, Dundon and Wilkinson's (2000) illuminating research into 'ConsultancyCo', a software production company, provides a telling case study of how 'culture managers' work to stimulate loyalty and enhance productivity under the guise of introducing workplace 'fun'. In 'ConsultancyCo' the culture manager's role was to 'organise play' with the express intention of enhancing employees psychological commitment to the company and encouraging 'social rather than contractual relations within the firm' (ibid., p. 103). More co-operative and sociable internal relations were seen by managers as crucial to competitive advantage. The company culture was developed through various gaming, training and social events (usually conducted in employees' 'own' time) including:

> weekends away (with families invited), nights out in pubs, sporting competitions (in which men competed and the women, dressed as cheerleaders supported them), 'dress down' days in the office and charity fundraising events. A surprisingly large number of activities involved staff wearing some form of fancy dress, encouraging perhaps, a more complete immersion of the self...[e]mployees were expected to want to participate and to actively enjoy themselves when they did. (2000, pp. 102–103)

Grugulis and colleagues reveal that attendance at these events was only notionally voluntary, and strong pressure was applied to ensure that staff fully participated. More perniciously, the 'voluntary' inclusion of families helped further erode the boundaries between work and home, and anyone who resisted such effacement, or absented themselves, was not only subjected to suspicion but, in some cases, disciplinary action. As the culture manager put it, such events were deliberately designed to ensure that everyone was able to develop 'a sense of belonging which makes them loyal' (ibid., p. 102).

In addition, a key role of the culture manager was to take part in recruitment and selection to ensure that the 'right' kind of 'ConsultancyCo' person would be employed. It was revealed that candidates were selected primarily for their likelihood to 'fit in' with the company culture, and only once this was established would their job skills and professional qualifications be assessed. The ideal type that the company envisaged tended to replicate the appearance and characteristics of the managers and founders of the company; what Grugulis and colleagues refer to as the 'homosocial reproduction' of the model employee:'Almost all ConsultancyCo staff members were white, male and aged between twenty and forty. Of the 150 employees only 23 were women...the majority [were] assigned to low-level administrative posts... [ethnic] minority staff were even more poorly represented' (ibid., p. 106).

The homogeneity and strict control of the social aspects of work stood in marked contrast to the lack of bureaucratic control over work tasks. As many of those interviewed revealed, workers were afforded autonomy and creative latitude in their work, with only minimal interference from managers.[5] Indeed, it was shown that 'ConsultancyCo' deliberately eschewed a traditional approach, whereby managers sought to specify and regulate tasks, in favour of management through 'normative control'. As Kunda notes, this involves 'the regulation of the employees self, rather the work they are engaged in' (1991, p. 2 cited in Grugulis et al., 2000, p. 97), that is, managers direct their efforts towards managing employee's emotions, feelings and personal and social relationships. In all (not just cultural) industry sectors 'culture managing' has become a popular method for guaranteeing loyalty, retention and a moral orientation to work through offering the illusion of autonomy through the 'decontrolling' of tasks in craft production.

It is difficult to judge the 'colonisation of self' and the commodification of social and interpersonal relations in a positive light. Even in firms where material rewards are high, it is rare for this 'corporate culture' to be unambiguously welcomed by workers or accepted entirely by free choice – long hours and a lack of free time, tacitly enforced attendance at events and a compulsion to be a 'company person' often prove to be uncomfortable impositions. What, then, is the price of creative freedom at work? Davis and Scase (2000) suggest that the creative and highly skilled nature of labour in software (and other sectors of cultural) production ensures that workers now enjoy considerable autonomy, in that they are more able to organise and plan their own work, relatively free from managerial constraint. While this is taken as evidence of the decline of managerial authority, Grugulis and her colleagues show that managerial power does not disappear but simply takes on new guises. Creative workers may well obtain more freedom in their work, but, for some, this comes with the cost of accepting encroachments into non-work time. Indeed, the colonisation by work of the non-work realm has become a widespread concern in the cultural economy – and when this extends into the broader colonisation of the self through the dictation of personality, the erosion of free time, the encroachment into family life and the commodification of friendship relations, then it becomes difficult to defend the work of 'culture manager' and the growing desire of firms to extend their workplace privileges into non-work contexts.

The necessity of having a creative team that 'pulls together' has been routinely emphasised in my own interviews with managers. As one owner-manager of a new media marketing company put it 'bad apples, I can do without'. The casual and informal nature of cultural work, particularly in small firms, often means a failure to follow fundamental, legally proscribed equal opportunity and diversity procedures – and here, perhaps more than in any other sector, managers will appoint in their own image. One manager I interviewed in a small new media marketing company revealed his thoughts on recruitment when he specified that 'you've got to have anoraks' which he proceeded to define as sci-fi buffs and guys (always guys) who spend a lot of their leisure time surfing the net, reading up on the latest software – guys like him in fact.

Even if the team does not quite gel, given the temporary, informal and 'disorganized' nature of cultural work, it is often quite easy for firms to shed excess or troublesome labour. The same manager revealed that one guy had to be 'let go', mainly because he insisted on leaving at 'five on the dot' to catch his train home, and refused to work unpaid overtime; it was offered that he 'did not fit into the culture'. In the same way that labour is now required to be innovative, flexible and amenable to enforced changes of career or employer, so individual workers must themselves be 'company persons', quick to 'join in' and uncritically accept the prevailing work 'culture' (Martin and Wacjman, 2004). Offering an alternative or conflictual understanding of ones own self in relation to work is frequently deemed intolerable by managers. Thus, failure to be properly creative may turn out to be (at least economically) fatal.

Summary

In the new economy the prevailing fetishization of creativity is illustrative of a shift to a mode of post-industrial production that now appears to value more 'flexible', 'aesthetic' and 'soft' workplace cultures. The more upbeat accounts of life in the cultural workplace continually emphasise the promise of individual emancipation and attest to the benefits of engendering a 'creative culture', enthusiastically endorsing both the personal and corporate advantages that it can provide. Such accounts are seductive, not least for the possibility that alongside money and status, cultural industry firms might offer a work environment to cherish and savour; one that provides a long-overdue sense of sociability and self-fulfilment in creative labour (Ross, 2003). The buoyant expectations of creatives have led many to anticipate a future where 'unhappy work' (McRobbie, 2002a, p. 521) could be circumvented by a more creative, reflexive and fulfilling form of production. The utopian tenor of this discussion tends to disassociate itself from traditional notions of what might make a good workplace (order, planning, efficiency, democracy, mutuality, security and stability) in favour of an emphasis on the personal and individual freedoms now able to be exercised within the loose confines of a more 'enabling', playful and decentred set of work relations.

In reality, however, the sweet the taste of 'freedom' can quickly turn sour. Cultural industry firms are amongst the most enthusiastic disciples of what we might term 'creative governmentalization', a process that promotes artistic and creative freedom while at the same time regulating identity and ensuring conformity to rational corporate objectives. Here, rather than achieving creative fulfilment, workers become preoccupied with maintaining their positions as 'valued objects in the eyes of those in authority, [so] subordinating their own subjectivity in the process' (Collinson, 2003, p. 536). Further, more broadly, as it is progressively 'normalized' into economic development discourse, the idea of creativity as a critical challenge to orthodoxy is diluted by its re-appropriation as useful or productive resource able to be harnessed to capitalist imperatives for growth. Creativity as a source of *criticism* is compromised when such management incitements as 'thinking out of the box' or 'blue skies development' are directed only towards appropriate tasks of corporate economic development. Bilton and Leary (2002) support this utilitarian definition of culture when they define creativity 'something innovative but also useful' (2002, p. 53), a process through which chaos and contingency crystallize into something functional and fit for a (business) purpose.

Yet, despite the evidence I have presented to the contrary, the idea that cultural work is an innately rewarding world populated by an array of self-determining and self-directed fast-thinkers, risk-takers and project-makers remains pervasive. This is testament to the power of firms, managers (and policy-makers) and their abilities to skilfully promote and apply their own discourses of creativity and enterprise in multiple organizational and social contexts. Yet while firms and managers offer a seductive narrative of creative liberty, it seems, at the same time, they are constructing new 'soft' forms of governmentalized control. While they may preach individual freedom, they appear to close down the creative possibilities of selfhood. In their eagerness to construct the creative and corporate 'family', they arguably undermine non-work based identities and social bonds. While they may extol the virtues of flexibility they may simultaneously undertake local strategies of repression. These days, it seems, somewhat paradoxically, that to be a 'creative' is to be more manipulated and controlled than ever before.

5
Choice, Reflexivity and 'Alternative' Cultural Work

Critical theory and governmental approaches suggest that cultural work has come to be dominated either by the consolidation of the 'culture industry' (through industrialization and the degradation of independent craft production) or through neo-liberal discourses of 'enterprise' that enable the administration of creative endeavour. In these scenarios, cultural workers are seen to be deprived of autonomy and bereft of meaningful identity as a consequence of their increased alienation from the conditions of production, or through the conformity and discipline now imposed by governmental 'mechanisms of rule'. Furthermore, as both approaches identify, the increasingly 'uncreative' cultural work that remains will become pervasively more precarious as the shift to a flexible and globalized economy leads capital to further rationalize its commitments to labour through programmes of institutional 'delayering', introducing casual, non-standard and unstable forms of employment and dismantling collective systems of recognition and reward. It is additionally argued that increases in the relative strength of capital over labour will further reduce opportunities for workers' resistance to temporary insubordinations and 'tactical' interventions of limited impact. Now, for both critical theorists and governmentalists, the cultural worker appears a fully *individualized* subject, one who must endure artistic disaffection and the constant stress of self-reliance under prevailing conditions of enhanced economic uncertainty. According to such sombre assessments, the prospects for progressive cultural work now appear fatally contaminated.

Yet, while these critics have strenuously emphasized some of the 'negative' aspects of cultural work, the aim of this chapter is to explore more 'positive' theories of cultural industry labour. Initially, such theories are not hard to find. As was discussed in the previous chapter, a whole slew of neo-liberal commentators, politicians and capitalists have attested to the virtues of cultural work – routinely presenting the cultural industries as some kind of artistic Eden; a weightless post-modern utopia populated by free, creative subjects (see Löfgren, 2003). Academic commentators also appear to have embraced this rhetoric, with many now arguing that creative, culturally focussed work represents some kind of blueprint for a better kind of (market-driven) society (Seltzer and Bentley, 1999; Florida, 2002; Howkins, 2001; Leadbeater, 1999). While these studies have their virtues, a critical perspective on capitalism is not one of them. The freedoms imagined in such works are the neo-liberal freedoms of unfettered production and pure exchange, where (ultimately) individuals exercise creative autonomy, but only in the interests of accumulation. But what if artistic and creative cultural work contains within it the possibility of *another* kind of freedom? A freedom that seeks to moderate or challenge market culture rather than simply reinforce it? Exploring such a possibility is the aim of this chapter.

This chapter explores the work of theorists who argue that individualization processes may be cultivating the conditions for an *expansion* (rather than retraction) of creative agency and 'alternative'[1] cultural work practices. Given the apparent total dominance of the neo-liberal 'culture industry', this might seem a contentious claim. Yet, in what I term the 'liberal-democratic' readings of modernization (ones principally occasioned by Beck and Beck-Gernsheim, Giddens, Keat and Lash and Urry) it is proposed that a *renaissance* of alternative production may have occurred as a direct consequence of expanded opportunities for self-expressivity and biographical self-organizing amidst now demonstrably more individualized and 'reflexive' social environments. Central here is the liberal–democratic idea that individualization leads to 'not just a flattening, but a deepening of the self' (Lash and Urry, 1994, p. 31) as avenues of self-reflection and choice are opened up by detraditionalizing impulses and modernity's ambivalent effects (Smart, 1999).

In terms of 'alternative' economy, I first explore how individualization has arguably led to a revival of artistic and creative cultural production, marking a resuscitation of the long-standing interest in the 'aesthetic' as a field of contrast or opposition to capitalist rationality (Williams, 1958, 1980; Wolff, 1993). Such a revival represents a clear turn back towards 'art' in the context of the 'art–commerce relation' and an attempt to reinvest cultural production with those elements of creativity, beauty and magic (apparently) denuded by the commercial imperative. Here, creative cultural production is primarily understood as a search for *meaning*, rather than a means to accumulation.

Second, while it is noted that the 'pure' aesthetic domain provides the *primary* refuge for those opposed to calculation and disinterested exchange, I examine how cultural workers have also begun to hitch their artistic impulses to more evidently 'social' or 'political' economizing practices. The search for new forms of 'alternative' cultural work is, therefore, not simply to be judged as an expression of some latent (and now remobilized) *aesthetic* tendencies, but might be more broadly seen as an attempt, on the part of individuals and groups, to initiate *ethical* forms of production that attempt to re-embed and re-moralize economic life (see Heelas, 2002; Keat, 2000; Sayer, 2004b). So while the 'art–commerce relation' remains central in cultural work, this dichotomy is also somewhat problematized by the apparent intrusion of 'social' values into the ordinary contexts of cultural production.

To support these claims, I suggest that 'alternative' cultural production might be broadly categorized into three kinds of aesthetically driven production, namely the 'pure-artistic', the 'practice-led' and the 'ethical'. While based on readings of the literature, and derived in part from observations made in the context of my own empirical research, these categories should only be read as loose, schematic and provisional. However, I also suggest they offer a useful approximation of the character of post-industrial and individualized 'alternative' production, particularly (if not exclusively) within the context of small, independent firms, artists, freelancers and sole entrepreneurs operating at the margins of the mainstream economy.

Individualization and choice

Beck and Beck-Gernsheim have described individualization as an entirely 'new mode of societalization' (Beck, 1992, p. 127) one that is primarily defined by the 'disintegration of previously existing social forms' (Beck and Beck-Gernsheim, 2002, p. 2). This disintegration, however, is not necessarily to be viewed negatively since individualization is also understood as the catalyst for releasing 'individual creativity...under conditions of radical change' (Beck and Beck-Gernsheim, 2002, p. xxi). Such a view contrasts markedly with critical theorists who understand individualization as a force that largely diminishes the creative capacities of individuals in society. Further, Beck and Beck-Gernsheim also appear more optimistic than theorists of governmentality, who, while recognizing the necessity of 'active' subjectivity for the reproduction of social life, have yet to offer clear guidance as to how individuals might consciously evade their everyday 'governmentalization'. Indeed, we might suggest that a clear point of contention between Beck and Beck-Gernsheim and other critics of the neo-liberal order is how far contemporary societies confer the possibility of actual and progressive *choice*. For Beck and Beck-Gernsheim, the 'necessity of choice' is fundamental condition of 'second modernity',[2] and is one foisted upon actors, partly by the retreat of tradition, partly by radically transformed institutions that set new ground rules for social engagement. Choice is idealistically understood as both real and a potential pathway to new and better world – not simply as a manufactured illusion of the 'culture industry' or as a Trojan horse for enhanced governmentalization.

How does choice operate? While individualization might at first appear to signify the 'death of the social' or even the opening up of a purely indeterminate space in which to play out one's life, as Beck and Beck-Gernsheim aver, the opposite is in fact true. The new arenas of choice are neither about 'atomization' nor unfettered sovereignty.[3] Indeed, a key aspect of individualization is the emergence of new kinds of *institutional* frameworks, ones that eschew traditional guidelines and prohibitions yet impose a more provisional, but not less influential set of social and structural arrangements. Beck and Beck-Gernsheim (2002, p. 11) refer to this as *institutionalized individualization*. The argument proposed here is that institutional frameworks must necessarily continue to ensure the provision of civil and legal rights, health services, education, employment, mobility and the like, but the accelerated 'rolling back' of the state and the liquidation of traditional social structures now ensures that responsibility for the effective *deployment* of these frameworks is placed more firmly within the hands of the individual user. In short, citizens must learn to 'help themselves' in the new institutional climate.

Thus, as its name suggests, 'institutional individualization' is based on something of a paradox. While the individual is increasingly 'individualized' through the dissolution of traditional social ties and relationships (such as those based around the nuclear family, class, gender, ethnicity and traditional neighbourhood community) they are at the same time being forced into nascent relationships with transformed institutions that both encourage and compromise the ability to live a 'sovereign', autonomous and unfettered existence. Beck and Beck-Gernsheim summarise this more succinctly:

> You may and you must lead your own independent life, outside the old bonds of family, tribe, religion, origin and class; and you must do

this within the new guidelines and rules which the state, the job market, the bureaucracy etc. lay down. (2002, p. 11)

Structures, then, do not disappear but take on a more provisional form. Furthermore (and crucially), unlike critical theorists or neo-Foucauldians, Beck and Beck-Gernsheim (like Giddens) do not see individuals as wholly passive, or as shackled by these new structures. As they argue, a decisive aspect of individualization is that the new institutional rules are founded on the premise that outside of the 'old bonds' individuals must *assert* themselves in order to obtain the life they crave. The necessity of making choices is thus double-edged. While the compulsion to make ones' life in a more fluid, open-ended and indeterminate institutional landscape has become a decisive characteristic of the current ('governmentalized') modern phase, because it is based on *self-application* and what Giddens (1991, pp. 28–29) dubs 'extreme reflexivity', it is one that contains within it a progressive potential for critical social action. Crucially, for Beck and Beck-Gernsheim, as tradition fades, individualization leads to *active reflection* on ones' positioning within systems and, indeed, on the very nature of systems themselves – and it is this that contains the promise of freedom. Individualization does not necessarily mean, as some critics aver, the 'death of the social',[4] but its reconstitution sufficient to permit radical patterns of interaction and choice – including, as I will explore, the possible formation of 'alternative' practices in environments of cultural industry production.

Progressive choice?

The opening up of new avenues of possibility and the urgent necessity of making choices characterize the condition of accelerated or 'extreme' reflexivity. But in the wake of 'institutional individualization' and receding guidance from traditional social structures, how are actors able to decide in a world of unstable 'flows'? (Castells, 1996).

As Beck (1992) and Giddens (1991) have argued, what enables new forms of reflexivity to flourish in the now post-traditional situation is the sense of 'freedom' generated by the flight from the past but also, more substantively, developments such as enhanced travel and social mobility, the remarkable growth of formal and self-directed education, and the (related) rapid dissemblance of uncritical belief in the 'truths' offered by government, science and other 'experts'. Such transformations, it is argued, have prodigiously expanded the horizons of social possibility. For Beck and Giddens, actors now need to rely less on 'received wisdom' and can instead tap into the new global circuits of knowledge and information, and forge ahead in seeking out their own local truths. Indeed, Lash and Urry argue that it is *precisely* these new information and communication structures that give characteristic shape to what Beck calls 'institutional individualization', and contain within them the possibility of a remade social subjectivity:

> [R]eflexivity is often seen to be a matter of individualization via the decreasing importance of social structures, such as the family and class, and the concomitant freeing of social agents. This individualization however entails a lot more than just the relative retrocession of social structures. It entails the replacement of social structures by information structures. Without the presence of information and communication structures...reflexive individualization is impossible. (Lash and Urry, 1994, p. 111)

For Lash and Urry, enhanced information and communication structures provide the vital means through which to (re)construct the self and, it is argued, prompt the *re-embedding* of social and economic subjects. Implied here is the reconstruction of both a *moral* and a *creative* subject – one able to elaborate judgement on the necessity or desirability of different socio-economic practices, and equipped with the ability, it seems, to fashion a new life politics. Crucially, for us, it is in the context of the cultural industries that many of the resources from which to create this new, more reflexive and critical subject are now being forged,

> the flows of signs of the various culture industries also provide the materials for aesthetic critique. On the reception side this is conducive not just to niche-marketed individuation, but simultaneously to authentic aesthetic-reflexive individualization. On the production side this opens up and helps reproduce a space disintegrated from culture-industry behemoths from which meaningful aesthetic critique can be launched. (Ibid., p. 143)

In contrast to the claims of critical theorists, it is offered that the exponential expansion of media and information structures (including the 'culture industry') has not closed down subjectivity but provided the raw materials for more self-reflexive, and critical world-views.[5] Whether cognitive or aesthetic,[6] the growth of 'reflexive modernization' (Beck, Giddens and Lash, 1994) and the possibility of new social structures is now underpinned by an expanded 'universe of discourse', new information structures and increasingly *mediated* worlds of choice – a clear inversion of the 'culture industry' critique.

Thus, while some of the previously discussed critics of cultural work have, to some extent, argued that there is no *real* choice under a neo-liberal, market-led culture, it is contended in the liberal–democratic model that heightened reflexivity and the necessity of choice open up opportunities to break away from social prescriptions that would seek to contain individuals in traditional roles largely determined by, and beneficial to, capitalist institutions. Indeed, Beck and Beck-Gernsheim's theory helps turn the idea of 'enterprise' against itself, suggesting that while corporations, governmental 'discourses' and 'mechanism of rule' might exert strong conformist pressures, the idea that individuals are somehow locked into their prescribed fate and that 'resistance is futile' (as the critical theory and governmental critics of cultural work would increasingly appear to suggest) does not take into account the innate instability of discourse nor the potentials for change brought about by systemic inducements to act *in particular* as a free-thinking, self-determining and autonomous individuals. In short, encouraging people to 'be independent' and 'think for themselves' runs the risk that one day they may actually do it – in ways unanticipated and unwelcomed by government.[7]

Thus, in order to fully comprehend the contours of cultural economies it is necessary (since I have already examined their more deleterious impacts) to explore the terrain where the active promotion of free choice and self-determination may have led to some unleashing of the ambivalence and 'potential subversiveness' (Beck and Willms, 2004, p. 66) that Beck argues underpins radicalized modernity. In particular, as I now show, this subversion has apparently materialized in the context of varied, 'alternative' tendencies in cultural production, ones that (at least initially) appear to go beyond 'tactical' insubordinations and offer more substantive challenges to 'pure' (only profit-driven) capitalism.

Alternative cultural work

Individualization is argued to have a profound 'liberating' effect on the social totality – but how specifically does it impact on cultural work? In the following sections I identify three schematic – yet closely intertwined and often correspondent – 'progressive' tendencies in cultural work that appear to have come further to prominence in ambivalent individualization. These tendencies appear to be premised on a rejection of 'pure' capitalistic practices, and while evident within the kinds of mainstream firms discussed in Chapters 2–4, are perhaps more prevalent amongst small, independent firms, artists and entrepreneurs, operating outside or at the margins of the conventional capitalistic cultural economy:

- First I examine how the growth of 'aesthetic reflexivity' (Lash and Urry, 1994) in cultural work may have led to an expansion in traditional, 'pure' artistic ('bohemian' and 'avant-garde') cultural production – a revival of the apparently faded and compromised critical hermeneutic tradition of Modernity. Here a more fulsome penetration of the 'realm of the senses' into personal biographies and strategies of life planning may have enabled a reinvigorated pursuit of 'aestheticized' life projects based around cultural production and ars gratia artis.
- Second, drawing on the work of MacIntyre (1981) and his use of the concept of 'practice', I show how individualization appears to have encouraged a renewal of interest in not only aesthetically based but also 'authentic', artisanal and craft-based cultural practices and forms of production that can generate internal rewards and benefits for communities of creative practitioners (Becker, 1982; Keat, 2000).
- Third, I move beyond the 'pure' aesthetic sphere and the internalized 'economy of practices' in order to demonstrate how far various forms of 'social' or 'ethical' cultural production appear to have persisted and even become expanded in the apparently 'desocialized' cultural industries context. While not particular to cultural industries – the growth of 'social enterprises' in the cultural sector is evidence perhaps of the how the economy's mooted social or moral 'turn' (Amin et al., 2002; Heelas, 2002; Lash, 1994) may now be affecting workers in even the most (apparently) superficial and demoralized arena of cultural production (McRobbie, 2002a,b).

Workers operating in *all* these categories emphasise the art dimensions of the art–commerce relation, in so far as they prioritize creativity, self-expression and the pursuit of the aesthetic over and above the purely rational pursuit of profit and accumulation. This might be conceived of in absolute terms (art is a timeless, essential and superior value) or in relative terms (art is non-essential but preferable to pure commerce). Yet, also, in two of the three categories, it is noted *ethical* as well as aesthetic values are becoming increasingly important to the cultural worker – and most obviously converge in the context of more 'communitarian' or 'social' environments of production. It seems that the simple dichotomy of the art–commerce relation – where workers appear to be only implicated in social relations of *either* an aesthetic *or* a commercial form (Molotch, 2004; Ryan, 1992) – is becoming complicated by the rapid importation of social values into realms of production (Amin et al., 2002). In such instances, the hitherto neglected ethical or *moral* dimensions of cultural production become more visible and pronounced.

'Artistic' economies

In contrast to the claims of orthodox critics, it appears (for others) that social creativity and independent artistic production are actually on the *increase*. Indeed, the recent rapid growth in the number of individual, self-employed artists and craft producers (Arts Council of England, 2003; DCMS, 2005), and the expansion of artistic occupations more generally would not *just* appear to reflect the apparent coming together of art and commerce in the corporatized cultural industries, but more positively support Lash and Urry's claims for the revival of 'aesthetically reflexive' and autonomous forms of independent production in reflexive modernity. It now appears *all* forms of art are on the increase[8] – not simply those which are geared or amenable to commodification. Where specifically has the impetus for this alleged renaissance of independent creativity come from?

As discussed in Chapter 1, one of the distinctive features of cultural production is its artistic or aesthetic foundation. Cultural industries generate goods and services which contain within them some essence of beauty, style or creativity; a component that appeals to the 'realm of the senses' and not just to functional needs and utility. Cultural workers and artists are themselves often seen to be the embodiment of aesthetic virtues and imperatives. In terms of the art–commerce relation, an overt emphasis on art has often provided workers with a sphere of relative autonomy where they could experiment and explore often counter-rational and radical creative impulses. For many workers, the daily defence of the absolute or relative autonomy of the aesthetic is a necessity for preventing the total corruption of art in the service of commerce (Molotch, 2004). Traditionally, of course, even before 'culture industry', the aesthetic realm provided a creative and spiritual counterpoint to the rationalizing tendencies of the new modernity. The consolidation, from the eighteenth century, of conceptions of 'culture' and the 'aesthetic' marked a Romantic and idealist riposte to the invasion and blight of calculative rationality (Williams, 1980); an attempt to preserve and promote the virtues of self-expression, creativity and art. While philosophers and sociologists of art and culture have long debated whether the aesthetic actually exists as a separate and essential domain, in opposition to economic rationality, or whether it is itself merely the *product* of economic class relations and bourgeois ideological interests (see Bourdieu, 1993; Wolff, 1993), it is clear that the aesthetic has continued to act as a rallying point for all kinds of creative, spiritual and political opponents of unfettered economy.[9] While today, for some, the convergence of the cultural and the economic appears to undermine the possibility of an aesthetic 'outside', it remains the case that the aesthetic continues to provide resources and inspiration to a whole range of social actors, not just artists and creative cultural workers, as Negus and Pickering here remind us:

> The aim of self-creation requires appropriate models, and chief among these is art. The link forged between artistic creation and self-discovery or self-making remains important as an alternative resource to religious faith, or to scientism and the 'iron cage' of reason. Ideas about creativity have become integral to the modern sense of individuality because the sense of being ourselves implies expressing ourselves, in speech and in action, and so arriving at what is special and distinctive about us, or what it is we strive towards. (2004, pp. 8–9)

Regardless of the extent to which academics or critics can identify any 'specificity' or separateness for the aesthetic realm (Frith, 1996; Garnham, 2000; Williams, 1980; Wolff, 1993), a *practical belief* in its autonomous existence has proved persistently inspiring to artists and creative cultural workers. How, then, might we more fully account for the apparent *revival* of interest in the practices of aesthetic 'self-creation' in individualization?

Initially, Featherstone's (1991) argument that the 'aestheticization of everyday life' has become a characteristic feature of contemporary societies is suggestive of the possibilities now opened up for alternative forms of cultural work to flourish in individualization. In a detraditionalized epoch, marked by the rise of a more pronounced 'consumer culture', Featherstone identifies the growing use of cultural or symbolic resources as sources of identity and as bases for social differentiation, and suggests that this process of 'aestheticization' occurs in three main ways:

- First, through the effacement of the boundaries between art and everyday life, a process of 'de-auraticization' of art in a manner consistent with the practices and ambitions of the avant-garde of high modernism (Benjamin, 1970). The dismantling of a clear distinction between 'high' and 'low' culture is illustrative of the way in which art and aesthetics appear to have become more central to lived experience of ordinary people. In what are contended to be 'post-modern' societies, this effacement has now entered a more pronounced phase – witness for example, in the United Kingdom, frequent attempts to demystify and popularize opera, classical music and conceptual art (such as the popular media furnishing the movement of radical 'Young British Artists' into the mainstream of popular culture) and, in the other direction, the ways in which popular music, television and so on become consecrated in the traditional manner of 'high' culture. Art, it seems, is now for everyone and to be found everywhere.

- Second, there is the idea that life itself can be lived as a 'work of art' – this has a long history. As Featherstone traces, the coming of modernity afforded the flaneur, the dandy and those 'curious of new sensation' the opportunity to indulge in the search for new passions, tastes and indulgences (see also Tester, 1994). The viewing of one's life as an aesthetic project, a drama to be played out, is no longer the special preserve of the bohemian, the intellectual or aesthete but is now affected by a more diverse range of consumers and class fractions. Similarly, the modern obsession with bodily practices, in terms of the pursuit of new sensations and experiences, augmentations and presentations is indicative of the dispersal of a more self-conscious aesthetic attitude (Giddens, 1991). Importantly, with the democratization of aestheticization comes a corresponding intensification of the urge to display ones' taste and distinctiveness regarding the myriad ways in which culture can be 'handled', displayed and reproduced (Bourdieu, 1984). It appears culture has become more central to self-identity.

- Third, 'aestheticization' is evidenced in the proliferation of mediatized, communicative and informational goods and images that now circulate in the dizzying realm of real and virtual social space (Baudrillard, 1988). Today, advertising, television programmes, films, magazines, websites and so on are designed directly to appeal to our subjective and emotional needs, cultivate our tastes and provide us with 'dream-images' which stimulate our desires. Yet, these channels of information and communication provide us with the raw material with which to fashion new selves – arguably underpinning the formation of a more widespread critical, self-reflexive attitude (Lash and Urry, 1994).

Thus, we can read the aestheticization of everyday life as an effacement of traditional boundaries between different social realms; art and everyday life, production and consumption, fantasy and reality. The social effects of these are ambivalent. As we saw in Chapter 2, the opening up of the aesthetic realm provides new opportunities for commodification – capitalism has become extremely adept at packaging new aesthetic experience and lifestyles and commodifying established forms of cultural production (Bell, 1976; Harvey, 1989; Jameson, 1984). Indeed, as Lloyd identifies, the ethic of experimentation, creativity and insecurity that traditionally characterized 'bohemian' culture now exhibits such a clear 'elective affinity' (2006, p. 241) with the demands of post-industrial capitalism, that it is no surprise that, for some, capitalism and bohemia now appear mutually reinforcing.[10] Yet, in contrast, as argued, a combination of the aestheticization of the self in everyday life, harnessed to the 'potential subversiveness' that underpins radicalized modernity, has apparently revived the desire amongst a wider constituency of creative cultural producers to 'live a life of one's own' in a self-consciously stylized and artistic manner – one that still seeks, in utopian fashion, to avoid incorporation into a bourgeois (or perhaps now, corporately controlled) 'mainstream' (Lloyd, 2006)[11] and create a new oppositional politics.

Arguably, the increase in self-reflexivity identified by Beck and Beck-Gernsheim and Giddens (and others) may have helped re-energise the desire amongst the aesthetically inclined to pursue the 'art-life' in ways that seem to not only echo the distinctive affectations of the flaneur, dandy or aesthete of the past but also point towards new avenues of political self-expression and modes of aesthetic reflexivity. As Lash and Urry (1994) further argue, aesthetically reflexive production is on the rise and is concerned with bodily, emotive and creative modes of being, and not simply with what is economically rational or calculable. In a context of 'institutional individualization', amidst the need to remake meaningful personal bonds and social configurations, the cultural economy provides opportunities for strong artistic and aesthetically reflexive tendencies and forms of 'restricted production'[12] to flourish that, we might argue, provide a source of values inimical to a neo-liberal market rationality. Indeed, despite the machinations of the culture industry, Lash and Urry retain some degree of faith that the aesthetic domain will continue to provide a critical counterpoint to the dominant strain of rational, utilitarian and bureaucratic modernity:

[The] heremeneutic tradition of modernity provides a key foundation, a moral source for contemporary post-organized capitalist oppositional politics ... It is reflected in the rejection of the abstract, bureaucratic centralization for the immediacy of locality; in the rejection of the abstract commodity form and of consumer capitalism in general; in the rejection of highly mediated forms of material culture for an empathy with nature; in the rejection of cold abstract logic for feeling and empathy; in the rejection of abstract politics of the public sphere for a politics of the personal. (Lash and Urry, 1994, p. 49)

The apparent growth of various kinds of art-led, avant-garde and independent cultural practices – even amidst what appears to be a total triumph for commodification – suggest that reports of the death of the artist may have been somewhat exaggerated and that the search for the aesthetic 'outside' continues (see Blazwick, 2001; Carducci, 2006; Featherstone, 1991; Hall, 1998; Kit-wai Ma, 2002; Lash and Urry, 1994; Martin, 1981; O'Connor, 2006; Purves, 2005; Ray, 2004; Reynolds, 2005; Wilson, 1999, 2002). As individualization has imposed the 'necessity of choice', more and more actors appear to have chosen to pursue the art life in preference to more conventional life projects. In individualization, the necessity of 'self-creation' encourages more detailed explorations of the aesthetic domain. Contrary to McRobbie's (2002a, b) assessments, it seems that the promise of radical art as 'one of the last imaginable refuges of autonomous subjectivity' (Ray, 2004, p. 568) may remain (at least partly) intact – despite the growing 'elective affinities' between art and commerce.

While traditional artistic attitudes may have become more widespread as the 'aesthetic reflexivity' of the social individual has increased; the enhanced stimulation of desire, aspiration and a sense of style has encouraged the pursuit of other aesthetic, non-rational or non-linear modes of being (Lash and Urry, 1994). Indeed, if the role of the artist or bohemian was/is to occupy a critical space outside of the mainstream, to promote and preserve the value of art and creative cultural production in defiance of markets and modernization, a new breed of sub-bohemian grouping has emerged in the urban contexts to promote the virtues of art and culture, albeit, it seems, in more ambiguous fashion. Bourdieu (1984) famously refers to the now enhanced role of the 'cultural intermediaries' – the artistically inclined sub-group of the 'new petit bourgeoisie' whose role involves insinuating new patterns of cultural meaning, taste and style into the social fabric.[13] Bourdieu sees cultural intermediaries as mainly comprising media critics, commentators and journalists, but theorists such as Featherstone (1991), Negus

(1992), Nixon (2003) and Wright (2005) have since embraced the term and expanded it to theorize a whole variety of occupations and roles concerned with cultural promotion, brokerage, commentary or curatorship (for a critical note on this see Hesmondhalgh, 2007). In contrast to the more obviously outré or bohemian element, the cultural intermediary occupies an ambivalent terrain between art and commercial worlds. For instance, initially, Bourdieu (1984/2003, p. 326) is rather scornful of the efforts of these bohemians of the consumer age, labelling cultural intermediaries as 'moderately revolutionary taste makers', instrumental arrivistes engaged in 'controlled transgressions'; whose main role appears to be acting as promoters of new forms of capitalist cultural production, servicing the demands of the culture industry for those who can translate and mediate new products to various markets and 'taste publics'. Others, however, have more enthusiastically adopted the notion of the cultural intermediary to demonstrate the capacity of cultural producers to set new and diverse patterns of taste and lay the foundations for paradigmatic shifts in the social and political tenor of cultural production activity (Featherstone, 1991; O'Connor and Wynne, 1996b). For instance, using the example of Manchester's popular culture economy (particularly the economic and physical renewals associated with the 1980s 'Madchester' music scene), O'Connor and Wynne argue that cultural intermediaries can exert a diverse range of effects, transforming cities and culture in progressive ways unanticipated by the political and commercial mainstream, creating new opportunities for alternative and vernacular forms of cultural expression to flourish beyond or alongside market culture; here they demonstrate cultural intermediaries' political potential. They argue that while the culture industry's constant and expanded demands for translation, promotion and promulgation of specialized aesthetic experiences has led to significant expansion of cultural intermediary occupations in mainstream market contexts, such a shift has also opened the door for alternative – that is more 'oppositional', 'local' or 'experimental' forms of cultural intermediation to develop (see also Kit-wai Ma, 2002; Milestone, 1996; Ward, 2000).

In summary, while (echoing Adorno) many critics have alluded to the creeping commodification and industrialization of art and culture, and the degrading effects of capitalism on artistic, bohemian and cultural intermediary practice, for others the ongoing expansion and dissemination of aesthetic/art practices (within and without the context of capitalist firms), alternative art forms and the growth of cultural intermediation beyond market culture suggest that the possibilities of autonomous production may have, in some part, been *enhanced* by the individualizing dynamics that now underpin the social structure of contemporary societies. Underpinning the growth and diversification of cultural production is a retention of belief in the autonomous potential of the aesthetic realm, where the concerns of art and culture are considered to be of equal or greater merit to that of the economic, and where utopian possibilities are explored in the context of a post-traditional culture that 'is not a singular narrative...but a set of relationships, possibilities, open moments [and] potential becomings' (O'Connor, 2006, p. 99; see also Frith, 1996). Of course, while an aesthetic 'renaissance' and an increase in the volume and spread of art and cultural production provides no guarantee of its political efficacy, it seems reasonable to hypothesize that autonomous production and its apparent democratization and dispersal may be providing *some* opportunities for new kinds of cultural work identities to emerge that offer a challenge – not only to existing cultural or artistic orthodoxies but also to market-led forms of cultural work.

Now, having identified the possible endurance of an aesthetic 'outside', I want to examine what happens when aesthetics and ethics collide. While social scientists continue to puzzle over the differences between the aesthetic and the non-aesthetic (see Wolff, 1993), it is clear that at the level of practice, cultural workers are becoming increasingly (re) engaged in economic practices that seek to combine both aesthetic and more evidently 'social' and 'political' impulses. The 'social turn' and the mooted 'remoralization' of economic relations (Heelas, 2002) appear to have had their impacts on even the apparently 'desocialized' cultural industries sector. In the following sections I thus examine two further alternative tendencies in the cultural industries sector – ones that seek to generate not *just* aesthetic goods or an aesthetic critique (since this remains central), but also develop more communitarian or socially oriented values in production. I refer to these as (in the first instance) 'practice-led' and (in the second instance) 'ethical' economies.

Practice-led economies

The assumption that the acquisition of *external* goods such as money, power and fame is now the primary motivator of cultural workers is implicit in the critical theory and governmental critiques. When workers are faced with constant exhortations to become more entrepreneurial, promotional, business-like and self-directed, could it realistically be anything else? But, under individualized conditions, others have argued that the pursuit of *internal* rewards can provide just as strong an incentive to (cultural) work than the accumulation of external goods. Taken as primary motivations, these internal rewards can not only moderate the extent to which the pursuit of external goods is prioritized but may also promote alternative forms of economic organizing with socially progressive potential. Arguably, under individualized conditions, we can identify something of a shift back to 'authentic' forms of production (local, traditional, 'natural' or 'organic') and a revalorization of craft production amongst cultural producers as they seek out the benefits of these internal rewards (Becker, 1982; Lash, 1994).[14]

In recent times, MacIntyre's *After Virtue* (1981) has done most to promote recognition of the importance of internal goods and rewards, mainly through his critical discussion of the declining role of *practices* in the reproduction of social and economic life. Practices, in MacIntyre's usage, refer to a very distinctive assemblage of activities:

> By a 'practice' I am going to mean any coherent and complex form of socially established cooperative human activity through which goods internal to that forms of activity are realised in the course of trying to achieve those standards of excellence which are appropriate to, and partially definitive of, that form of activity, with the result that the human powers achieve excellence, and human conceptions of the ends of goods involved, are systematically extended. (1981, p. 175)

For MacIntyre, the range of practices is wide, extending across the arts, humanities and sciences, and he suggests physics, architecture, football, painting, farming and gaming as illustrative examples. MacIntyre is clear that, regardless of their material specificity, practices are inherently concerned with internal rewards, that is, the production of goods intrinsic to the practice itself, rather than *merely* the pursuit of competitively acquired, external rewards. Practices, then, may generate wealth but are also worthy and good to do in themselves. The generation of goods 'internal to a practice' is explained here through the example of the practice of chess-playing:

> There are thus two kinds of goods possibly to be gained by playing chess. On the one hand there are those goods externally and contingently attached to chess-playing and to other practices by the accidents of social circumstance...goods such as prestige, status and money. There are always alternative ways of achieving such goods, and their achievement is never to be had only by engaging in some particular kind of practice. On the other hand there are goods internal to the practice of chess which cannot be had in anyway but by

playing chess or some other game of that specific kind. We call them internal for two reasons: first, as I have already suggested, because we can only specify them in terms of chess or some other game of that specific kind ... and secondly because they can only be identified and recognised by the experience of participating in the practice in question. Those who lack the relevant experience are incompetent thereby as judges of internal goods. (MacIntyre, 1981, p. 176)

Internal rewards, then, are those unobtainable elsewhere; they are practice-specific. Moreover, they can only be fully realized through dedication and immersion; that is, when practitioners establish a knowledge and appreciation of a given practice's interior qualities, and an intimacy with its specific demands, rhythms and routines – what we might call a true 'feel for the game'. Internal goods tend to derive from respect, perhaps even love, of the practice, and recognition of its fundamental virtue in providing an ethical centre and a culture of embedded moral sanctions. The practitioner who wishes to acquire internal goods must seek to reproduce the practice and serve the community of practitioners.

In contrast, external goods/rewards (such as money, power and fame) tend to be practice-independent and rather more exclusive because, as MacIntyre and also Keat (2000) argue, those who possess them do so at the expense of those who do not. External goods are the property and possession of individuals and circulate in the economy as objects of competition, which, for MacIntyre, encourages the cultivation of selfish and acquisitive tendencies. While internal rewards also stem from competitive tendencies (to emulate or exceed the efforts of others), they differ from external rewards because their successful achievement provides 'a good for the whole community who participate in the practice' (1981, p. 178), leading to (say) a general standard of technical improvement or a collective raising of consciousness regarding the creative possibilities of future practice – they are not *primarily* pursued for personal advantage or material gain. The crucial point is that competition in the context of practices is 'conducted in relation to the shared standards of the practice concerned' (Keat, 2000, p. 24), ensuring that success is enjoyed in a non-exclusive form.

Why are practices important? For MacIntyre, the prevalence of practices is one indicator of a morally coherent and stable society. The exemplary case cited is the pre-modern society where economic production (it is argued) was predominantly undertaken in a practice-like manner and so provided the moral guidance and existential certainty necessary for societal reproduction of a common order (Booth, 1994; Scott, 1976). In *After Virtue*, McIntyre's claim is that the shift from a 'moral' economy, embedded in community contexts, to a more abstract and disembedded system of market exchange has been the catalyst for the relative erosion of practice-like social relations and a subsequent demoralization of society. More specifically, because market-led societies have placed greater emphasis on the acquisition of external rather than internal goods, (indeed the pursuit of wealth, fame and status is often an end in itself), this has then overpowered the virtues internal to practices such as pursuit of the 'common good' and the valorization of rigour, excellence and integrity. This, in turn, has disastrous consequences for the individual, as correspondent with this estrangement from the virtues of generating and sharing in community benefits comes the undermining of individuals' well-being, self-respect and sense of security, strongly argued by MacIntyre to be amongst the innate qualities of personality to be obtained through working in practice-based communities.

MacIntyre's argument would appear to uphold (rather than challenge) an orthodox critique of cultural work – that is, the pursuit of external goods is overpowering the virtues of community development associated with reflexive production. However, there are good reasons to reject MacIntyre's pessimistic analysis. Keat's (2000) re-articulation of MacIntyre's ideas moves us towards a more sanguine view of the fate of practices; indeed, Keat develops his own line of argument to suggest that practices not only endure within modern economies but may also be intrinsically supported by the move towards a more institutionally complex as well as individualized economy.

Keat's critique rests on a disagreement with MacIntyre regarding the role of institutions in modern societies. While MacIntyre (rightly) argues that practices cannot survive without the guidance and legitimacy provided by institutional settings (example of institutions may include markets, firms, schools, hospitals, football clubs and so on), he is sceptical that the pursuit of practices is, in the long run, able to be maintained within the context of such institutions. This is because, MacIntyre argues, institutions tend to be concerned with obtaining external rather than internal goods, indeed, he sees their express function being to accumulate money and other material goods, to obtain power, status and standing, and to discriminately distribute these goods as rewards. The pursuit of external rewards is, for MacIntyre, inimical to the long-term cultivation of practices, for external goods (usually justified in terms of the pursuit of 'public standing', 'commercial interest' or meeting the 'demands of the market') can overshadow and diminish the autonomy of practices, or as MacIntyre puts it, 'the cooperative care for the common goods of the practice is always vulnerable to the competitiveness of the institution' (1981, p. 181). Keat (echoing Beck's view of the ambivalent potential of institutional individualization) rejects this argument as overlooking some essential variety in the dynamics of institutional life:

> What might then be suggested ... is that there is a significant degree of (actual and potential) variability in the extent to which firms may possess [practice-antithetical] characteristics, and likewise in their possession of practice-like ones. On this view, what is wrong with their standard theoretical depiction is not that this bears no relation to reality, but that it misrepresents as universal, unvarying and necessary what may in fact be specific, variable and contingent. (Keat, 2000, p. 117)

For Keat, institutions and the pursuit of external goods are not necessarily inimical to practice-like activity. For example, even amongst firms most dedicated to cultivating external rewards, practices may endure. This is because often it is simply not in the interests of firms to behave as 'rational' organizations and eradicate 'irrational' (non-competitive) elements of practice. For instance, firms may find that that employees engaged in 'non-practice' activity, are, in Keat's terms, 'a manager's nightmare' (ibid., p. 118), simply because their single-minded pursuit of self-interest over and above the concerns of the organisation may 'play havoc in any organization requiring high degrees of co-operation, mutual respect and commitment to its collective goals' (ibid., p. 118). Indeed, the cultivation of external rewards may well be *more likely* to occur if a firm employs the character of a practice and tries to implement a culture where colleagues value one another, and the community in which they are embedded, as well as take pride and show concern to meet practice-like standards of quality and excellence in their work. This idea is now realized in the ways managers routinely attempt to transform firms into 'communities of practice' (Amin, 2000; Grugulis et al., 2000; Wenger, 1998) and adopt 'culture change' programmes, so getting employees to value themselves, their work and identify as member of a practice-like community (see Chapter 4). Thus, firms may legitimately seek to cultivate both external and internal rewards, and, indeed, may see them as self-supporting. While this *appears* to offer progressive potential, the endurance of practices under such circumstances does not necessarily mean, of course, that these practices contain any radical or ethical commitment other than those deemed permissible by managers working under market conditions – we should not celebrate too soon.

However, the endurance of practices in institutions is crucial for a second, potentially more progressive, reason. While the will to obtain external rewards may well override a commitment to internal rewards, or external rewards and internal rewards might be seen as commensurable and symbiotic (the 'communities of practice' approach), it is also the case that the desire to derive goods internal to a practice can more substantively displace the pursuit of external rewards and the adherence to market imperatives. That is, practices can flourish at the *expense* of non-practice based, market-led imperatives. As Keat observes, firms and organizations may well act as profit–satisfiers rather than profit maximizers, and entrepreneurs and workers may be more strongly motivated by internal rather than external rewards, not least by the love of the practice, respect for others and the concomitant sense of well-being and security that practice-like activities can potentially generate. The phrase 'I do it for the love and not the money' is commonly heard in these institutional contexts.

While, as we saw in Chapters 3 and 4, such sentiments may leave workers open to (self)-exploitation, they can also lead to counter-capitalist initiatives. For Keat, modern institutions always contain within them the possibility of practice-like behaviour, for not only do economic actors remain more socially embedded than MacIntyre appears to allow but they are also motivated by a diverse (and often unpredictable) array of non-economic rationales.

While practices are not specific to cultural work, there is (as we have seen) a clear affinity between embedded forms of craft production and cultural work, indeed (industrialized) craft production remains the dominant form of cultural work organization (Becker, 1982; Ryan, 1992). Craft values and modes of organization are so central to the design and manufacture of cultural goods it is no surprise to find practice-like values *particularly* prevalent in environments of cultural industry production. For example, Toynbee (2003) appears to confirm the persistence of practices in cultural work in his account of workers' motivations in the music industry. His reflections on the reasons why, despite the strong possibility of economic exploitation or failure, many musicians, bands and labels continue to write, produce, perform and promote their own music resonate strongly with Keat's arguments:

> Popular music production is a form of capitalist enterprise in which money and labor are conjoined so as to produce star commodities.

Yet it also constitutes a creative arena in which people come together on a mutual basis to make symbolic artefacts. Certainly these two zones are imbricated. But it is wrong to see the latter simply as a function of the former....Exchange does go on in proto-markets. People buy and sell records and they pay to go to gigs and enter clubs. But what defines the proto-market is that music-making cannot be explained solely by economic factors. Musicians produce and perform to small audiences for the love of it, for the esteem and also, of course, because they hope to be recruited by the music industry [but] the very weakness of the imperative to accumulate in the proto-market facilitates a strange mixture of experiment, hybridity and parochialism. (Toynbee, 2003, pp. 52–53)

Many musicians and DJs I have interviewed also appeared to embody this community-focussed, practice-like approach; as one here commented:

I like playing in Manchester because you know who's going to turn up and your friends are there...I like small club nights...I think if you want to make money from it you've got to have a really tight conventional night, like you've got to do a student night, pack it with students play mainstream numbers. You see [club] nights [that] start small, they start underground, and then they just get bigger and bigger and kind of lose it a bit, do you know what I mean? They become more mainstream and it's not what they're about originally and I never want that to happen to what I was doing, I just wanted to keep it how I always wanted it, otherwise I wouldn't bother doing it.

Despite the ever-present dangers of commodification by the culture industry, craft values and creative impulses remain vital motivations for action, and can support conditions where music production continues relatively autonomous of market imperatives. In contemporary dance music in particular, with its emphasis on the 'tunes' rather than their (usually faceless) author, on creating 'authentic' clubbing environments and through the 'strong connectivity between music-makers within the genre', Toynbee identifies a commitment to aesthetic and autonomous production that has clear echoes with MacIntyre's understanding of the constitution of a practice. MacIntyre would no doubt approve of dance music's emphasis on 'shared creativity' and the production of 'beautiful gifts' (Toynbee, 2003, p. 52–53). For Toynbee, the embedded nature of dance music is the latest example of how 'making music, in all its contradictions, offers an example of the virus-like persistence of mutual and democratic practice within capitalism' (ibid., p. 53), and while not indifferent to the more deleterious intrusions of the market, he is, nonetheless, convinced that cultural production is an environment where 'both conditions pertain', that is where both creative/autonomous and market imperatives coexist in a related tension (see also Becker, 1982; Hesmondhalgh, 1998; Molotch, 2004).

Thus, we might surmise that cultural firms (and institutions in general) are diverse constituencies, composed of groups and individuals that display considerable variability in the way they value and work to obtain, both internal and external rewards. The musicians studied by Toynbee (and myself), tend to support Keat's argument that individualization, rather than *only* producing desocialized or self-driven egoists (as recently suggested by Bourdieu, McRobbie, Sennett and so on) also provides enhanced opportunities for critical self-reflection on the part of economic subjects, and can lead to a more judicious and evaluative attitude regarding ones' involvement in the competition for obtaining internal or external rewards:

> there are other and more positive ways of interpreting and evaluating the 'separation of individuals' in modern society. In particular, one might view these separate identities as conditions of individual autonomy, and hence also as associated with the possibility of more reflective and critical modes of judgment on the part of individuals. What is then distinctive about modern morality is not so much its attempted solution to the 'new' problem of egoism, but its insistence that rules of conduct and principles of social action should commend themselves to critical judgement. (Keat, 2000, p. 127)

This supports Beck and Beck-Gernsheim's observations that flexible economic restructuring and individualization processes generally have helped create new and differentiated institutional settings and enhanced the possibilities for critical self-reflexivity. Keat's work supports the idea that in advanced societies, characterized by diffuse range of internally complex institutions, the prospects for an expansion of not only aesthetic but also moral – that is, *socially embedded* – practices may be in part revived: ones founded upon hard-to-destroy communitarian sentiments that continue to underpin the execution of economic responsibility. Indeed, I now explore how the social embeddedness of cultural workers also appears to be generating, not only a relatively closed occupational economy of craft practices but also more explicitly public, civic-minded or *ethical* forms of cultural work.

Ethical economies

The virtue of the idea of practices is to reawaken us to the enduring *social* basis of economic production.[15] This runs contrary to the impression given in most discussion of cultural industries where one side of the 'art–commerce' relation is usually given priority, and social values are either marginalized or only residually considered. However, cultural production, like all economic production, is also socially based – and always has been (see Booth, 1994; Sayer, 2004b). Because, as Lash and Urry (1994) argue, the 'socially-embedded' worker in the cultural economy of 'signs and space' is not simply a relatively benign mediator of capitalist social relations (as implied by Granovetter, 1985) but an active, self-reflexive and critical subject (Lash, 1994), I want to explore here how this active subjectivity now extends into more explicitly ethical (as well as aesthetic) critique in cultural work. While the pursuit of the good and the pursuit of the beautiful have not always been considered desirable or compatible, I argue here that an increasing number of cultural workers and firms are now attempting to merge the two.

From where do these ethical impulses derive? While, for Lash and Urry, it is new information and communication structures that provide the principal means for creating the reflexive self, here I explore how such structures may merely be helping to remobilize some *already existing* deep-rooted desires for social and ethical re-embedding amongst worker–subjects; ones that are given distinctive expression in the context of an emergent 'ethical' cultural industries economy.

While capitalists (and neo-liberals particularly) argue that the 'natural' pursuit of self-interest derives from some firmly rooted psychological and social impulses that help reinforce an inclination towards instrumental independence, simultaneously there are those psychosocial impulses that incline us strongly towards communal and collective (and essentially non-economic) forms of sociability. If we accept that humans are driven by a psychological and social need to belong and to both give and receive such virtues as love, recognition, affirmation and respect – in this way we may be able to understand how, despite the undoings of the individualization process, actors can remain committed to moral and ethical commitments associated with family, community, work, religion and politics, even as these undergo radical reconstitutions in form.[16] Indeed, in liberal–democratic fashion, we might argue that this deep-rooted and durable search for meaningful social bonds has been (at least partly) revivified and refocused by the individualization process.

While, as Beck notes, in the interests of competition and choice, markets may attempt to unglue social bonds, so removing people from the secure foundations of tradition, it nonetheless appears that actors feel compelled to reinvent and re-establish forms of solidarity and attachment, even if such bonds seem often more precarious or unrecognizable from those which have gone before (Beck and Willms, 2004). Beck identifies that the compulsion to commune with others is strong. As long as people strive for love and other rewarding emotional relationships, work to create new forms of community, 'do their bit' for a 'better society' and pioneer heterodox models of 'family' life, so the individualized subject cannot merely be seen as a generalized *homo economicus*, but as fully rounded human actor who, at one and the same time, must balance the pursuit of self-interest while seeking self-fulfilment and upholding the moral obligations that derive from their own psychological needs and (unavoidable) embeddedness in the social world (see also Booth, 1994;[17] Sayer, 1999). Indeed, the extent to which one is able to achieve self-fulfilment is not easily reducible to ones' ability to exercise profitable market choices, but may be more closely correlated with how far one is able to balance economic needs with the ability to socialize and commune with others, for as Beck understands it, a strongly entrenched belief (at least amongst European democracies) is in the 'duty and necessity of reinventing social arrangements' (Beck and Willms, 2004, p. 75) while simultaneously living a self-chosen life. This not only means people feel regard for others, and act in relation to this, but they must also co-operate and consort with others if they are to achieve the levels of self-fulfilment consummate with becoming what we might term a fully rounded and self-realized *character*.

What is character? For Sennett (1998, p. 10) it is concerned with 'the personal traits which we value in ourselves and for which we seek to be valued by others', and is expressed in 'loyalty and mutual commitment' and is defined, not by those interior preoccupations that 'fester within' but by an orientation to the social world. Character is that which endures beyond immediate satisfactions and self-interest – in this way it is resolutely incompatible with the idea of the rational market subject. Indeed, in his invective against the autarkic subject of market societies, O'Neill (1998) argues against the view that people who can adopt and discard social roles for instrumental purposes can represent fully self-realized subjects – true autonomy, as he puts it, 'requires serious commitments which are non-contractual in nature' (1998, p. 76). He argues that even in market-dominated societies, autonomous individuality is not meaningful if understood as the mere freedom to exchange contracts. For O'Neill, autonomous individuality is a *combination* of both free-choice imperatives and the embedded moral legacies of norms, values and obligations; it is this amalgamation that enables the formation of meaningful character, in his terms 'a set of settled dispositions born of deep commitments to lasting projects and relationships which organizes one's experience of the world' (1998, p. 82). The figures of the calculating and rational market subject (and, also, the post-modern notion of the playful and autonomous self-creator) are rejected by O'Neill as equally impoverished notions of the self:

> The person who could move in and out of commitments has no clear identity of character at all. The commitments and loyalties to other persons and projects that make up a person's life, that make it her own life, could not exist in the person who with ease could move out of them. The person who shifted his ties to projects, to a community, to ideas and values, with the ease with which an individual changes clothes with the changing fashions lacks an identity. They are in Mill's sense characterless. (O'Neill, 1998, p. 75)

From a liberal–democratic perspective it is possible to argue that 'self-insufficiency' (Beck and Beck-Gernsheim, 2002, p. xxi) and the search for character can act as important catalysts for social re-embedding. Character comes through socialization with others, and provides the possibility of self-fulfilment on a more emotionally complete and existentially rewarding level beyond that offered by markets. Of course, as Sennett (1998) has argued, markets can 'corrode' character, but amongst those vouching for its robustness and relative autonomy from market strictures is Berking, who argues that regard for forms of non-instrumental sociality remains vital and enduring, for even in individualized societies:

> [O]ur everyday knowledge continues to distinguish strictly between market-governed relations and social relations, between the principles of equivalence and reciprocity, between contract and the non-contractual conditions of any contract, the latter being cognitive, norm-like and emotional competences which anything but reduce interest in the other to the mode of a merely strategic interaction. (1996, p. 192)

Echoing Beck, Berking suggests that meaningful forms of self-realization cannot be achieved outside of interaction with others; for it is only in recognizing the value and importance of non-market social relationships that true self-realization (a fully rounded character) can be attained, as he asserts: 'The ego's identity, its claim to self-realization, or put more banally, its well-being, is not worth a rap without the care for and attention to the 'others' and nature' (Berking, 1996, p. 201).

While, for personal or structural reasons, the attainment of character may prove elusive, for many, in recent years, the diffuse constitution of contemporary politics, no longer simply conducted at the level of class and nation, has seen a concern for oneself, for others and, indeed, for the global commons, take root in the private and familial sphere, find articulation in discourse on local and global 'issues', and take on a more integrative and extensive form in the guise of 'life politics' or the 'new social movements' (Berking, 1996; Giddens, 1991; Maffesoli, 1996). Arguably, the rise of alternative political movements has come hand in hand with individualization, so expressing modernization's radical impulse for eroding 'old' (class-based) political alliances whilst simultaneously carving out new axes of discrimination and conflict, 'expanding the scope of the expressible and giving new normative impulses to the struggle over the definition of the social' (Berking, 1996, p. 200). For Beck, the arena in which re-embedding occurs, that is, where social–political values and moral obligations may be re-established, is referred to as the realm of 'sub-politics', that is, the institutional space created by individualization pervasively 'tearing down the borders that separate the arena of specialized politics from a depoliticized society' (Beck and Willms 2004, p. 98). Subpolitics is defined as political activity both beyond and within the formal political systems of first modernity, that is beyond the nation state, the party system and passive adherence to ones' inherited fate and prescribed identity. Notwithstanding appropriate concerns regarding their effectiveness, as Holzer and Sorensen (2003, p. 95) confirm, contemporary societies are now widely populated by 'active subpoliticians who refuse to restrict themselves to the channels provided by formal politics', who have moved to take control of their fate across the full range of social spheres. For example, the recent proliferation of 'social enterprises', various forms of environmentally friendly and ethical business and the growth of more aesthetically and spiritually directed 'slow' or 'soft' capitalism suggest that alternatives to the neo-liberal market model already pervade economic discourse and practice (Amin et al., 2002; Heelas, 2002; Honoré, 2004; Leyshon et al., 2003; Williams, 2005). Indeed, just at the point where neo-liberalism appears to have achieved a 'natural' supremacy (Smart, 2003) writers such as Crossley (2003), Kingsnorth (2003) and Klein (2000) point to the emergence of a wide array of social relations and movements opposed to the dogma of free-market fundamentalism, impelled to make new social and economic relations based on sustain-ability, mutuality and a sense of moral obligation.

The social or moral turn is not specific to the cultural industries, but now the explosion of ethical fashion houses, socially responsible graphic designers and new media entrepreneurs, community film projects, pub-lic access media channels and so forth evidence an expansion of social rationales in cultural enterprises (see for example Carducci, 2006, Drake 2003, Klein 2000; Ray, 2004) – and contradict increasingly abject read-ings of cultural industry's 'demoralized' character. To provide an illus-trative empirical example, Amin et al., (2002) in their study of the 'social economy' identify a number of art-based, ethical enterprises, such as the Art Factory in South Wales, a highly successful community organization specializing in the training of local people in arts and environmental crafts, lifelong learning and creative enterprise, serving one of the poorest parts of the United Kingdom. To give an illustration from my own locality, in Manchester, the Ultimate Holding Company is an art collective and not-for-profit design company whose work is premised on a radical motivation:

> their explicit aim is to identify and seek to operate outside established political consensus, to seek to establish equal relationships on the basis of collaboration. It is not they want to form alternative coali-tions; rather they explicitly work against the government and instead seek to have a direct relationship with communities. Their artistic and political engagement is based on the fundamental idea that UHC opposes...the cultural decay created by neo-liberalism. Art on a collective, not for profit basis is used as a tool to directly challenge commercial primacy. (Vloeberghs, 2006, p. 33)

Indeed, amongst the cultural workers I have interviewed, a conver-gence of aesthetic and social–ethical tendencies has often been noted; a desire to undertake cultural production that generates not only eco-nomic profit but also artistic *and* social–political benefits and impacts; as here first, a digital artist and curator, and then, second, a new media entrepreneur and former music promoter, articulate:

> What I do at the moment is much more politicised ... and that's what really interests me, turning round the idea of gallery art not having political potential [just] because its a self contained system, and I would always argue the other way round; that [is] the artist can put

on ... political activities which otherwise would be outlawed so to speak, so I'm trying to ... work on the interface between culture and political action, that's my motivation.

I was putting on shows. They were mainly for global things, like anti-apartheid, anti-racism generally; the biggest one we did was in Albert Square [in Manchester] called 'Jammin' for Jobs', it was about the city being forced to shed workers. There were quite radical political movements meshing with the cultural stuff.

The durability in modernity of arts organizations that are both aesthetically *and* socially oriented has been acknowledged for some time (Byrne, et al., 2006; Sharon, 1979). While it is of course difficult to specify the exact numbers of those involved, for optimists like Ray it is clear that 'oppositional convergence' as he calls it, is now in the ascendancy, with socially and politically motivated production and what he terms 'catalytic art' now identified as a widespread means for producing 'other desires and other imaginaries' (2004, p. 565–569) in a whole variety of social and spatial contexts. As he identifies, there is now a *global* coming together of the radicalized cultural worker and organizers of social–political initiatives, increasingly interacting in new kinds of rhizomatic production network, such as the GALA Committee, Critical Art Ensemble, Electronic Disturbance Theater, Superflex, Raqs Media Collective, Nettime, Institute for Applied Autonomy and the Bureau of Inverse Technology, all of which seek to mobilize social change and challenge some complacencies of the 'institutionalized art world' (Ray, 2004, p. 570).

Additionally, Holmes (2004, p. 551) identifies something of a (re)convergence of artists and creative cultural workers with other social and occupational groups committed to ethical forms of economic production:

A deepening consciousness of personal stakes in the contemporary economy has more recently led young and not-so-young artists and theorists to participate in the self-organization of flexible workers, giving rise to a new kind of urban event, the Mayday parades,[18] first organised in Milan and then in Barcelona.

As he further comments, buoyed by such initiatives, the 'anti-precarity' movement has, in turn, helped re-inspire the direct actions of cultural workers; to give one example:

In France, direct attacks from the right-wing government and the employers' organization have resulted in the struggle of the part-time theatre and audiovisual workers to defend a special unemployment regime that helped shield them from the conditions of flexible labour, and so allowed them to practice their art outside the conditions dictated by the market. (2004, p. 551)

While we should be cautious about over-emphasizing the waves generated by these radical interventions, I would agree with Ray (2004) that we should not too airily dismiss the valuable impacts of these concrete efforts to instantiate social and ethical forms of cultural production – nor the prospects for their continuation in individualization.

Summary

In contrast to previous chapters, here I have examined the progressive, liberal–democratic possibilities of individualization in cultural work. Positing the possible revival (rather than the repression) of active agency in individualization, underpinned by the durable persistence of an aesthetic tradition and an intrinsically socially embedded or 'moral' economy (Booth, 1994), I have identified how the new 'necessity of choice' appears to have underwritten a renascent search for heterodox forms of (cultural) economizing. Outlined were three schematic responses of the individualized cultural worker:

- First, I examined how enhanced 'aesthetic reflexivity' and the mooted 'aestheticization of everyday life' may have re-energized the efforts of artists, bohemians and cultural intermediaries to seek out new social utopias. Despite ever-present dangers of commodification, the possibilities for critical forms of 'restricted production' appear open and durable and have arguably been enhanced by individualizing dynamics (Lash and Urry, 1994). Implied here is some assumption that modernity's aesthetic domain continues to exhibit some relative autonomy from capitalist conditions that seek to contain it (Frith, 1996; Williams, 1980; Wolff, 1993).
- Second, I have examined how a quest for not only aesthetic but also more 'authentic' and 'meaningful' forms of post-traditional identity may lie behind the ongoing pursuit of 'internal goods' and practice-based communities in craft-based cultural work (Becker, 1982; Keat, 2000). While it has long been accepted that the unique feature of craft-based cultural production is that it is motivated by certain intrinsic (artistic, creative, aesthetic) values as much as by the pursuit of external rewards, it has been recently assumed by critical theory

approaches that the diminution of craft production has proceeded in line with market development and the consolidation of the culture industry (Ryan, 1992). This chapter has explored the opposite view, that, in fact, practice-led craft production *can* actually flourish in detraditionalized and individualized social environments character-ized by the necessity of choice and the ongoing search for meaning. Indeed, the revival of craft production amongst amateurs, artisans, small firms and enterprises is becoming a more prominent feature of late-modern life (Becker, 1982; Crafts Council, 2004).

• Third, I have explored the mooted growth of socially directed, ethical rationales in cultural work, ones that derive not only from the freedoms of choice imposed by individualization but also from the enduring socially embedded (moral, normative) character of eco-nomic life (Amin et al., 2002; Beck, 2000; Berking, 1996; Booth, 1994; Sayer, 1999, 2004b; Wilber, 1996). As long as people strive for values that markets cannot provide, they will work to (re)construct socially embedded structures that furnish them with these values, which can involve developing forms of social or ethical economizing, and it seems that in contrast to their conventional image as 'depoliticized' – cultural workers are often at the forefront of such initiatives (Holmes, 2004; Ray, 2004).

This chapter has attempted to summarize some of the more visible traits of 'alternative' production now evident in the cultural industries. It describes, however, only some overlapping and integrated *tendencies*; schematic approximations of the varied *possibilities* for alternative or 'progressive' practices under conditions of economic flexibility and enhanced individualization – and so does not claim to provide any fixed or immutable categories. The schema suggests that while a general sense of the aesthetic underpins all these interventions, some enduring and emergent social values are becoming increasingly important in cul-tural production. Within this classification, no prioritization is implied; the 'pure' aesthetic is not judged as being superior to a compromised utilitarian or 'social' production model, nor is communitarian or socially 'useful' production prioritized over the abstractness or 'frivol-ity' of the aesthetic – the identification of contrasting forms of cultural production is, at this stage, merely empirical. Cultural economies and individual firms and producers may, therefore, be seen to be driven by varied combinations of what I have crudely termed 'pure-artistic', 'prac-tice-led' or 'ethical' motivations – or perhaps none of these.[19] As Paperstergiadis (2002, p. 74) otherwise puts it, 'the recruitment of art in the politics of oppositionality does not fall into a pre-set position'. What *has* more *generally* been suggested is that the acceleration of individuali-zation – that is, the rapacity with which modernization breaks down social forms – while appearing to secure the hegemony of the 'free' mar-ket by eroding traditional non-market structures, and privileging only capitalistic 'enterprise', can also lead to enhanced opportunities for reflexive critical judgement, and the development of alternative forms of economizing. When coupled to deep-rooted aesthetic impulses and hard-to-destroy (moral) desires for social re-embedding, this can prove a powerful impetus towards economic diversity and remoralization.

While critics of individualization see only the retreat of institutional alternatives in the midst of market advancement, here I have explored the alternative view that individualization may actually lead to further hybridization and social re-embedding as individuals and firms radi-cally explore the possibilities of detraditionalization (and retradition-alization) amidst the enhanced 'necessity of choice'.[20] Thus, I have sought to expose the ambiguities of individualization and suggested the possibility of more 'progressive' cultural work futures. But before we subject this new model to the required critical analysis, in the next chapter I want to detour in order to examine how the contrasting 'critical theory' and 'liberal-democratic' models of cultural production have become re-articulated in the context of a new and compelling discussion on the emergent *geography* of the cultural industries.

6
Space, Place and Cultural Work

In industrial societies, while capital emerged as an 'abstract', 'mobile' and 'de-territorializing' force, in order to be effective, it required grounding in the material world. Indeed, it was largely (if not exclusively) through the process of investment in relatively *immobile* plants, machinery, infrastructure, labour and land that new commodities were produced and surplus values extracted. In creating profits from these fixed resources, capital was then remobilized to seek out new spaces, so garnering further profits and insuring against devaluation crises and recession. Thus, as various spatial theorists have since argued, it was only through the production of space could space be conquered (see, for example, Harvey, 1989; Lefebvre, 1991). Yet, paradoxically, it was also the case that while the creation of spaces and places may have helped provide capitalism with development *opportunities*, the social structures that inhered within places had an erratic tendency to generate certain 'local variations' (labour alliances, community structures, governments, cultural norms) that offered a *threat* to capital's effective operation. Places, then, contained hidden surprises; populated by capricious forces, they were unpredictable and irregular; always fluid and never fixed, to use Massey's (1993) conceptualization. It is this duality of place that I keep in mind as I examine here the spatial organization of cultural industries and cultural work.

First, following on from Chapter 2, I analyse the apparent globalization of industrialized cultural production. A number of theorists have sought recently to argue that the 'culture industry' now operates most efficiently across trans-territorial space, as barriers to the free flow of cultural commodities evaporate, and production systems seek to integrate materials, systems and labour from all corners of the globe (Bourdieu, 1998; Debord, 1967; Hardt and Negri, 2000; McRobbie,

2002a,b; Miller et al., 2003; Rifkin, 2000; Scherzinger, 2005). The geography of cultural production is understood here as singular, integrated and neo-liberal – a 'de-localized' space inhabited by workers subjected to internationally applied standards of 'flexible' labour control. I then outline a more nuanced version of the globalization thesis which identifies the growth of 'decentralized accumulation' (Wayne, 2003) in embedded production contexts, yet continues to stress that even apparently 'independent' and '(re)localized' production remains dominated by the strategic interests of powerful corporations.

Second, in contrast, I explore how various theorists of social and spatial embeddedness have sought to stress the relative *autonomy* of the 'local' in these ostensibly globalized times. Here, critics understand the geographies of cultural production to be more substantially composed of particularized agglomerations, organizations and social processes – where, crucially, small, independent firms and local 'clusters' appear to be surviving on something like their own ethical terms (Florida, 2002; Fujita et al., 2000; Porter, 1990; Scott, 2000). Here, place is identified as crucial to not only the production of distinctive commodities but also the reproduction of embedded and harmonious social and workplace relations. However, as critical theorists have countered, while the mooted shift towards more reflexive 'clusters' of (cultural) production might appear *initially* to be socially progressive, promising more place-specific and emancipated forms of work, in actuality, the renaissance of sociality remains regressive since it continues to be dominated by global corporations driven by conventional goals of capital accumulation and underpinned by an instrumental and corrosive 'network sociality' (Wayne, 2003; Wittel, 2001). Thus, it is surmised, the 'localization' of cultural production may not necessarily lead to more radicalized or autonomized workplaces.

Yet, finally, and in contrast, moving away from the mainstream contexts conventionally studied by economic sociologists, geographers and other 'cluster' theorists, I explore how some reflexive agents operating in geographically embedded production contexts appear to be more effectively working to generate critical alternatives to (or moderated versions of) capitalistic cultural work. The argument is made (following on from the previous chapter) that individualization may have provided some context for the resuscitation of artistic, practice-led or ethically focussed forms of cultural production – and that these initiatives should not be understood as merely *social* but also discretely and distinctively *spatial* in character. Here, the term 'mixed economy of clusters' is used to highlight the variegated character of local production – and to further highlight the ambivalence of individualized, reflexive modernity and its diffuse economic forms.

The globalization of 'cultural industry'

The discussion and debates around the subject of globalization are both vigorous and extensive (for one comprehensive overview see Held et al., 1999). We can define globalization as increases in economic and social interactions across trans-territorial space, fuelled by the development of cheaper and more rapid transport, travel and telecommunications and enhanced capacities for capital to integrate (and switch between) different production locations. Given these developments, it is no surprise that many critics now claim that globalization has led to the hegemonic consolidation of cultural industry 'mega-corporations' with enhanced monopoly powers (McChesney, 1998; Miller et al., 2003; Scherzinger, 2005; Wayne, 2003). While, in Adorno and Horkheimer's day, cultural industry firms were largely nationally based and *unintegrated*, producing a singular or limited range of commodities for mainly domestic audiences, now, for example, the competitive arena is dominated by giants such as AOL-Time Warner, Disney, EMI, Sony, Viacom and News Corporation which can all boast a complex of 'flexibly integrated' television, film, music, publishing and new media interests. AOL-Time Warner, as Scherzinger details, now 'owns magazines, book publishing houses, film studios, television networks, cable channels, retail stores, libraries [and] sports teams' (2005, p. 24). For these conglomerated companies the strategy is clear:

> When Disney produces a film, for example, it can guarantee the film showings on pay cable television and commercial network television, it can produce and sell soundtracks based on the film, it can create spin-off television series, it can produce related amusement park rides, CD-ROMs, books, comics and merchandise to be sold in Disney retail stores. Moreover, Disney can promote the film and related material incessantly across all its media properties. In this climate, even films that do poorly at the box office can become profitable. (McChesney, 1998, p. 14)

> Companies like Disney are in a position to produce films, promote them across a variety of subsidiaries, screen them on an owned network, and generate television replicas – not to mention CDs, reading material, toys and branded apparel – and all with an eye to external profits. (Miller et al., 2003, p. 196)

The importance of obtaining stakes in different forms of culture, media and communications should not be underestimated; cross-platform integration ensures that firms obtain a breadth and depth of market presence and alleviates risk by allowing the production and circulation of products to be more effectively integrated and managed (Bustamente, 2004; Wayne, 2003). Additionally, firms are increasingly coming together to form strategic alliances that further enhance market position, as Scherzinger (2005, p. 24) notes 'Disney has equity joint ventures, equity interests, or long-term exclusive strategic alliances with Bertelsmann, NBC, TCI, Kirch, Hearst, DreamWorks, Canal Plus, American Online and so on.' Thus, through such efforts, monopolies and effective cartels can be created and operating costs and risks substantially reduced – supporting consolidation and enabling further expansion. It is, therefore, unsurprising that, for many, the new globalized cultural economy appears as an Adornian nightmare writ large (Rifkin, 2000; Scherzinger, 2005). It should be also be noted that (as was discussed in Chapter 2) for workers employed by the consolidated corporations of culture industry, employment is now increasingly individualized and precarious, often poorly paid, short-term and contract based – and the very nature of this kind of work strongly undermines the possibility of workers protecting themselves from the capriciousness of firms and the exigencies of the integrated global market. Further, as Miller et al. (2003, p. 53) contend, in the 'New International Division of Cultural Labour' corporations are aided by the state which continually 'undermines the union movement on behalf of capital through policies designed to "free" labour from employment laws'.

Alliance capitalism

Globalization does not necessarily mean, however, that only large corporations survive. While, various critics have identified that the enhanced efforts of cultural industry corporations to construct and monopolize global regimes of production, circulation and consumption has seriously diminished the economic opportunities for small, independent and local firms (Bourdieu, 1998; McRobbie, 2002a; Meiksins, 1998; Scherzinger, 2005), the true picture is perhaps more complex. It seems that for such firms survival *is* possible – but, increasingly, appears dependent on precarious collaborations with the 'majors'. For example, using the case of the independent fashion design sector, McRobbie (2002a,b) argues that the possibility of stable and secure employment in independent production has been overshadowed by the efficiency with which larger companies can now move in to co-opt, diminish or dissolve small producers. The UK fashion sector is dominated by large retailers (for example, the Arcadia Group with over 2000 stores in its Burton, Dorothy Perkins, Miss Selfridge, Wallis, Top Shop and Top Man brands, high-volume discounters such as Matalan and Primark, and supermarket brands such as Tesco and Asda-Wal Mart) that strongly determine the terms and conditions of any sub-contractual collaboration they have with independent designers and manufacturers. Independents who do secure contracts with the majors for retail concessions, design or manufacture are highly vulnerable; first, because competition to obtain these deals is now so intense given that few alternative outlets exist, and, second, because there is a constant threat from overseas producers in low-cost labour locations (such as Eastern Europe, China, Indonesia, Bangladesh and India) that are able to supply retailers with cheap and high quality manufacturing and designing services. As McRobbie makes clear, in this new globalized fashion economy, small agglomerations of independents may continue to survive – but they have become precarious and eminently dispensable.

Hesmondhalgh (2007) rehearses a similar narrative of expansion, consolidation and control by media industry corporations and a corresponding diminution of the power of local independent firms. Like McRobbie, Hesmondhalgh suggests that while certain 'flexible' changes in the organization of cultural production (notably the shift to 'post-Fordist' systems) have enabled and, indeed, encouraged small firms or local agglomerations to survive and develop, rarely do they operate under conditions of their own choosing. As he notes, the growth of 'alliance capitalism' (2007, p. 176, see also Castells, 1996) has been one of the striking trends underpinning the globalization of the cultural economy. While the past 20–30 years have witnessed a marked intensification of media mergers, take-overs, collaborations and conglomerations, there has simultaneously occurred a vertical disintegration of functions within firms, and a substantial shift towards subcontracting and outsourcing of production sufficient to underwrite the growth of independent production complexes across a range of industry sectors (music, television, film, new media and so on), ones often constellated at the local and regional level. 'Alliance' capitalism appears predicated on a principle of mutual benefit: for the major corporation, subcontracting or outsourcing enables the off-loading of risk and developmental costs to the independent while maintaining control over distribution and intellectual ownership – the key profit centres.[1] It also allows the corporation to remain 'cutting edge' and 'credible' providing them with a conduit to new trends and developments at the creative 'grassroots'. For the independent, benefits accrue from avoiding the bureaucracy and constraint of a larger organization and retaining the autonomy to seek out new alliances and exercise choices regarding which future projects to undertake or reject.

Yet, arguably, despite the illusion of mutuality and partnership, the power relationship in alliance capitalism is profoundly asymmetrical. As Hesmondhalgh puts it, alliance capitalism is in effect 'another sign of corporate take-over' (2007, p. 176) as small independents are co-opted and constrained by the demands and contractual obligations imposed by the larger firm. It is common for small firms to be offered 'take it or leave it' deals by their paymasters, or forced to accept prescriptive conditions that restrict the activities of the independent while providing maximum control, flexibility and protection for the larger firm. Also (as I discussed in Chapter 2), many so-called 'independents' are now placed under strong pressure to reproduce familiar formats, successful genres and standardized scripts that can be then artfully (re)packaged as 'new' cultural products to a mass or niche market (Ryan, 1992; Scherzinger, 2005). Critics thus conclude that despite the growth of the 'indies', the idea that alliance capitalism leads to secure, stable and *autonomous* production is highly questionable (Bourdieu, 1998; McRobbie, 2002b; Meiksins, 1998; Ryan, 1992). Indeed, Wayne (2003) refers to the prevailing policy amongst cultural industry corporations as one of 'decentralized accumulation', whereby large firms may adopt an apparently 'disintegrated' and flexible corporate structure, so creating a space for the 'indies' and localized subcontracting, but still ultimately ensure (through an elaborate system of relationships, partnerships and contractual arrangements) that profits and power remain firmly in their grasp, as he comments here:

> [T]his deconcentration of capital turns out on closer inspection to refer not so much to concentration of ownership, with which it is confused, but such contingent features as a shift away from large plant sizes towards smaller plant sizes and the geographical relocation of capital around the world (often developing countries where labour supply is cheap) as opposed to its regional concentration under Fordism. (Wayne, 2003, p. 93)

As we have seen, in this apparently 'decentralized' and 'localized', but, in fact, strongly corporate-controlled and conglomerated regime, workers are now inveigled into an internationalized division of labour where they can expect to be further exposed to precarious work regimes that suppress wages, disavow unionization and compromise 'local powers'. Indeed, through 'decentralized accumulation' global corporations have managed to turn flexible economic restructuring to their own advantage, brokering a complex, trans-global web of strategic alliances where a panoply of large and small firms provide production, distribution and ancillary services and systems. This enables the majors to absorb any threats that local production systems, independent competition or increased worker autonomy might pose, mainly through tying independents and freelancers into restrictive contracts, or by buying out or out-competing the opposition.

Thus, it appears that while there have been significant changes in the geographical *organization* of production since Adorno and Horkheimer's day, there is little evidence to suggest that the *ownership and control* of cultural industries and concentrations of wealth and power first highlighted in the culture industry critique have been arrested by globalization and post-Fordist transformations. For critical theorists, the shift towards globally integrated but 'decentred' production systems, while *appearing* to engender organizational diversity, preserve geographical uniqueness and enhance worker autonomy serves only to reinforce those traditional monopoly powers, relations of spatial exploitation and workplace alienation associated with the industrial society's 'culture industry'. Thus, even within decentred production regimes, the idea that 'place' can persist as an independent realm of economic action and as a distinctive repository of meaningful and autonomous social and workplace relations appears irredeemably undermined.

The embedded economy

In contrast to this rather pessimistic assessment of life under globalized 'alliance capitalism', a number of more liberal critics have argued that the capacity of firms to nurture genuinely autonomous production has been somewhat *reinvigorated* by the high transactional demands of the 'new' economy and the turn towards 'decentred', geographically embedded production.

As we saw in the previous chapter, the likes of Granovetter and Lash are amongst those who have sought to stress the social 'embeddedness' of the economy, emphasizing its co-operative, transaction-dependent and (for Lash) 'reflexive' nature. Alongside this work, a number of theorists have also sought to emphasize the importance of place to the effective embedding of (now, particularly) post-industrial production. Indeed, the recent revival of interest in geographical agglomerations and localized production complexes builds on efforts first made in the 1980s by economic geographers, whose work on 'industrial districts' attempted to make sense of the disintegration of Fordism and the apparent emergence of regionalized pockets of 'flexibly specialized' production that appeared to eschew traditional organizational formulas (Amin, 1994; Malmberg and Maskell, 1997; Markusen, 1996; Piore and Sabel, 1984; Saxenian, 1994; see also Martin and Sunley, 2003 for a review). In this literature, emphasis was placed on how firms were attempting to innovate and adapt to new flexible production processes, and respond to more specialized patterns of consumer demand, by resuscitating traditional forms of craft production in embedded geographical contexts (frequently cited examples included craft and hi-tech production complexes within areas such as Boston, Baden-Württemberg, Cambridgeshire, Emilia-Romagna, Grenoble and San Francisco). Here, place was seen as central to the operation of firms, not simply because proximity reduced transaction costs, but because it also provided the social and cultural repertoires necessary for the harmonious production of specialized, distinctive and 'quality' goods. As Harvey (1989) identifies, further implied in this analysis was the assumption that work in such contexts was based on principled attachments to place, and was therefore more likely to be locally managed, communitarian and democratic – and so appeared to offer a more optimistic vision for industrial organization; one where more harmonious and co-operative work relations triumph over dominant and repressive forms of management and control.

Recently, these ideas have been popularized in the context of a more prominent thesis that has sought to detail how social relations in discrete places have now coalesced to create distinctive 'clusters' of post-industrial production. Inspired, mostly, by the proselytising work of Porter (1990), the cluster concept has provoked much academic debate, and somewhat cornered the market as a model for local economic development (see Bathelt et al., 2004; Cooke, 2002; Cumbers and MacKinnon, 2004; European Commission, 2002; DTI, 1998; Martin and Sunley, 2003). Porter has defined clusters as a 'geographically proximate group of interconnected companies and associated institutions' (Porter 2005, p. 261), enthusiastically proposing that 'the presence of a well-developed cluster provides powerful benefits to productivity and the capacity to innovate that are hard to match by firms based elsewhere' (ibid., p. 267). As an economist, Porter's straightforward business-friendly style contrasts with the more critical and analytical approach of economic sociologists and geographers (see Martin and Sunley, 2003) yet the differences are not so great as to obscure a shared interest in promoting the importance of socially and spatially embedded work relations to the effective operation of the post-industrial production complex. In such literatures, contrary to the global pessimists, work, it seems, remains both a *humanized* and *place-specific* activity.

The geography of cultural 'clusters'

Correspondingly, drawing on these diverse literatures, a number of observers have now proposed the idea that there exist close linkages between *cultural* firms and place, with many identifying emergent 'clusters'[2] of locally embedded cultural production seemingly characterized by more embedded, democratic and autonomous social and workplace relations (Banks et al., 2000; Crewe, 1996; Drake, 2003; Florida, 2002; Mommaas, 2004; O'Connor and Wynne, 1996a; Pratt, 2000; Verwijnen and Lehtovouri, 1999). Perhaps most notable amongst these is Scott's *The Cultural Economy of Cities* (2000) which provides a compelling account of how local clusters of cultural production are emerging at the leading edge of post-industrial urban transformation. His argument works from the premise that

> since the core elements of capitalist industrial systems are invariably organized as networks of producers bound together in dense criss-crossing relationships, there will always be a tendency for at least some of the individual producers tied together in this manner to converge locationally towards a common geographic centre of gravity. (ibid., 2000, p. 18)

In the case of cultural production, the 'centre of gravity' tends to be larger 'core' cities that possess a critical infrastructure of actors and organizations involved in the emergent media and culture industry sectors – such as London, Los Angeles, New York and Paris. The clustering of sectors and producers is stimulated by three principle factors:

- the need to obtain economies of scale and/or access to external production functions (suppliers, training, support agencies, shared facilities and so on);
- the need to tap into the accelerated rate of 'cultural', symbolic, informational and knowledge flow to be found in cosmopolitan urban milieux;
- the need to exploit 'transactionally-based modes of social solidarity' (Scott 2000, p. 18) deemed necessary for creative cultural production.

Thus, for Scott, the emergence of localized zones of cultural production marks not only a period where the organizational conditions for the production of cultural goods and services have been transformed by corporate decentralization and revived interest in agglomeration economies but also one where the capitalist colonisation of cultural field has intensified, heightening the importance attached to (often place-specific) symbols, knowledge and information in the composition and value of (post) industrial products. Furthermore, and crucially, the effective production of cultural goods is seen to be amplified by the local existence of agents working in *co-operative social networks* with embedded *communitarian values*. In the following passage, describing historical forms of cultural production complex and their analogue with contemporary film clusters of Paris and Hollywood, Scott captures the kind of idealized social arrangements he perceives to underpin cultural production in place:

> The examples cited ... already hint at one of the representative features of such communities, namely, that they are less constituted as miscellaneous jumbles of individuals following many different and disconnected pursuits, than they are comparatively homogenous collectivities whose members are caught up in mutually complementary and socially coordinated careers. A major factor binding such collectivities together is the traditions and conventions that invariably come into being in any localized social group that has subsisted over a period of time. As such, they are the repositories of an accumulated interpersonal cultural capital connecting generations of workers to one another through time and serving to orchestrate each collectivity's internal and external relations. (2000, p. 33)

Scott's argument is that the competitiveness of production clusters rests substantially on the ways in which creative agents, local social relations and spatially embedded forms of 'cultural capital' operate (see also Ettlinger, 2003). Within this, it is assumed that solidarity and harmony are both necessary and naturally occurring elements of a local social complex. Such 'soft', 'human' attributes are judged to contribute significantly to the success of cultural industry clusters, and so (we surmise) help provide rewarding, richly socialized and meaningfully embedded identities for their constituent workers.

The importance of social and spatial embeddedness is also identified by Florida (2002) in his discussion of the economic activities of the emergent 'creative class'. While recognizing that the clustering of creative industries is driven by the conventional economic imperatives of reducing transactional costs, accessing shared facilities, developing economies of scale and so on, Florida, more so than Scott, argues that social solidarity and community connectedness provide the *primary* underpinnings for a successful production complex. Creative class workers not only create networked structures that are conducive to efficient and successful production – this social dimension is, in itself, the principal component of local economic value. Indeed, Florida argues that it is the actions of individual workers *themselves* that create the cluster; for, as he puts it 'regional economic growth is driven by the location choices of creative people' (2002, p. 223), rather than firms, global economic systems or capitalistic market structures. Creative clusters thrive not for 'traditional economic reasons' (ibid., p. 218) but because 'creative people want to live there' (ibid., p. 218) and it is they who make the cluster by creating an 'integrated eco-system of habitat where all forms of creativity – artistic and cultural, technological and economic – can take root and flourish' (ibid., p. 218). Florida appears to attribute workers with untrammelled powers to create their own social structures and clusters – almost independent of the wider structural contexts within which they are conventionally seen to be embedded. Here, economic determination fades from view, and governments and planners are recast as humble attendants who must seek simply to provide these mobile and aspirational creative class workers with the institutional climate required to develop their own autonomous neighbourhoods, community structures and work environments – from this, economic benefits will inevitably follow.

   In fairness, Scott (and Florida) are not unaware of how firms may be embedded in impersonal, instrumental and 'far-flung global networks of transactions' (Scott, 2000, p. 13), that can undo these local economic configurations – but, more generally, both are inclined to emphasize the autonomous capacity of localities and workers to 'negotiate their way' (ibid., p. 13) through the global, neo-liberal minefield, at least partially on their own ethical terms. Particularly in Florida's work, the cluster is fully utopianized – presented as the wholly constructed fancy of free-thinking members of the 'creative class'; an idealized community where work is no longer the site of exploitation, oppression and alienation but an intrinsically rewarding environment where workers can freely 'validate their identities as creative people' (ibid., p. 218). Such a utopia is now presented as intrinsically *local*; for now, 'place' – as Florida puts it – has become the central organizing unit of our time' (2002, p. 6).

Critique of 'clusters'

The theory of cultural 'clusters' and 'embeddedness' is an inversion of the 'culture industry' thesis – since craft production, creativity and local autonomy remain vital and prevalent. However, not everyone understands the emergence of clusters so positively. More sceptical critics continue to identify an underlying logic of capitalistic disembedding that pervades even (apparently) liberalized and autonomous agglomerations of local production.

First, for many, the notion that the cultural industries economy is organized into self-sustaining and socially harmonious clusters appears somewhat far-fetched. Indeed, enhanced *de*-autonomization and *dis*-harmony are perhaps more likely to be evidenced in an economic situation that, despite the apparent institutionalization of 'embedded' social relations, remains highly dependent on externalized market relations (Amin and Thrift, 1992). Indeed, as we have seen, one reason why rivalry amongst small firms in core-city clusters remains so intense is that many of these 'local', 'independent' and 'networked' firms are struggling to compete with – or existing in contractual hock to – larger or multinational corporations, in relations of 'alliance capitalism'. As Wayne has argued, for the major cultural industry conglomerates, the use of local firms and networks may merely expedite corporate growth through the principle of 'decentralized accumulation'. Thus, while some identify a kind of progressive localization involving more autonomous and reflexive cultural firms, others see a conscious and deliberate *strategy* amongst post-Fordist corporations to outsource risk by off-loading burdens of manufacture, design, innovation and R&D to pockets of highly competitive small, independent and subcontracted firms – while continuing to exert control at arms length by acting as the dominant node in the production network. It should be noted that small firms themselves may well be innately competitive and acquisitive, irrespective of their 'local' status, and so may well seek to become as large and commercially successful as their corporate counterparts. Places (and the firms and social networks they contain), then, are often to be instrumentally and efficiently *utilized* for conventional economic ends – and while certain forms of non-economic obligations, relationships and transactions may be stimulated by localized agglomerations and clustering (as, for example, Scott demonstrates in his discussion of the vitality of kinship ties amongst Bangkok gem industries), such concerns are increasingly secondary to (or vehicles for) the principal goals of profit maximization and growth (Harvey, 1989). Indeed, it seems likely that in core-city clusters the overwhelming focus on commercial growth and meeting the rigorous demands of ever-more competitive economic conditions will continue to overwhelm small firms' ethical commitments to places, non-economic obligations and forms of (non-market oriented) practice – resulting in a decline in distinctiveness and local autonomy, and, as the likes of Bourdieu, McRobbie and Rifkin have forcefully argued, some serious degradation of the cultural realm.

Second, the promotion of local clusters as models of economic development is seductive and plays heavily on the perception that such initiatives serve the interests of both capital and labour. It is argued that through such 'embedded' and 'networked' development, both economic efficiency and workers' personal freedoms and social connections can be enhanced. Yet, despite the optimism of policy-makers and some academics, critics have argued that the existence of intensive and close-knit social relations in cultural clusters does not automatically lead to more sociable, ethical or (as we might hope) radical forms of production. For example, contrary to industry claims, the core-city clusters studied by Scott are not especially known for their radical or enlightened working practices.[3] Indeed, in order to survive, firms in the 'close-knit' media, fashion, advertising, design and music industry clusters of London, Los Angeles and New York must operate as aggressive and agile capitalists and remain always focussed on the prime motivation of making money in a competitive market – instrumental utilization of networks (and the workers that comprise them) is standard (Harrison, 1992; Miller and Yúdice, 2002; Nixon, 2003; Rantisi, 2004). Scott and Florida recognise that localities do not always engender productive or progressive cultural economies, yet there is a tendency (particularly from Florida) to understand local social relations as innately progressive and conducive to the 'social solidarity' that both identify as prerequisite for the efficient functioning of a local production complex. Thus, while tension and conflict are not absent in Scott's or (even) Florida's account, they do tend to be elided in favour of a view of embeddedness that prioritizes only the co-operative aspects of proximate sociality, rather than its more insidious articulations. Simply put, the dysfunctionality of clusters and networks (such as forms of protectionism, favouritism and nepotism), the potential for malfeasance and the dangers of lack of external regulation and accountability beyond the locality are not fully addressed. As observers such as Amin and Thrift (1992) and Sayer (2001) have argued, there is a widespread but misguided belief that embedded, networked interactions are intrinsically inclusive and egalitarian, since they are more likely to be based on personal or face-to-face interactions.

While there is an innate attractiveness about this argument, it does not bear close scrutiny. Social ties can constrain as well as enable, and when firms find themselves in a highly competitive situation the pressure to utilize networks to more readily protect economic interests will inevitably be strong. This may involve sourcing new network 'nodes' (contacts, suppliers, collaborators, markets) and withholding information, it may mean utilizing knowledge to outbid or undercut a rival firm in the network, it may involve hiring and firing staff as new opportunities for cutting costs or sourcing new creative/knowledge inputs are revealed; in short, network activity can encourage an intensification of instrumental behaviour rather than alleviate its more deleterious effects. As Sayer puts it, 'the metaphor of embeddedness sounds soft and comforting, and possibly sends our critical faculties to sleep, but what it describes can be harsh and oppressive on occasion' (2001, p. 698).

Finally, critics have begun to question what is life *really* like for those working 'reflexively' under conditions of intense inter-firm rivalry and 'alliance capitalism'. The social relations of embedded production in core-city clusters has been more closely analysed by Wittel (2001) who identifies in the cultural economy the emergence of new kind of social commons premised on what he dubs an individualized and instrumental 'network sociality'. In contrast to traditional 'narrative sociality' based on stability, positive embeddedness, shared concerns and mutuality, network sociality is imagined as an emergent form of association reflecting the shift towards instrumental social relations conducted over multi-dimensional economic space. While attributes of network sociality have socio-historical antecedents, the cultural industries, and new media in particular, are seen to be the vanguard industries ushering in what Wittel hypothesizes will become the 'paradigmatic social form of late capitalism' (ibid., p. 71).

Taking the view that the expanded emphasis at work on such 'assets' as flexibility, creativity and self-management has profound consequences for human conditioning, Wittel suggests that (new media) workers have become more self-interested, instrumental and emotionally detached from others. Systemic pressures to adapt to market imperatives, to key into the global 'space of flows' (Castells, 1996, p. 376), undermine the premises of community with its emphasis on embedded social and moral relations, continuity, shared history and common goals and fortunes; as Wittel notes:

> Network sociality is not based on a shared history or a shared narrative. Instead it is defined by a multitude of experiences and

biographies. The new media field contains subjects with a diversity of educational and geographical backgrounds. People are, so to speak, 'lifted out' of their contexts and reinserted in largely disembedded social relations, which they must at the same time continually construct. (2001, p. 65)

On the one hand, network sociality is explained through the potential for *dis*embedding through the rise in use of e-business, the Internet and telecommunications in cultural work, as well as enhanced transports and automobility in general (Urry, 2000). The concept of 'virtual' community, the setting up of discussion and mailing groups, videoconferencing, the circulation of 'hot' websites, mobile, online and email information transfer and long-distance travel are all, of course, crucial to a new, reconfigured, impersonal global sociality. But network sociality is also localized and 'embedded', in the sense that it relies upon 'real' – as much as virtual – networking spaces (such as cultural districts, workspaces, bars, clubs, galleries etc.) and is thus heavily reliant on proximity and clustering. Locality, therefore, still matters. Yet, while firms may be 'locally embedded', the basis of this communion is, for Wittel, morally suspect, since while managers and workers may congregate and connect, it is only for the purpose of securing opportunities for personal or corporate gain. Network sociality is thus seen as a structured, evaluative response to a society where market values dominate and where social bonds are under constant threat of annihilation. Where profit takes primacy, deep emotional investments are risky and insecure, foregrounding the necessity of conducting ephemeral and fleeting relationships with colleagues, acquaintances and strangers within both local and global environments. In this case, individualization leads to withdrawal and self-directed behaviour – not to liberation or an opening out of the self to others.

In order to evidence his claims Wittel provides some compelling data from his ethnographic excursions into the London new media sector. Here he identifies a number of formal and informal groups, networks and organisations, each attempting to plug into the grid of information, knowledge, capital and contacts that circulate in this vertiginous world of frenzy, rumour and spin; here, more than ever, time is of the essence:

First Tuesday for example, a network to connect ideas and money, entrepreneurs and venture capital, found a particularly efficient way to enforce networking practices. Internet entrepreneurs wear green badges, investors have red badges and service providers get yellow ones. In this way, nobody loses time accidentally talking to the wrong person. (ibid., p. 56)

Despite an appearance of traditional and non-instrumental sociality – networks may meet at pubs and clubs, restaurants and parties – the social element is wholly secondary to the instrumental need to establish a coterie of usable contacts, set deals in train and earmark future opportunities. This is, for Wittel, a prime example of the ways in which clusters and embedded personal relationships have become commodified in the new economy, and he reveals how effectively instrumental, rational-economic goals have colonized the social, partly, it seems, through adopting the camouflage of traditional forms of sociability:

> On the one hand the commodification of social relationships (doing a pitch, getting funds, finding work) is highly obvious, on the other, it is important to hide this commodification by creating a frame (music, alcohol, etc) that makes people feel comfortable, that suggests a somehow 'authentic' interest in meeting people. (ibid., p. 56)

One of Wittel's informants describes the social intercourse at networking events as 'promiscuous' in so far as participants must be prepared to constantly 'check people out' and be ready to move on to the next relationship when their needs have been met. Throughout, Wittel emphasises the abject nature of this new sociality in so far as it fails to service non-instrumental and non-economic imperatives, and he offers little prospect that this trend will not extend into other sectors, accelerating a more widespread commodification of human social relations. What occurs in London cyber salons today, will, it seems, be found everywhere else tomorrow.

Thus, in contrast to more optimistic theorists of 'embeddedness', Wittel shows that reflexive and local cultural clusters, held up by liberal–democratic theorists as paradigmatic units of post-Fordist production, offer only a thin veneer of meaningful and sincere sociality.[4] Here, while 'active agency' and a commitment to social 'networking' are required, both remain subordinate to, and controlled by, capitalistic imperatives.

Overall, many critics now conclude that localized and reflexive agglomerations of cultural producers, while offering the superficial promise of self-fulfilment and autonomy, will continue to generate neither as long as they are organized in accordance with the principles of 'decentralized accumulation', temporary and opportunistic trust-relations and a socially corrosive 'network sociality'. For such critics, the primacy of economic values, over all others, will ensure that in the final analysis, instrumental and profit-related motives will take priority over any 'social' or 'community' sentiments or relations identified at the local level.

A mixed economy of cultural clusters?

The evidence appears to indicate that the kind of 'local' and 'independent' clusters championed by embeddedness theorists and economic geographers are dominated by capitalistic imperatives, and so remain reliant upon (and vulnerable to) instrumental and externalized economic flows and processes. Thus, the hope that such clusters are somehow more conducive to creative and autonomous working practices – simply by virtue of their 'embeddedness' – is somewhat misplaced. Regardless of any prospective social value, embeddedness is first advantageous to the flexible operation of post-industrial firms – not the liberation of workers. The clusters that economic geographers and sociologists hold up as blueprints for more locally democratic and rewarding production appear simply to reinforce conventional patterns of ownership and exploitation – albeit ones glossed with the promise of more 'reflexive' and 'autonomous' social relations for those willing to accept the precarious and flexible workplace freedoms now on offer.[5]

But are all clusters like this? What happens if we move outside the corporate mainstream, beyond the clusters and network organizations at the hub of core cities, into the peripheral zones and less celebrated margins that lie within urban cultural economies? Here, in amidst the recessed terrain of capitalism, is it still possible to locate various critical and creative communities, sub-political interest groups and other radicals committed to experimental or alternative forms of production – all operating within distinct geographical milieux? Maybe so. But even if we find such collectives, a conventional Marxian critique would seek to dismiss these 'superstructural' coalitions as mere epiphenomena of the economic landscape – countercultural relics too easily suppressed beneath capitalism's strong hand to effect any meaningful long-term 'resistance'. But is this pessimism justified?

Clearly, Zukin's (1982) seminal analysis of the transition of New York's SoHo from a bohemian enclave of cultural production to a commodified landscape of cultural consumption has been widely drawn upon by critics as evidence that the life of the independent cultural cluster tends to be nasty, brutish and short. Her account details how, in the 1960s, the original, pioneering recolonization of SoHo's derelict and abandoned industrial spaces by marginal artists and cultural producers led to physical and symbolic renewal as well as a strong re-embedding of community, and so appeared to mark a significant victory for forces of autonomous cultural production. However, as she further details, this triumph was somewhat short-lived. Hot on the trail of the artists, in flight from the suburbs, followed a new affluent swathe of the young, professional middle class, eager to breathe in the revalorized urban aesthetic and keen to establish their own bohemian credentials. This invasion further attracted a whole cadre of property ('loft') developers, commercial landlords and a more market-oriented infrastructure of 'high' art and established cultural businesses, ones equipped for servicing the tastes and expectations of the upwardly mobile middle-class. The new relations of supply and demand quickly ensured that the poorer and more marginal artists were squeezed out, and the contours of the 'landscape of power' (Zukin, 1991) re-established. Arguably, the SoHo experience has since been replicated in many de-industrialized Western cities, where grass roots cultural zones in the city fringe have been pervasively gentrified and sanitized by local authorities seeking to attract middle-class residents and consumers, often through a generic mix of upmarket chain stores, corporate bars, expensive boutiques, designer galleries, themed restaurants and the like (Atkinson, 2003; Crewe et al., 2003; Harvey, 1989; Hollands and Chatterton, 2003; Jones and Wilks-Heeg, 2004; Lloyd, 2006; Wilson, 1999, 2002). The lesson of Zukin appears to be that artistic clusters are always susceptible to the incursions of market culture, resulting in cities being widely robbed of their critical and creative infrastructure and socially vital elements of autonomous production.[6]

While Zukin offers a powerful critique, Mommaas (2004) proffers an alternative view, suggesting (in liberal-democratic fashion) that clusters take on a 'great variety of forms and rationales' (ibid., p. 530) and cannot be presupposed (as Zukin does) to have a particular orientation or permeability to market forces. Mommaas suggests a world of more open social formations where certain types of cluster may be more or less amenable to corporate domination – and this is especially the case in Europe where the effects of neo-liberalism are tempered by residual attachments to social, welfarist values and where the state and non-economic institutions play a more interventionist role in cultural and economic development (Beck, 2000). For example, Mommaas describes here the *Westergasfabriek*, a cultural industry complex located in the Amsterdam city fringe:

> In the course of the past 7–8 years, the place has developed into a distinctive cultural site, housing a broad and vivid mixture of short and long-term cultural activities. It includes amongst other things a stylish café-cum-restaurant, a movie theatre especially dedicated to Dutch cinema; rehearsal, production and performing spaces for theatre companies, visual artists, a small film production company, designers and spatial planners ... [it] is based on a clever centrally controlled management scheme, aimed at producing as much cultural variety, change and openness as possible. Its success is also based on a carefully maintained ambience of historicity and marginality. (2004, p. 511)

More radically, Ploeg (2006) reports that the former industrial plant of The Landbouwbelang in Maastricht has recently been granted community 'arts centre' status by the local state in defiance of corporate plans to develop commercial entertainment venues; a deliberate 'choice in favour of creativity' (ibid., p. 4) as he describes. Groth and Corijn (2005) detail successful efforts made in Berlin, Brussels and Helsinki by artists and 'informal actors' to develop 'free', creative production spaces. First, then, cultural initiatives of this nature are able to flourish because of the mixed approach taken by (European) planners and governments to their 'strategic' economic development (Groth and Corijn, 2005). Second, however, as Mommaas contends (echoing Lash, 1994), the expansion of a more 'reflexive cultural attitude[s]' (Mommaas, 2004, p. 527) amongst producers and consumers themselves (see also Banks et al., 2000) is also highly significant– the creative *agent* continues to play a vital and autonomous role in the development of cultural clusters and spatial interventions.

Thus, the degree to which clusters are oriented and open to markets will significantly vary. Indeed, Mommaas suggests (for example) that some clusters (in Amsterdam, Tilburg and Utrecht) are led by pockets of reflexive cultural producers who explicitly eschew the ethos of market culture, and are aided in this endeavour by local government regimes that seek to preserve autonomy and independence in the cultural sphere, and look to cultural clusters as a means to incite new kinds of communitarian relations or promote a distinctive 'breaking away from the established arts-policy regime and opening up an urban cultural platform for otherwise marginal tastes and groups' (Mommaas, 2004, p. 525) (there are clear echoes here with the ambitions of the Greater London Council in the 1980s see Garnham, 1987; Hesmondhalgh and Pratt, 2005). While these more hybrid 'social' clusters are not immune to the impacts of the market, it is nonetheless evident that significant steps are often taken to 'protect' cultural activities from mainstream commercialization, with emphasis placed on providing sustainable conditions in which these locally specific combinations of cultural and economic practice might flourish (see, for example, Hoyler and Mager (2005) on state-backed arts centre formation in federalist Germany or Puype (2004) on *Kunst in de Buurt* projects in Ghent). Clusters then can emerge for a variety of purposes and, as Evans notes, not all are designed to expedite market processes:

> Clusters can therefore be seen as examples of mutual co-operation through formal and informal economies of scale, spreading risk in research and development (R&D) and information sharing via-socio-economic networks; as reactive anti-establishment action (avant garde artists' squats); and as a defensive necessity, resisting control from licensing authorities, guilds and dominant cultures artistic and political. (Evans, 2004, p. 75)

While recognizing their precarious nature of such interventions, Evans (2004) shows how, even in the more market-driven USA context, cities such as Philadelphia and Boston have created state-practitioner partnerships that seek to protect and stimulate artist communities, and he provides further examples of how in the European context cites such as Munich and Paris have made considerable efforts to develop a diverse mix of cultural clusters and activities.

For these critics, creative and radical cultural production is both more resilient and sustainable than Zukin's model would appear to suggest, for, even now, it continues to generate clusters underpinned by a whole admixture of aesthetic, social and economic motivations – despite the prevailing neo-liberal hegemony. The identification of particularistic and hybrid types of cultural cluster, with mixed orientations to the market, would appear to provide some hope that alternative models may persist and be sustained. Mommaas concludes that the ability of local cultural economies to create and protract a small but significant level of cultural production and consumption activity, beyond or in tandem with the 'mainstream', should not be underestimated. Additionally, in similar spirit, others have highlighted the persistence of scenes or clusters that are not deliberately 'planned' at all, ones that have emerged more organically or 'convivially' (Shorthose, 2004) from determined agents working at the 'grass roots' (see, for example, O'Connor and Wynne, 1996b on Manchester's Northern Quarter; Shorthose, 2004 on Nottingham's Lace Market) rather than (at least initially) being reliant on state support. Again, while potentially open to the incursions of corporate capital, such initiatives remain widespread and operate as 'independent' clusters in areas where local democracy persists, where creative impulses thrive and where capital has thus far failed to adequately isolate and exploit a cluster's more marketable or commercial qualities.

Cultural work and sense of place

I now address more explicitly how a 'sense of place' may underpin these 'alternative' agglomerations. In an 'institutionally individualized' epoch, with an emphasis placed on self-coping and resourcefulness in order to provide anchors for self-development, the turn back to place has become a fundamental feature (Harvey, 1989; Sennett, 1998). Indeed, the search for place appears an important dimension of the attempted remoralization of social and economic practices I identified in Chapter 5. As actors struggle to re-embed life projects and biographical narratives, the desire to do so in particular *locations* becomes more pronounced. While this can generate social reaction, we might also suggest, for cultural producers, that the feel or sense of a place might provide a focus or inspiration for alternative forms of cultural production based on aesthetic, practice-based or social/ethical endeavour. Evidently, special 'atmospheres' or senses of time and place should not be seen as inherently market-antithetical, for, as we have seen, such phenomena may simply be used to assist the generation of commercially oriented goods that exploit and traduce local tradition (Harvey, 1989, 2001). Places are hugely marketable constructs. Yet, equally, it is arguable that a sense of place may help temper the extent to which market forces are applied to the production and distribution of cultural goods. It might be suggested that the value attached to art, 'internal rewards' or a desire to contribute to a 'better society' often goes hand in hand with a strong, intrinsic sense of attachment to a particular community of *place*. Developing on the previous chapter, I first address how place appears to underpin the enduring search for more alternative ('bohemian' or 'avant garde') artistic communities and clusters amidst a more markedly individualized and aestheticized social climate (Featherstone,

1991; Lash and Urry, 1994). I then examine how cultural workers' strivings to undertake more 'practice-led' and, finally, 'ethical' forms of cultural work can appear strongly informed and motivated by geographical attachments and senses of place.

Artistic clusters

While, as Marshall (1890) first observed, places can generate industrial 'atmospheres' that aid economic productivity, place can also exert a profound atmospheric effect on the aesthetic or artistic sensibility. Indeed, critics and commentators have long traced the development of artistic communities, and assessed their contributions, not just to the autonomous world of art but to the broad and intricate development of cities and civilization as commonly experienced and understood (Evans, 2004; Hall, 1998; Miles, 2004; Lash and Urry, 1994; Lloyd, 2006; Reynolds, 2005; Savage, 1991; Wilson, 2002). The communities of cultural producers that have periodically populated the landscapes of modernity (often most evident in, but not restricted to, core cities such as Paris, London, Vienna, Berlin, New York, Tokyo and so on) have not only conventionally generated art and cultural goods and markets but have also offered the city new conceptual panoramas and creative vocabularies that have inspired political, social and cultural change. At one level this has been manifest in the galvanization of artists, commentators and critics prior to and in the wake of major civil upheavals,[7] on the other it has led to a more general, low-key 'revolutions of everyday life' (Vaneigem, 1967) in the durable form of artistic or anarchistic clusters (such as in the 'free' city of Christiana in Copenhagen, various European squatter communities – see Pruijt, 2003); or it has more simply been registered in artists' spirited refusals to bow to the demands of city authorities for formally regulated and governed cultural practices (Flusty, 2000). Indeed, we might suggest that the contemporary survival of artistic communities is not only supportive of Lash and Urry's observations regarding the durability of the hermeneutic tradition, and the enhanced democratization of 'aesthetic reflexivity' under more individualized social conditions but is also reflective of the city's historical tendency to irrupt consciousness and act as an 'incubator for revolutions' (Blazwick, 2001, p. 9). There is sufficient evidence of ongoing critical and reflexive activity in the artists' districts, colonies and communes of Amsterdam, Copenhagen, Helsinki, Hong Kong, London, Los Angeles, New York, Paris, Stockholm, Sydney and in second-tier cities beyond – such as Antwerp, Marseille and Rotterdam (Ploeg, 2006) to suggest that autonomous zones of creative dissent continue to crop up even amidst the more cleaned-up and commodified spaces of neo-liberal cultural economy. Currently, the economically and socially transitional Berlin is being promoted as Europe's leading bohemian, creative city with its marginal districts (such as Prenzlauer-Berg) becoming widely touted as epicentres of a renascent European artistic sensibility (Luetgert, 2006). Thus, while capital's efforts to commodify bohemian space may appear unstoppable (Lloyd, 2006; Zukin, 1982), the persistent failure of markets, partnered with the durable compulsions of radical artists to evade commodification and assimilation into market culture, should not too easily be overlooked or dismissed.

It is possible to imagine that a sense of place may be used to inform aesthetically directed, counter-rational production – a desire to evoke or celebrate ones embedded being at the expense of commercial expediency. Just as Hall comments how, in radical nineteenth century Paris, 'the streets and slums of the city played a crucial role in shaping the consciousness of the artists who lived and worked in them' (1998, p. 233), so today, as Kit-wai Ma (2002) demonstrates (for example) in the context of a genealogy of underground rock/hip-hop music scene in Hong Kong, the construction of alternative spaces (various kinds of local, trans-local and hybrid production and performance spaces) can be underpinned by values that actively resist 'local governmentality and the work-and-spend culture of transnational capitalist discourse' (Kit-wai Ma, 2002, p. 150; see also the music scenes variously detailed in Whiteley et al., 2004). In similar ways, Drake is concerned to reflect on the importance of being-in-place to cultural production, and in particular 'how individuals may use locality to extend their imaginative capacities in ways other than through close contact with other creative workers' (2003, p. 515). That is, place *itself*, in terms of its built form, its emotive effects, its specific experiential textures, shifts and rhythms, may provide a special inspiration that lies beyond conventional, rational (i.e. cost-minimizing) motivations for 'clustering'.

O'Connor and Wynne's (1996a) collection similarly suggests that places can have a special energy and creative atmosphere that stimulates cultural workers to pursue a bohemian or creative lifestyle in conjunction with like-minded others. They identify a key incentive to undertake cultural work lies in the chance to savour the culture and atmosphere of the city and reproduce it through ones own patterns of cultural production and consumption. Work and the pursuit of profit are not necessarily the principal criteria for integration – to be a part of something meaningful, life affirming, or even 'cool', exciting and unique may be more important than obtaining external rewards. Others have similarly suggested that places have a characteristic 'buzz' or 'noise' that attracts creatives and stimulates creative activity (Bathelt et al., 2004; Crewe et al., 2003), a phenomenon that appears (to me) as much rooted in unspoken elements of atmosphere and a located sense of being, as in the realms of conscious and rational calculation. Indeed, my own interviews with cultural workers have suggested that one of the primary attractions of cultural work lies in the opportunity to dwell in the city and to become absorbed by its wealth of cultural opportunities, as this graphic designer from Manchester intimated:

> As I said I came to college and stayed here. I'm emotionally attached to the city, I like the city, it accounted for most of my evolving from some spud who was at school to a human being...The city contains all the elements I require personally and professionally and it has evolved with me, or I have evolved with it. There's a natural magnetism for people to come into Manchester.

In similar ways, Williams' (1973, 1977) tantalising concept of 'structure of feeling' might also usefully be invoked in order to describe some of the ambient, atmospheric elements and embedded modes of being that attract workers to the cultural cluster. Williams famously defined structure of feeling as socially shared elements of meaning and experience, observable as the 'culture of a period', but which defy a logical, formal classification. Structure of feeling is realised as 'embodied, related feelings' (Williams, 1973, p. 10), qualities of 'impulse, restraint and tone' (Williams, 1977, p. 132) that shape the character of a culture – not as formal as an 'ideology' or 'world view', nor a coherent discursive project, but, simply, a particular sense of life unique to a time and place. While Williams conceived of such a collective sense of life to be implicitly bound by a national geography, both Longhurst (1991) and Jackson (1991) have since offered that structure of feeling offers theorists a potential tool for dismantling some of the complexities of local social formations, in so far as it offers a way of thinking about localities as more than simply 'labour markets', but as places possessed of more intangible and ethereal socializing structures. Indeed, without explicitly discussing the term, O'Connor and Wynne's (1996a) collection offers some glimpse of how certain elements of a 'structure of feeling', such as a creative atmosphere and a collective attachment and orientation to place, were crucial to the development of a cluster of pop cultural producers in 1980s Manchester. In this collection, Milestone evocatively reflects on how Manchester's 'pop culture bohemians' came together in the late 1970s driven by a sense of collective energy and creative possibility, not motivated by rational calculation but by (as Williams would no doubt recognize) certain embedded and affective elements of social relationship that cohered around shared experiences and inspiring visions of place:

> The hard-edged grimness of a declining industrial landscape was in many ways inspirational in generating the angry post-punk sounds. The destructive aspects of punk and post-punk echoed the destruction of the landscape, the disused warehouses and factories provided ideal backdrops ... these spaces were daunting, sinister and sometimes brutally beautiful ... [bohemians] renegotiated these elements to construct something that was cool, frightening, imposing and urbane. (Milestone, 1996, p. 101; see also Reynolds, 2005 on other post-punk movements and landscapes)

While structure of feeling remains an elusive concept (though see Taylor et al., 1996 for one of the more substantive attempts to apply it empirically) it at least hints at how artistic clusters might form as a discrete but loosely articulated community, as a 'scene', subculture or lifestyle group, or as a local social formation that trades on and develops its own sense of uniqueness and specialness in the face of perceived homogenizing market forces (as in Milestone's fiercely independent Northern pop bohemians, for example). To be part of a creative place, one with an embedded and reproducible 'structure of feeling', where an aura of possibility and belonging can be palpably experienced, is not just conducive to effective cultural production, but is beneficial and supportive of a sense of well-being and life-affirming affect. While evidence of such sentiment is clearly not necessarily incompatible with firms also seeking to maximise commercial opportunity (in the United Kingdom even those archetypal Northern 'pop culture bohemians' like The Beatles and The Smiths eventually moved to London),[8] it might be argued that 'sense of place' and 'community feeling' can act to restrain the pursuit of external rewards at the expense of internal ones. Indeed, the prevalence and durability of place attachments might be argued to have the potential to underwrite – not just purely aesthetic – but certain kinds of practice-led and social–ethical forms of cultural production that vitiate directly against economic rationality.

Practice-led clusters

Alongside these local 'aesthetic refusals', it is possible to identify a prevalence of practice-led forms of place-based production. For example,

Drake's (2003) interviews amongst Birmingham's metalworkers and jewellery designers evidence typically the existence of practice-like and craft-based communities that, in the MacIntyre sense, may seek to obtain both internal and external rewards, but adamantly refuse to sacrifice the necessity of the former for the pursuit of the latter. The importance of continuing the long tradition of jewellery making, the awareness and value attributed to that tradition, and the sense of reward gained from ensuring its reproduction acts as a crucial element of workers' identities, ones given additional significance by their association with locality and place (though see Pollard, 2004 for a contrasting account of this sector). Drake thus alerts us to the important possibility that social values, expressed in the desire to participate and contribute to a specific and geographically located community of practice, have not yet been fully attenuated by the principles of neo-liberal, market-led exchange.

Similarly, in my own research amongst Manchester's popular music communities, significant attachments to place, a 'craft pride' (see Becker, 1982) and commitments to produce work that spoke of (and to) Manchester and its diverse range of communities was a commonplace observation. One record label owner, committed to developing ethnic minority musical talent, when interviewed, remarked with passion:

> We're proud Mancunians we didn't call our record label Rainy City Music for nothing, we actually did it to say we live in Manchester and we're proud it rains here, we're proud of this city...we need to create a positive image of Manchester full stop....England needs Manchester, Birmingham to stand on their own two feet and give their own individual vibes to the nation. That's one of the reasons we set up our label because we believed in Manchester itself and our music as well.

Since the late 1970s a number of the UK's provincial cities have seen the growth of independent labels, bands and musicians, DJs, clubs and club nights, festivals and so on that have created a rich and diverse economic landscape of popular music production (Brown et al., 2000; Cohen, 1991, Hesmondhalgh, 1998; Reynolds 2005; Savage, 1991; Webb, 2004). While many of those involved are committed to the orthodox pursuit of external rewards ('making it big'), a significant number are motivated by the love of music and the chance to support and develop an embedded community of musicians (see also Finnegan, 1989; Toynbee, 2003; Whiteley et al., 2004). This commitment achieves spatial expression in the desire to contribute to a 'scene', a 'movement', to build on a local musical tradition – to indeed engage in activities that articulate the very essence of practice development and the creation of goods internal to a practice.

Ethical clusters

Finally, to give only an indicative example from my own research of how moral attachments to place can inspire cultural workers to more explicit social or ethical interventions, recent years have seen some significant involvement by cultural workers in Manchester in the work of voluntary Northern Quarter Association (NQA), a community group lobbying for environmental, social and cultural renewal in one part of Manchester's traditionally 'bohemian' city fringe (see Wansborough and Mageean, 2000). This organization has had some success in shaping and occasionally resisting the plans of the city council and developers to gentrify and further commodify the Northern Quarter – though the efforts of capital to impose standardized models of middle-class residential and retail development may at times prove difficult to fully resist (Banks, 2006; Leeming, 2007). While, on the one hand, it might be argued that 'helping the community' or 'improving the neighbourhood' is motivated by an instrumental need to preserve a 'unique' (marginal) local environment that provides the necessary countercultural cachet required for cultural businesses to flourish, on the other hand entrepreneurs' motivations for joining the NQA seemed to be less concerned with instrumental gain or with negotiating a position as a regeneration 'mover and shaker' (Harvey, 1989; Tickell and Peck, 1996), and more about attempting to reinforce cultural pluralism and an ethical commitment to place in a city increasingly subject to generic patterns of property-development and gentrification (Peck and Ward, 2002). Here, one member of the NQA articulated his commitment:

> I think we've got a big challenge at the moment to infiltrate what is happening at the larger scale and I think the signs are we're doing that quite well right now, but again very under-resourced. I don't think I'd like the NQA to be a very big organisation at all: it could be bigger and better resourced ... but its got to watch it doesn't become 'Establishment' itself, I think its role will always be somewhat anti-establishment ... its more about ideas and creativity than money you know.

Such initiatives belong within a noble historical tradition of artists directly contributing to the regeneration (or preservation) of the built environment (see Ashton, 1972; Blazwick, 2001; De Salvo, 2001; Fowle and Larsen, 2005) – and, indeed, despite their fragile nature, such interventions appear to be on the increase (see contributions in Purves, 2005). To give another example, Drake (2003) in his discussion of the work of new media/digital design entrepreneurs in Sheffield reveals the efforts made by theoretically 'desocialized' (McRobbie, 2002b, p. 111) workers to undertake work that contributes to social development of the community, and indeed improves the physical regeneration of marginal 'inner city' environments. In Manchester, I came across a similar group of new media designers and providers of ICT services espousing no less an aim than to 'bring about social change through our actions'. This was seen to be achieved through servicing the design and ICT needs of community organizations, charities and social and cultural organizations at non-commercial rates. In this firm, contribution to local community development was prioritized over rationalistic demands for disinterested exchange and accumulation. Another organization encountered, in Salford, has emerged as (one of a clutch of) hybrid 'social enterprise' organizations dedicated to providing small businesses and community groups with film-production services and facilities in the Salford and Manchester area; on their website working principles are articulated:

> Within the community [we] also provide commercial services for small businesses. Thus supplying the local community with low cost and socially responsible video production … Our long-term vision is for a sustainable community film making enterprise that can provide skills to all disadvantaged sectors of the community and encourage other community members to be involved with film projects of their own.

Such actions can be seen as merely indicative of a growing movement to develop more pluralized, democratic and non-commercial applications for media, design and new media technology in local places (Best, 2003; Lee, 2005; Uricchio, 2004) – itself part of an accelerated 'convergence' of new forms of reflexive cultural and political production amidst the economy's broader social turn (Amin et al., 2002; Heelas, 2002; Paperstergiadis, 2002; Ray, 2004).

In this respect, and in contrast to Wittel's nomadic and desocialized new media entrepreneurs, devoid of 'common and shared history' (2001, p. 67) and McRobbie's (2002b, pp. 111–112) 'despatialized' and 'desocialized' cultural workers, these workers appear committed to a more traditional and embedded notion of 'community action' and sense of place. Once, McRobbie argued that cultural work opened ethical 'desires for social transformation...too easily dismissed as marginal, merely cultural and politically insignificant' (1999, p. 30), and I would maintain that these desires can persist and remain significant. The compulsion to undertake autonomous (aesthetic, practice-led, social/ ethical) production is strong and is often distinguished by its principled commitments to place and by its uncompromising attitude to the demands of 'disembedding' forces such as planners, property developers and corporations – such initiatives illustrate the ongoing possibility of alternative forms of cultural work persisting even amidst substantially market-driven and commercialized cultural industries. Indeed, in Western economies, it is possible to identify a panoply of new linkages and alliances being forged, ones that seek to *combine* economic ambitions with artistic, practice-based and social goals within discrete geographical milieux.

Summary

How are we to characterise the geographies of cultural industries and cultural work? At first glance, globalization appears to fundamentally undo local cultural formations, shoring up the power of culture industry corporations and the unstoppable move to a 'single global market'. Yet, it is clear that locality remains important – offering vital 'landing points' for capital in the form of distinctive and exploitable arrays of materials, labour, production systems, commodities and markets. The benefits for the cultural worker are, however, dubious. 'Alliance capitalism' and 'decentralized accumulation' are just two of the terms critics have applied to describe the ways in which individual places and producers are now inveigled into the global cultural economy (Hesmondhalgh, 2007; Wayne, 2003).

In contrast to this pessimistic critique, the likes of Porter, Scott and Florida more positively emphasize the renaissance of embedded economic practices, and the attendant renewal of 'embedded' or 'autonomous' place-based production. Localities, in the form of clusters of production, are now seen as providing 'the essential economic backbone of thriving cities and regions' (Scott, 2000, p. 16) with cultural clusters in particular, cited at the leading edge of this local economic renaissance. The media, art, design, music, advertising and fashion clusters of London, Los Angeles, New York and Paris are widely hailed as new models for cultural industry organization, paradigmatic configurations of post-industrial production that fuse the local and the global and offer seductive new agent-centred and 'reflexive' working environments that offer creativity and freedom (Florida, 2002; Lash, 1994; Lash and Urry, 1994; Scott, 2000). Yet, the reality is often somewhat less revolutionary, for while reflexive and localized production may appear emancipatory, it remains the case that it is somewhat traditional patterns of capitalistic growth and labour exploitation that continue to underpin 'local' economic activity in core-city clusters – and workers now (through compulsion or choice) find themselves strongly embedded within relations of 'network sociality' (Wittel, 2001).

The conventional cluster study tends only to focus on regions and sectors of production that remain locked into the 'mainstream' capitalist economy – it is therefore unsurprising that any progressive social relations or non-economic values detected in the contexts of these studies will tend (eventually) to become shackled to the interests of capital. Yet, outside of core-city clusters and central hubs of London, New York and Los Angeles, geographically clustered communities remain important foci for more *critical* elements of aesthetic, practice-led and ethical cultural production – ones that deny the *total* primacy of profit. A combination of state interventions (or non-interventions), market failures, fluctuating land rents, cheaper and more accessible technologies of production, political incitements to self-determination and, most crucially, the resurgence in individualization of creative and self-reflexive communities of like-minded practitioners (including both proximate and more dispersed forms of online or 'virtual' communities), have arguably ensured that the possibilities for autonomous cultural work have been sustained. As this chapter has detailed, the longing for place, a yearning for rootedness and depth in the midst of dislocating social and economic change, can also be cited as an explanation for the endurance of local production complexes that stress cultural independence and local autonomy. Arguably, while the commodification of such places is likely it is never inevitable. It is clear that at the margins of core cities, in the fringe districts, alternative production persists. In regional, provincial and second-tier cities, off-centre places peripheral to the main thoroughfares of the 'space of flows' (Castells, 1996, p. 376), small – but vital – cultural economies may survive.

What I have termed the 'mixed economy' of clusters is further evidence of the ambivalent character of modernization and individualization; transformations that promise to render obsolete traditional forms of social association, yet at the same time provide agents with the opportunity to resuscitate or revive social (and also spatial) bonds.

However, while I have suggested here (and in the previous chapter) that such 'moderated' or 'alternative' forms of capitalistic cultural work appear to thrive and *co-exist* alongside the 'pure' market-led variant, I have not yet ventured into any assessment of the relative strength of these alternatives, nor appraised their prospects as political models for the *future* of cultural work. A pressing concern must be, what prospects are there for alternative rationales to obtain a foothold sufficient to effect widespread or radical social and economic change? The final chapter considers this question.

7
Cultural Work and Moral Futures

For many, the freedoms unleashed by processes of 'reflexive modernization' would appear to have imbued a vast array of creative workers, counter-capitalists, bohemians and community-minded cultural entrepreneurs with fresh impetus to fashion worlds in their own image. But before we retire to celebrate the revival of art and the new-found freedoms of the cultural worker, it is clear there remains much to be discussed. Rather than accept these 'alternative' interventions as inherently progressive, the first aim of this chapter is to more thoroughly question how far such initiatives present a serious deviation from, or significant challenge to, the capitalistic practices they purport to subvert. Indeed, for a body of renascent sceptics, while so-called 'alternative' cultural economies are seen to provide some palliative to the virulent excesses of neo-liberal 'culture industry', as long as the efforts of artists, firms and entrepreneurs remain contained within a capitalist framework – where, ultimately, profit and accumulation remain necessary for underwriting the *continuation* of alternative production – then attempts to moderate or check capitalism are unlikely to succeed. Thus, the chapter begins by providing a summary of more recent critical responses to the idea of alternative production – and the real freedoms of liberal–democratic individualization are finally assessed.

The second part of this chapter is concerned with the *future* of cultural work. The aim here is to reflect on how certain forms of radical cultural production may be emerging, ones that appear more *fundamentally* opposed to capitalist exchange than the moderated or restrained forms of capitalism currently championed in the liberal–democratic model. The emergence of various forms of barter and gift economy and some nascent attempts to create 'digital democracy' are chosen as illustrative examples. I ask, how far do these utopian formulas offer the prospect of new kinds of *post*-capitalist cultural work emerging?

Critique of 'alternative' economies

While I have explored the argument that individualization opens up the potential for a renaissance of alternative (various art-based, practice-led and social/ethical forms) of cultural production, a number of critics have fought back to raise objections to the idea that capitalist values can be so easily evaded. Indeed, many observers continue to emphasize the total-izing hegemony of capitalist social relations, and their innate capacity to undo these 'alternative' economic configurations.

The power of the market

While the economic landscape is now more widely inhabited by creative cultural workers engaged in noble efforts to subvert or 'hold out' against 'pure' capitalist values – by creating alternative record companies, art studios and galleries, fashion houses, cafes, graphic design agencies, bookshops, new media firms and so on – at the same time, we should recognize that this kind of alternative production is highly vulnerable, not least to the formidable power of capital to appropriate for itself 'without permission' whichever elements of the 'alternative' it so desires. The inevitable diffusion of any form of avant-garde or alternative production will eventually bring it to the attention of mainstream cap-italists who may attempt to exploit markets for goods and services that furnish desires for the autonomous and authentic. Indeed the compel-ling evidence of cultural history is that almost all radical innovations are destined to be appropriated and absorbed into the commercial world. Everyday, regardless of the wishes of its practitioners, oppos-itional art is decontextualized, commodified and thus (arguably) divested of its critical power (Bell, 1976). The transgressive sounds of jazz, punk, rock and rap are reworked into soundtracks for advertising cars, supermarkets, bank accounts and holidays (Scherzinger, 2005); left-wing, revolutionary and situationist ventures are turned into tour-ist experiences, trendy T-shirts or coffee-table volumes (Swyngedouw, 2002), independent fashion retailers find their alternative styles easily absorbed into the lines of mainstream corporations (Crewe et al., 2003; McRobbie, 2002a). Capitalists employ specialist 'cool hunters' to delve into the recesses of transgressive cultures in order to retrieve signs, symbols and texts that can be refashioned into new commodities or used to sell existing ones to the segmented panoply of youth, middle-youth and baby-boomer markets (Heath and Potter, 2004; Klein, 2000). Beyond individual styles and commodities themselves, the radical philosophies that underpin counter-cultural production are also vulnerable to appropriation, as, for example, when the moral templates of ethical, independent fashion designers reappear in Nike's promotion of its 'code of ethics' in dealing with international suppliers, or when the civic-minded inclinations of those dedicated to 'digital democracy' are reworked by profit-hungry companies such as Microsoft.[1] The whole idea of radical and reflexive self-autonomy is itself requisitioned by the likes of Ikea, whose advertisements suggest that buying furniture provides the means to 'design your own life'. Clearly, the search for remoralized economic practices and the ideas and experiences that underpin the quest for more 'authentic' and 'alternative' ways of life are now rich seams of opportunity for the resourceful capitalist (Holmes, 2004).

Additionally, the search for a *spatially fixed* alternative may in itself be no defence from the commercial imperative. Indeed, just as radical symbols, texts and lifestyles are able to be so readily appropriated and commodified, so too discrete places become objects of fascination for capital. Re-branded as 'cities of culture' or internally as creative or bohemian districts (Lloyd, 2006), Chinatowns, Little Italies, Moroccan quarters and so on (Harvey, 1989, 2000, 2001), 'alternative' places often appear as organic, fully formed commodities in themselves, ripe for commercial cultivation. Thus, while the previous chapter identified the enduring existence of a 'mixed economy of clusters' outside of the 'core-city' cluster and mainstream economy, the inevitable power of market forces to undo or exploit even those *marginal* geographical configurations that seek to resist the sweep of market culture has been re-emphasized in recent Marxian accounts. Harvey (2000), for example, while recognizing that opposition to the excesses of capitalism has helped stimulate the formation of myriad anti-capitalist economies, forms of labour re-organizing, cultural retraditionalization and popular place-based and social re-embedding movements remains sceptical that the search for a geographically fixed point of resistance to capital is likely to be successful given the 'raw fact that the global market implies that there are hardly any places now left outside of market influences' (ibid., p. 67). As he continues:

> The geographical bounding being striven for and the numerous inventions of tradition that are occurring indicate that this is a dynamic field of human activity which is moving in somewhat

unpredictable ways. Yet I think it is also undeniable that all of this is being strongly driven (albeit in different directions) under the impulses of capitalist globalization. (ibid., p. 67)

The pursuit of tradition and the search for re-embedded forms of economizing remain fragile and uncertain endeavours, prone to calamitous rupture as the forces of global capital hone in on the commercial potential of even the most marginal, 'authentic' or non-marketized forms of community and place. Thus, for many critics, despite individualized (and some collective) efforts to re-embed social and economic life in the sensuous and affective terrain of place and locality, the possibilities for doing so *effectively*, appear to be fast diminishing. Increasingly, it seems, there is no longer any critical 'outside' from which to repel the advances of capitalist social relations.

The false grail of individualization

While we should remain cognisant of how, at the macro level, market forces can systematically undo alternative enterprises, it is further necessary we remain alert to the ways in which, at the micro-level, individual 'potentials' embedded in the now (ostensibly) more 'open' individualization process are being directed towards the reinforcement of capitalistic values. While the ambivalence of individualization, has, of course, long been a concern of critical social science, many practitioners (such as critical theorists and governmentalists I have discussed) remain sceptical that individualization in the present contains within it the potential to provide those growing powers of autonomy so often claimed on its behalf. Indeed, most recently from critical theory, Honneth (2004) has offered a direct riposte to the optimistic reading that implicitly underpins liberal–democratic accounts of the individualization process. While Honneth (like Beck) acknowledges that it is 'indisputable' that processes of individualization have forced members of Western societies to 'place their very selves at the centre of their own life planning and practice' (2004, p. 469), he is less certain that this has led to demonstrable increases in autonomy or, indeed, the cultivation of an effective political terrain outside of the parameters of capitalism. Indeed, his provocation is that the demands and potentials of individualization 'do not in any way conflict with the functional requirements of the capitalist economy' (ibid., p. 471) since the pursuit of individual autonomy has itself become a 'productive force' underwriting the further expansive colonization of the lifeworld by impulses of commodification. Furthermore, he argues, the pursuit of autonomy and independence has in itself, somewhat paradoxically, become an ossified ideological standard. For Honneth, we inhabit a curious world where everyone is simultaneously and collectively attempting to be individual – yet the means to achieve this are becoming ever more strongly standardized and prescribed.

Indeed, Honneth (2004) argues that individualization leads to a kind of 'organized' quest for self-realization. Echoing Foucauldians, he avers that the structuring of individualization stems from the 'interpellation of individual workers, who no longer [are] addressed institutionally as employees but rather as creative entrepreneurs or self-employed persons' (ibid., p. 473). But also, building on Adorno, he sees such a process determined by 'the cultural goods offered up to individuals by the advertising industry, with its calculated feeling for the variations of age, class and gender' (ibid., 472–473). Claims made about the autonomy of alternative production are, therefore, rendered invalid, given that the freedom to act is now so strongly constrained by the highly restricted parameters of 'free' action, determined not least by the culture industry. In this respect, for Honneth, unlike Beck, the freedoms of individualization in 'reflexive modernization' appear chimerical and suspect. We might surmise, therefore, that seeking to develop an individualized and autonomous cultural workplace career is to be in pursuit of a false grail – a tragic prize that promises emancipation but provides only tyranny and unfreedom.

In Honneth's view, those working in the diffuse panoply of artistic 'clusters', 'practice-led' communities and social or ethical enterprises would doubtless be identified as subjugated because of their supreme willingness to uphold the principles of 'self-determination' that underpin the socially dominant 'enterprise' culture. Indeed, in its description of the dutiful (and essentially duped) worker–subject, Honneth's analysis once again closes down on the ideal possibility of autonomous subjectivity and/or alternative production flourishing in individualized work contexts.

The spectre of economic interest

Thus, it appears that even in reflexive modernity cultural workers, as Adorno would have put it, continue to 'fasten on the culture-masks proffered to them and practise themselves the magic that is already worked upon them' (Adorno 1991, p. 82). But if Honneth sees the individualized subject as essentially undermined by his or her own well-meant strivings for freedom, Bourdieu takes a somewhat more cynical view of the reasons why the incorporation of radical subjects appears unstoppable. For Bourdieu, working 'within the system' actually persists (despite radical protests to the contrary) largely because creative cultural workers believe that it is in their own personal (and class) interests to do so. In his account of 'restricted production' (broadly synonymous with 'alternative' cultural production), Bourdieu sees even embedded, oppositional organizations as socially antagonistic and competitive, in that workers are invariably engaged in 'position taking' activity in an effort to secure various forms of social status, advantage and prestige. While, in restricted production, this competition is not necessarily oriented towards conventional economic goals of profit and wealth accumulation, and may be focussed instead on the acquisition of internal community goods, such as development of the practice and accumulating the respect of ones' peers, as well as obtaining the consecration, by other producers and critics, of one's artistic endeavours (thus ensuring what Bourdieu calls the accumulation of 'symbolic capital'), Bourdieu is sceptical that even in the most avant-garde art communes there can be a full disavowal of economic imperatives. There is, in his view, a spectre of economy that 'always haunts the most 'disinterested' practices' (1993, p. 75), and thus never a 'complete repudiation of economic interest' (ibid., p. 76). So while young, nascent artists and cultural producers may *appear* to disavow the trappings of wealth and fame acquired by their more established peers, there is rarely any significant or widespread attempt on their part to challenge the logic of a system that (as Bourdieu assumes they know) provides avenues for those endowed with prestigious symbolic capital to convert this (in time) into conventional economic capital. Bourdieu reinforces the notion that a familiar pattern, in all cultural disciplines and fields, as trends and fashions evolve, is that the marginal eventually becomes mainstream and that avant-gardes are translated for mass consumption – thus, as Bourdieu has it, radicals have an interest in playing the game to try and insure future rewards. This explains why '[art] revolutions are only ever partial ones, which displace the censorships and transgress the conventions but do so in the name of the same underlying principles' (ibid., pp. 83–84). Thus, while not entirely ruling out the possibility of some form of radical opposition and catalytic social change in what he calls the cultural field's 'space of possibles', his tendency to reiterate the largely conservative nature of the world of art and culture, and the self-reproducing strategies employed by creative cultural workers, does tend to imply that artistic endeavours in embedded social contexts will primarily (if not entirely) be driven by instrumental, status-seeking (and economically acquisitive) social actors. For Bourdieu, (similar to MacIntyre's prognosis) self-interest will eventually outweigh community interest. Indeed, a cursory glance at the economic landscape now reveals an abundance of individuals and firms who have diluted or abandoned their 'progressive' or 'alternative' stance when faced with the innate pressures or seductive temptations of market culture. 'Selling out' appears endemic as 'independent' record labels become bankrolled subsidiaries of the majors, 'authentic' retailers coyly mask their corporate ownership and dynamic and 'grassroots' Internet companies are bought out by more established competitors. Thus, one problem with the ostensibly 'moral' (i.e., aesthetic, practice-led or social–ethical) forms of cultural production that I have identified is that their morality is too often easily bought.

A further example of the way in which the 'spectre of economy' haunts ostensibly non-economic practices is evidenced in the ways in which even the most radical of avant-garde or anti-capitalist philosophies have now sought to 'capitalize themselves' and embrace their *own* forms of commodification. While, as we have seen, the mainstream capitalist will attempt to commodify 'alternative' economies (the branding of radical chic, the appropriation of authenticity) it is notable that even the more outré elements of the counter-culture – such as emergent constellations of hard-line anti-corporate and anti-capitalist interests – are now not averse to adopting the tropes of commodity capitalism through their own efforts to promote 'ethical' consumerism. For example, as Carducci (2006) cites, the celebrated *Adbusters* magazine and website, supposedly an opponent of commodification, now stimulates consumption through providing links to its 'Culture Shop' where consumers can obtain more ethical and 'pro-grassroots' goods – such as the famous non-sweatshop 'Blackspot' sneaker, and various media subversion kits, posters, postcards and literature celebrating the culture of 'culture jamming'[2]. Thus, for critics, it appears the promotion of anti-capitalism has created its own market niche, ironically opening up 'new avenues of consumption through the pursuit of authenticity and the embrace of the natural' (Carducci, 2006, p. 125, see also Heath and Potter, 2004; Holmes, 2004; Klein, 2000). In short, it appears that the 'anti-brand' is becoming merely another form of branding[3]. Critics might be forgiven for thinking that, in the final analysis, despite radical intentions, the promotion of commodification and consumption remains undimmed.

Thus, in response to the liberal–democratic model, critics have sought to further reiterate that a combination of the enhanced ability of the market to out-compete or embrace 'alternative' economic practices and places, the enhanced standardization of individual self-directedness and the masked conformity of rebellion are amongst the real consequences of 'liberalized' individualization[4]. As 'resistant' actions now appear predetermined and wholly contained (and, in the last instance, reliant on moneymaking), the futility of any attempts by well-meaning cultural Canutes to turn back the tide of market culture is made apparent. Indeed, at the forefront of this drive towards 'autonomy', the culture industry actively encourages budding entrepreneurs and disaffected workers to seek out or from their own practical utopias (Bourdieu, 1984) – but in doing so they create, not freedom but merely, new commodities, taste publics and fields of consumption that capital will eventually colonize and conquer. Thus, despite the liberal–democratic impulses released in reflexive modernity, it appears that market-driven individualization (as the prevailing expression of the individualization impulse), with its destructive, de-socializing tenor, continues to hold the upper hand, and promises only further demoralization and dislocation, and a world where the possibilities for creative, independent work meet their final demise (McRobbie, 2002a).

Against pessimism?

Clearly, capitalism remains doggedly resistant to exterior challenge. Its capacity for undoing radical, ethical or local social formations is well-known. Further, through its own strategies of representation, capitalism has been able to construct itself as an autonomous logic, an independent force impervious to intellectual or practical contestation. The pervasive feeling that actors are 'condemned' to capitalism strongly undermines any efforts to repudiate it, to seek out new worlds beyond its limits. Thus, we might ask, in terms of cultural work, is there really any possibility of moving beyond its grasp? Surely, the widely held and deeply ingrained pessimism towards the 'alternative' efforts of individual worker–subjects is entirely justified? Capitalism, it seems, will always win. But maybe the picture is not so clear-cut.

First, we should not too readily discount the argument that alternative *aesthetic* production contains within it some *intrinsic* value, in the sense that it contributes to the continuation of human expressivity and vital aspects of 'symbolic creativity' (Willis, 1990, 2005; see also Wolff, 1993) that underpin quests for meaning and autonomy in modern life. Initially, quotidian aesthetics and symbolic cultural production have long been underestimated for the role they play in upholding 'sensuous and concrete practices and processes which allow the contextual *human* apprehension of wider structures and structural relations, their possibilities and potentials, *as locally experienced and explored'* (Willis, 2005, p. 76, his emphasis). For Willis, alternative (and indeed all) forms of cultural production, irrespective of whether they are mundane and 'invisible' (or visible in the sense of eventually become consecrated and/ or commodified) inherently enhance the possibilities for reflective self-comprehension and social action on the part of both producers and consumers. In this respect they are their own virtue. Alternative cultural production then, must in some way be credited for opening up possibilities for self-reflexivity, for engendering more creative and autonomous attitudes and for (at least potentially) furnishing possibilities for progressive social practices – even as these possibilities remain vulnerable to the incursions of commodification and marketization. In similar vein, Negus and Pickering (2004) drawing on the pragmatist philosophy of Dewey (1980), argue that art and culture continue to provide a sphere of relative autonomy away from the immediate concerns of the marketplace, a place where the creative impulse can lead not only to self-awareness but also to a more critical contemplation of both the ordinary and extraordinary qualities of everyday life[5]. Frith (1996) and O'Connor (2006) also stress the relative autonomy of the aesthetic dimension – and its capacity to ignite critical or alternative moral viewpoints in contexts of cultural production and consumption.[6] Thus, such critics remind us that while the realms of art and culture should not be essentialized, neither should they be reduced to the status of mere ideological effect.

While aesthetic and 'symbolic' creativity remain valuable for encouraging Macintyre-style practices and 'human flourishing', critics might remain sceptical of its effective ability to more substantially challenge capitalist hegemony – indeed, as many have argued, the prospects for it doing so appear somewhat unlikely. But perhaps there is something both churlish and misguided about this totalized bad faith in the efforts of the cultural worker. It is both easy and rather comfortable to shrug our shoulders and blame the power of 'the system', or even to criticize (what I have termed) alternative cultural workers for their apparent wrongheadedness, their complicities and accommodations, or even their lack of revolutionary zeal. Let us not discount how, in myriad global contexts, cultural workers are not only working to generate profit but also concrete political interventions and social benefits. Such work is immensely valuable in keeping alive the possibilities of a life beyond total commodification – however partial and precarious that life may currently appear. The post-1960s efforts of feminists, equality campaigners, anti-discrimination and labour movements alongside or in conjunction with socially motivated artists and cultural entrepreneurs to overcome inequalities and bring into existence more egalitarian and progressive workplaces *within* capitalism should not be dismissed – real benefits have been accrued (Miles, 2004; Papastergiadis, 2002; Ray, 2004; see also Webb, J. 2004). As Carducci (2006, p. 129) comments in relation to counter-cultural production, even such an ambiguous activity as culture jamming, while 'fraught with contradictions ... does lend itself to certain methods of social amelioration'.[7] It is to disparage and, perhaps more importantly, to empirically misrepresent the efforts of thousands of artistic, community-oriented and socially motivated practitioners to suggest that the fruits of their labour have served *only* the capitalist mode of accumulation which contains (and often constrains) their efforts.

Further grounds for optimism are offered by Gibson-Graham (2006) and Williams (2005), who suggest that the possibilities of alternative economies are only just beginning to be explored, and so argue we should avoid slipping into the register of dismissive pessimism that tends to surround the efforts of the traditional left (such as more conventional strands of political economy and critical theory) to dismiss alternative practices, subpoliticization and local ethical refusals as merely temporary, delusional and inadequate. As yet, it seems we simply do not know what the eventual possibilities of 'community economies' really are. Criticizing explicitly the left's obsession with a 'politics of the past', with its conventional faith that the path to emancipation lies *only* in the revolutionary potential of a collectively radicalized and unified industrial working class, Gibson-Graham rejects any 'stance that undermines efforts toward imagining and enacting noncapitalist futures' particularly 'that [which] Walter Benjamin called left melancholia, in which attachment to a past political analysis or identity is stronger than the interest in present possibilities for mobilization, alliance or transformation' (Gibson-Graham, 2006, p. 6). Indeed, it is arguable that the tirelessness with which the traditional Marxian left condemns the 'inauthentic' and fragmented radicalism of localized or communitarian subpolitics, with its small and seemingly inconsequential victories, has not led to an idealized rapprochement of radicals as the veil of false consciousness is lifted but to sclerosis in the 'politics of the present':

> The theoretical closure of paranoia, the backward-looking political certainty of melancholia and the moralistic scepticism toward power render the world effectively uncontestable. The accompanying effects of despair, separation and resentment are negative and repudiating,

inhospitable to adventure and innovation, at best cautious and lacking in temerity. From our perspective, these stances are what must be 'worked against' if we are to pursue a new economic politics. (Gibson-Graham, 2006, p. 6)

'Working against' market-fatalism, liberal-democratic theorists of individualization have stressed that intrinsic desires for social and spatial re-embedding (including the resuscitation of virtue and a rectification of the lifeworld) *can* lead to something better. I would want to (tentatively) support this view and reiterate that one of the 'unintended consequences' (in Beck's term) of neo-liberal globalization, with its credo of rationalization, a rolling back of institutions and the promotion of 'choice' is to facilitate conditions under which individuals may actually *choose to reject* those individualizing systems that place them at the capricious mercy of the market. Furnished with (as Lash and Urry identify) an expanded universe of discourse, a proliferation of media-communicative possibilities and, crucially, an enhanced ability to apply self-reflexivity to their own social situation, individuals may elect to evade their prescribed neo-liberal fate by invoking new modes of life that challenge market rationality and their own positioning within it. To put this in more Foucauldian terms, we can perhaps posit a clear disjuncture between the 'enterprise subject' and the potentialities of enterprise *itself*. Incitements to self-directedness can become uncoupled from programmes of government and, indeed, when (as Foucault himself noted it is prone to do) government fails, a window of opportunity for alternative or radical subjectivities emerges even (or rather *especially*) amidst the most strongly governed of economies, states and situations (Flusty, 2000). Hardt and Negri put this otherwise when they identify the incipient power of the labouring 'multitude' as arising paradoxically from the very structures of transnational economy and government ('Empire') that seek to suppress their agency:

Empire can only isolate, divide and segregate...however, it must be careful not to restrict the productivity of the multitude too much because Empire too depends on this power. The movements of the multitude have to be allowed to extend always wider across the world scene, and the attempts at repressing the multitude are really paradoxical, inverted manifestations of its strength. (Hardt and Negri, 2000, p. 399)

Of course, exercising 'free' subjectivity, individually or in 'multitudinous' form, is not a straightforward process. Given enduring power structures, deep-rooted social inequalities and entrenched forms of exclusion, only the foolish would suggest this option is open to all – it is never *simply* a matter of choice. But alongside, as Beck identifies, the prescriptions and promptings of radicalized social structures and institutions, and given actors' own enduring and deep-lying attachments to non-economic norms and social structures, the desire for radical choice can provide the engine power for re-embedding cultural work under conditions of advanced individualization. This may produce, in time, socially valuable and perhaps *entirely new* economic models that will offer significant alternatives to the tyranny of capitalism and (in this case) its apparently demoralized and disembedded culture industry components. As even sceptics such as Lloyd (2006) and Wilson (1999, p. 28) acknowledge in relation to art, 'it does not follow that cultural protest is rendered defunct or irrelevant by the reduction of the avant-garde, the bohemian and the 'shock of the new' to the latest consumer style' for certain breeds of artists and creative producers will always evade capture by market culture, particularly those whose pursuit of the 'carnivalesque, anti-authoritarian and self-sustaining' (ibid., p. 28) modes of social and economic life have proved difficult to assimilate into mainstream market culture. Wilson cites here the examples of New Age Travellers, environmental activists and more extreme elements of the artistic avant-garde – and so we should not rule out the additional utopian possibility that the seeds of future *workplace* revolutions are currently being sown by 'anti-authoritarian' or 'self-sustaining' workers even within apparently 'moderated' or 'system-friendly' forms of alternative cultural (or even non-cultural) production.

Thus, while we might broadly accept the argument that individualization has, to a significant degree, become a servant of capital and a pervasive global impulse that comes with certain prescribed governmental standards and subjective templates, it does not necessarily follow that all worker–subjects fall dutifully into line. Indeed, if we accept that more and more workers are 'choosing to reject' market-led capitalism is it possible a more radical subject may emerge, one more *fundamentally* concerned with 'breaking free' – both from 'moderated' forms of capitalism and the wider systemic apparatus of capitalist social relations?

Post-capitalist cultural work?

For Weber capitalism first appeared to present an 'unalterable order of things', (1930/2001, p. 19) and the current neo-liberal variant exudes a similarly inalienable supremacy. Yet, challenging the 'logic of the pure market' (Bourdieu 1998, p. 96) requires the imagining of new economic futures. While non-instrumental values appear to have been over-whelmed and discredited by the neo-liberal regime, critics have recently taken up the task of envisioning alternative societies that can re-establish social, political and cultural values at the core of social life. For example, critics such as Beck, Gorz and Harvey have each, in their own distinctive way, supplied us with sketches and route maps out of the demoralized terrain of neo-liberalism, suggesting new paths to more authentic forms of self-actualization and a renewed ethic of civic virtue. What these critics share is a conviction that the pursuit of instrumental ends has most effectively diminished moral guarantors of selfhood, work and sociability historically associated with traditional life. Indeed, these critics co-possess a broad antagonism to the expansion of market rela-tions and antipathy to capitalist notions of progress – and they seek to offer radical *utopian* solutions to prevailing crises. As Levitas (2001) argues, while utopias may appear detached from the realms of the pos-sible, they are useful in permitting a move beyond mere extrapolation from present situations to a critical space where we might consider an *ideal* solution, rather than what seems the best available one, given the current socio-economic climate. In similar terms, critical social science has turned again towards utopian theorising in order to propose ideal solutions to the problems generated by capitalist societies.

A common theme in much of this utopian writing is a rejection of the work ethic and paid employment as governing virtues of social life (Beck, 2000; Fevre, 2003; Gorz, 1989; Harvey, 2000; Illich, 1978; Levitas, 2001). For example, as technology and restructuring create unemploy-ment and part-time, functional and menial work and fragment the social basis of collective endeavour, Gorz (1982, 1989) has argued for the development of new societies where non-work 'autonomous activ-ities' assume an equivalent value and moral force to paid work. While recognising the social need to retain, and indeed develop, highly specialized 'heteronomous' jobs, Gorz argues that, for the most part, work increasingly only provides the powerful a means of occupying proletarian time, with employment no longer acting as the 'mode of insertion into a system of universal co-operation' but rather a 'mode of subordination to the machinery of universal domination' (1982, p. 71). He argues that useless, menial work is now deliberately engineered as a tool of social repression (see Ehrenreich, 2001 for echoes of this argu-ment) and suggests that only through a society-wide 'rejection of the accumulation ethic' (1982, p. 74) and the breaking of the sociological and psychological bond between paid work and meaningful self-identity can autonomous activities re-establish moral legitimacy and social value. In short, to break the primary bond we need to make heteronomous work less time consuming, less important and less necessary. Through a redistribution of work, Gorz seeks to 'share the labour' and imagines a world where *more* people are given the opportunity to work *less* – theoretically eradicating unemployment as a wider population undertake the decreasing amount of socially necessary, needs-based heteronomous work. A general reduction of working hours for all would thus free up time and energy to commit to other (equally necessary) non-economic activities – and, we might add, a revivification of art and cultural production would not be ruled out.

Echoing Gorz, Beck (2000, pp. 1–6) in his speculations on the 'post-work' society outlines a similarly utopian agenda for overcoming the problems of what he sees as a technologically advanced risk society characterised by informal, temporary and part-time work, endemic underemployment and the 'political economy of insecurity'. In an age when work becomes 'temporary and insecure' and characterised by 'discontinuity and loose informality', Beck sees opportunities for those enforced with idle hands to reinvigorate civil society through what he calls 'self-organized activity networks' (2000, p. 6) that eschew the hegemony of a paid work ethic and instead combine periods of paid employment with time out to undertake non-economic (social, environmental and aesthetic) 'civil labour' and community work. Gorz and Beck advocate seismic shifts that would require a wholesale ethical retooling of societies, and involve people being given the right to choose their own methods of working and not working, and negotiate a balance between work and undertaking projects and activities that upholster the civic good – clearly a big ask.

Similarly, Harvey (2000), in seeking to reject the 'craven and supine fear' (ibid., p. 195) that bedevils left-wing thinking on the subject of utopias, sketches out a vision of a remoralized future, one that attempts to avoid the nostalgic and tyrannical closures of utopias of spatial form, where universal principles are applied within a fixed and complete geography, and instead attempts to reconcile the tensions between the universal and the particular in the context of more dialectical and open-ended set of community relations. Striving for a future where there is 'sufficient stability of institutional and spatial forms to provide security and continuity, coupled with a dynamic negotiation between particularities and universals so as to force mediating institutions … to be as open as possible' (ibid., 242), Harvey imagines a post-apocalyptic utopia where openly democratic, self-directing and self-resourcing communities (*edilias*) populated by loose familial units (*hearths*) become embedded in federations of *regionas* (self-governing political units), themselves organized into fluid and mutable trans-spatial national alliances (*nationas*) developed for the purposes of barter and trade. In his vision, work is identified as socially necessary, but work for profit is rejected in favour of gift and barter economies and heteronomous production for community benefits, underpinned by a strong eco-conscious principles. But this is no nostalgic return to pre-modern simplicity, for media, technology, science, trade and economic specialization remain, but their use is now calibrated towards the service of the greater good and not individual gain. In this world, art and culture are divorced from instrumentality and rekindled as disinterested practices of 'amusement and self-betterment' (ibid., 273).

These visions of a remoralized future are seductive and especially compelling given the broad neglect of utopian thinking in the mainstream of critical social science. While many social scientists have come to accept market culture and neo-liberalism as inevitable, Beck, Gorz and Harvey remind us that 'thinking the unthinkable' and positing alternatives to prevailing structures remains an important job of critical social science, however fanciful and distant such visions might first appear. Buoyed by their creative spirit, but aware of my own imaginative shortcomings, my remaining intention is simply to address how far existing economies may *already contain* diverse examples of the progressive (utopian) interplay of economic and non-economic moral values in the contexts of cultural work. This has utility in so far as while Gorz, Beck and Harvey identify the progressive possibility of new combinations of workplace heteronomy-autonomy, their analyses fail to reflect on the existence of already non-capitalist work under existing conditions of modernization. While the mundane and often prosaic interventions I will discuss might be deemed insufficient to effect the necessary revolutionary transformations demanded by radicals such as Gorz, they nonetheless exist as significant utopian counterpoints to the dominant rationalities of market culture. Indeed, as I discussed previously, since economic life is already so intrinsically entwined with ideas of the social and the moral (Booth, 1994), it is reasonable to suggest that future utopian speculation might benefit from closer examinations of the ways in which economic actors already attempt to mediate and discharge responsibilities and regard for others, so striving towards utopias in the 'politics of the present'. Thus, by moving from utopian to extrapolatory method (Levitas, 2001) I want to conclude this book by assessing the ways in which existing and emergent forms of cultural production are providing the route-maps towards 'remoralized' futures beyond capitalism.

Barter, alternative currencies and gifts

The use of bartering – a system based on the exchange of goods without the medium of money – has long been a feature of (modern and pre-modern) economies, and, indeed, prominent amongst the economizing strategies of artists and creative cultural workers. In industrial societies, bartering provided a way for emergent artists to trade their works for food and other subsistence (and no doubt luxury) goods and services. The trend did not dissipate in advanced modernity, for as Time Magazine reported in 1956 'Many [Parisian] artists barter their works for art materials, do part-time drudge work painting lead soldiers, washing bottles, painting houses' (Time, 2006, no pagination) – bartering playing an important role in a mixed and marginal cultural economy. More recently, in Western, and, especially, non-Western economies (e.g., see Katel, 2002; Seabright, 2000), economic flux and uncertainty has underwritten a sharp rise in all forms of bartering – and artists continue to readily exchange their work for equivalent artistic and non-artistic goods. Indeed, in the cultural industries, it is increasingly common to find fashion designers, graphic designers, musicians, artists, promoters and web entrepreneurs undertaking reciprocal or non-monetized exchange of goods and services – particularly amongst more 'close-knit' cultural clusters. While there is not necessarily any radical intent in such transacting, it is noticeable that in recent years, the idea of goods-for-goods exchange has taken on a more evidently 'political' character, fuelled by concerns over the ways in which contemporary capitalism, driven, as it is, by states and global corporations operating within impersonal and disembedded financial systems, appears incapable of countering wealth inequalities or providing local communities and individuals with the means to sustain their own autonomous economic practices (Gibson-Graham, 2006; Leyshon et al., 2003; Williams, 2005).

Additionally, in seeking to challenge the tendency towards disembedding and economic abstraction, various artists and creative cultural workers have begun to experiment with alternative forms of currency exchange. 'Art-Money'[8] is one such example. The Bank of International Art Money (BIAM) was established in Copenhagen in 1998. Through it, artists can issue their own original art money bills, of their own design, which can be used to buy art from other member artists, or as part payment for non-art goods and services at conventional businesses that recognize art-money. The motivation of the founders is to provide a new kind of 'global currency', one that can not only be created and managed by artists themselves but also distributed according to communitarian principles of fairness and reciprocity, rather than accumulated and stockpiled to secure wealth and advantage. In similar vein, devised by artists in Providence, Rhode Island, 'Noney' is an alternative currency of individually, hand-designed pieces of art that can be traded for goods and services:

> Each Noney note has the same denomination: zero. This doesn't mean each note has no value... just relative value. There's no fixed exchange rate or location of operation. Noney's worth as both art and currency is something to negotiate through each individual transaction – anywhere. (http://www.noney.net/index.html, 2006)

The inspiration behind 'Art-Money' and 'Noney' appears to be a desire to counter the rational, dehumanizing tendencies that underpin the circulation of fiat money and institutionalized exchange and, in doing so, try and recover some sense of communitarian connection and interdependency within the economizing process. The bartering of art and the creation of art currencies represent an attempt to reintroduce some element of magic and humanity into the trading relationship – to re-embed the economy within a terrain of meaningful affect. In this sense they appear to contradict fundamentally the capitalistic principles of disembedded, mediated and impersonal exchange, driven only by the profit motive.

Motivated by a similar dissatisfaction with monetized and disinterested forms of exchange, Purves (2005) identifies a resurgence of interest in gift-giving and gift economies amongst artists and cultural producers. Listing over 40 recent projects, experiments and interventions in both Western and non-Western contexts, Purves and co-contributors emphasize how the principles of 'generosity' and 'hospitality' have become more central in radical art practice – fuelled by desire to make new art but also revivify social bonds. As they detail, the distribution of free paintings, photographs, theatre, food, clothing, shelter, transport, literature, magazines or labour is imbued with the utopian promise of a world beyond disinterested exchange, where the principles of generosity in gift-giving, and reciprocity in gift-returning are retained and re-established. In marketized societies, gifts, as Hyde (2006, p. 58) puts it, re-create a 'feeling-bond' between people, while 'the sale of a commodity leaves no necessary connection'. McIlveen (2005, p. 170) estimates that 'the last decade has seen an increase in artworks that use generous exchange systems', fuelled by artists and creative workers who wish to encourage audiences to recognize social and economic space as 'a moving network of rules/morals and social groupings/alliances that changes and responds to itself' (ibid., p. 170), one potentially composed of plural and more radical systems of non-capitalistic and non-monetized exchange.

Such anti-capitalist, utopian initiatives are part of a broader 'return of the social' (Amin et al., 2002, p. 7) now evident in Western economies, a process marked by the upsurge of interest and activity in alternative forms of economizing such as cooperatives, local currency and LETS schemes, recycling and gift economies, credit unions, self-help groups and various other 'Third Sector' organizations (Williams, 2005). While not every organization involved espouses anti-capitalist principles, many organizations do seek to position themselves as utopian agitators for alternative, non-capitalist economic futures; ones 'centred around the provision of socially useful services, meeting needs, ethical trade, and social/community empowerment and democratisation' (Amin et al., 2002, p. 116). Given their counter-rational credentials, it is common to see artists and creative cultural workers at the forefront of some of the more radical of these initiatives.

The new digital democracy?

It has been widely suggested that under conditions of pervasive individualization various 'subpolitical' groupings, 'neo-tribes' or 'new social movements' have become more prominent features of the social and economic landscape (see for example Beck, 2000; Crossley, 2003; Maffesoli, 1996). As Lacey argues here in relation to social activist networks in the United Kingdom, crucial has been the rise of new information and communications technologies that have helped fuse new circuits of both real and virtual community connections:

> The network of activists that exists around social centers and infoshops in Britain exists beyond the physical confines of their ndividual locations. Activists are linked in information networks, which in turn are woven together in a complex rhizomatic web of face-to face and virtual exchanges. Through their participation in these rhizomes of shared meaning and shared sentiment, in this case resistances to global capital, activists from loose, fluid communities.... It is not activists' proximities to one another that determines

connectedness; instead it is unquantifiable sense of vision and hope, and the desire to share these, that bring activists together in emotional communities. (Lacey, 2005, p. 289)

The rapid development of microprocessing and Internet-based broadband technologies has clearly opened up new horizons of possibility for the production, distribution and consumption of cultural goods. Amidst these transformations, two developments stand out:

• First, the remarkable rise of digital gift economies – through file-sharing communities and/or free software exchange. Here, consumers sharing music and video files by-pass and evade paying the premiums imposed by copyright protectors, or work to create new software systems based on free or 'open source' exchange. In these ways the benefits of technological advancement are shared outside of distributive market mechanisms.

• Second, new rounds of autonomous and non-corporate 'domestic' cultural production. A whole panoply of new producers are emerging as music, film, art and informational and symbolic goods are able to be manufactured locally and disseminated without recourse to the resources and 'expertise' traditionally provided by culture industry corporations.

Thus, while the mainstream cultural industries struggle to devise business models that can generate profits from the Internet (largely through seeking to co-opt new talent while protecting or promoting already existent intellectual property) it is clear that the Pandora's Box of 'digital revolution' has unleashed at least some potential for economic models that, in Uricchio's terms, 'hold the promise of radical reformulation, of an unknown but hopefully better future without the exploitative helping hand of large-scale corporate creative industries' (2004, p. 81).

Initially, a number of music (and also film and video) file sharing, peer-to-peer (p2p) networks have come to prominence in recent years, presented as an alternative means to disseminate cultural commodities amongst networks of fans, outside of commercial constraints. The well-known Napster system initially provided a template for the illegal sharing of music files, one since developed upon by the likes of Bit Torrent, Freenet, Gnutella, Morpheus, Kazaa, Limewire and Soribada (see Lee, 2005; Leyshon et al., 2005). Here the exchange of files serves as a kind of 'quasi-gift economy' (Leyshon et al., 2005) where through broadband-enabled downloads, consumers can access and exchange music rapidly and at minimal costs. The threats to the established music industry are obvious. The ability to obtain recordings without the necessity of buying CDs, DVDs and so on bypasses fundamentally current capitalist systems of production and distribution for profit, infringing systems of copyright designed to protect corporate interests and ensure accumulation. Leyshon et al. demonstrate how the rapid rise of file sharing has been identified by the mainstream music industry as a particularly nefarious form of piracy, threatening to denude the profits and monopoly control corporations have long enjoyed, and undermine the payment of royalties to artists themselves, who must suffer the consequences of falling corporate revenues from diminished sales of their recordings[9]. For Lee (2005) the rise of file sharing networks is politically important since it cuts against the grain of dominant systems of cultural production and emphasizes the radical potential of autonomous use of information. He predicts the implosion of the capitalistic music industry as consumers exploit the possibilities of a gift-based economy that is difficult to regulate and legislate against given the trans-national and mobile activities of service providers and consumers. In Deleuzian fashion, Lee sees users engaged in myriad 'lines of flight' that evade the grasp of regulation and legal control as they exploit the potential of a dispersed and anonymous technological medium (see Deleuze and Guattari, 2002). For Lee, file sharing is the alarm bell that awakens us to the necessity of developing a more sustained attack against the hegemony of corporations and copyright:

> To configure information–sharing in a socially oriented democratic model, it must go beyond a mere music-swapping tool, or else there is neither philosophy, nor movement, nor social and cultural resistance behind the current pattern of music swapping. The diminishing power of users, whose fate is dependent on the force of the market, needs to be underpinned by the kind of social movement that restrains the unlimited property rights of copyright owners and makes them abandon their proprietary rights on the internet. (Lee, 2005, p. 807)

Lee, like Hardt and Negri, has faith that the creativity of the 'multitude' now cannot be contained by the diffused system that has created it. His rallying call to arms is seductive – yet the practical steps required to mobilize this will to power remain (as yet) elusive.

More prosaically, the Habermasian principles of democratic exchange and unfettered access to informational goods and tools evidenced in file-sharing networks are more explicitly articulated through the activities of networks such as the 'Free Software Foundation' (see Best, 2003). The Free Software Foundation was formed in 1985 as a non-profit company and is a global organization committed to 'promoting computer users' rights to use, study, copy, modify, and redistribute computer programs'.[10] It acts as a network for the provision of all kinds of web architecture and services and through initiatives such as its Free Software Directory provides a resource detailing the availability of free software and operating systems. It actively campaigns against attempts by corporations to enforce closure of the digital commons through strategies of restricted copyright and 'digital rights management' (where the potential utility of digital products is artificially restricted to protect commercial interests).

It might be argued that workers, artists and entrepreneurs involved in such initiatives as the Free Software Foundation (FSF), and utilizers of its tools represent a challenge to the commodification of information and the capitalization of software labour through collective efforts to promote a public model of information and technology sharing. The uses of free software for the purposes of commodity production, community organization and knowledge dissemination are informed by a belief in a (digitized) public sphere, participatory democracy and a progressive politics of redistribution. As Best notes, the FSF seeks to bring forth a new utopian vision of a society populated by individuals freely engaged in information and knowledge exchange, committed, in a Gorzian sense, to both autonomous and heteronomous activities:

> The FSF idealizes the future in terms of a post-scarcity society, in which the inequities of resource distribution and workload will be evened out, and people will work fewer hours with more time for humanistic pursuits... In this sense the organizational model of free software is part of a 'vision and a plan' anchored in a public vision of value and collective decision making... The overall purpose of the movement is aimed at benefiting an imagined community, which consciously and consistently being worked towards. (Best, 2003, p. 456)

The FSF thus speaks the language of 'progressive' social reform through collective means and idealizes the virtues of digital democracy based on classical communicative principles. In this way, the FSF approach is motivated by an 'overt ideological position – even a sense of morality' (Best, 2003, p. 465) that 'characterizes old-style progressive politics' (ibid., 465). The FSF are, like Beck's 'sub-politicians', Lash's 'aesthetically-reflexive' workers and the other cultural workers identified in Chapters 5 and 6, 'active subjects' in the sense of progressively seeking to recover a sense of civicness amidst the unstable and detraditionalizing impulses of market culture.[11] Amidst the turmoil of cultural commodification, the FSF represent a return to tradition even as they embrace the possibilities of 'information society' and its attendant technoculture. Their efforts are predicated on the necessity of capturing the fruits of technology for the purposes of social re-embedding and the cultivation of ethical commercial production, practice-based communities and social and political goods.[12]

While the gift economies of file sharing and free software exchange by-pass capitalistic systems of distribution, helping to evacuate profit from corporate coffers, it is not obvious how cultural *production* is enhanced in any broad sense. Yet a second bequest of technological advancement, one coupled with the sense of political possibility opened up by radical individualization, is now evidenced in the emergent systems of autonomous art, film and music production being piloted through non-corporate means. With the accelerated development of new technological tools for the domestic (or rather non-corporate) production of music, film, art and other cultural forms, it has been mooted that the means of production of cultural goods is slipping out of corporate hands (Uricchio, 2004). The rise of an emergent 'bedroom culture' of music producers, digital artists, film-makers and so on, gives many observers grounds for optimism that the intermediary role of corporations, as investors, promoters and distributors of cultural texts, may be waning. Indeed, much excitement is currently being generated by the possible emergence of a 'second wave' Internet-based economy (Web 2.0, to give it its fashionable term) where emphasis appears to have switched away from corporations and experts (who populated the first dotcom 'boom' of the late 1990s) and their efforts to impose standardized business models and commercial protocols, to a model where users themselves become the authors of web content and the providers of what is dubbed 'social network' or 'MeMedia' – grassroots websites and services that rely upon ordinary individuals for their content and ultimately, economic value (Lanchester, 2006; Pareles, 2006). In this 'participatory culture' (Uricchio, 2004, p. 86), examples of 'MeMedia' or 'social sites' include Wikipedia (a free, user-created and edited online encyclopaedia), Friends Reunited (a site for tracking down old school friends – or enemies), MySpace (a form of Internet scrapbook where users can create personal pages showcasing their home-created music, poems, photographs etc.), YouTube (showcasing films clips and videos) and Flickr (an online photograph album). The exponential rise of 'blogging' (self-created online diaries, writings and commentaries) is a further notable feature of the production revolution, with (Lanchester estimates) around 175,000 new blogs created each day – two a second. The recent emergence of commercial blogging, authors selling their own e-books, and the use of sites such as MySpace to help pop bands promote themselves are taken as initial evidence that the days of the culture industry corporation may at last be numbered.[13]

The possibilities of cultural producers 'taking control' of the means of production, distribution, and harvesting the greater proportion of surplus value is further explored by Leyshon et al. (2005), who provide some intriguing data from their investigations into the activities of Internet-based music producers. Here they encounter pioneers committed to the idea that the future of cultural production will be more firmly based upon another kind of 'by-pass' model, one where artists are able to self-produce and distribute digitally their songs straight to consumers (and so receive a greater share of payments) without the need of costly services of intermediation (studio production, marketing, material production of CDs) provided by existing corporations. The possible removal of the need for investment in fixed capital costs of music production, reproduction and distribution, (it is theorized) will place control more squarely in the hands of individual artists. Clearly, in some form or other, any kind of computerized instantaneous and virtual 'streaming' system still requires capitalist firms in the shape of ISPs who can divert and filter individual artists to different taste publics (replicating the old A&R functions of record companies), take incomes from paid subscriptions, disseminate royalties and so on. Yet, while the formation of monopolies is possible as the big players seek to offer 'premium' streaming services with more rapid or diverse playlists, cheaper subscriptions and so on, it is arguable that the costs of executing this service pales in comparison to conventional music industry production and distribution, and the ease of market entry should enable the development of a more competitive and artist-friendly climate. So while this system does not repudiate a capitalistic mode (indeed, it might be seen by many as a further 'suspect' form of 'moderated' capitalism) it does offer the intriguing prospect of dismantling the traditional power of corporations and potentially, opening up a whole new system of production and distribution, one where 'the possibility of a middle class of professional musicians who will ... generate significant sums of money' (Leyshon et al., 2005, p. 198) appears more real than at present.[14]

The uncertain future

What are we to make of these utopian initiatives?

First, alternative currencies and the bartering or gifting of art and cultural goods remain marginal forms of economizing, and ones that (as yet) appear ill-equipped to serve the more substantial and complex social needs of community members. Indeed, it is notable that despite radical intent, proponents of alternative economies often remain dependent upon the mainstream capitalistic economy for a whole variety of resources – ones as yet unobtainable within a non-capitalist economic framework. For example, the provision of artistic 'gifts' is often reliant upon state and institutional financial support for artists in the form of grants, or artists themselves often rely upon conventional 'second' jobs in order to survive. Additionally, the production of alternative currencies may well rely upon resources obtained through fiat money purchases or conventional systems of commodity exchange. Furthermore, how far such alternative initiatives provide new models of social exchange that can stretch beyond the confines of the art world remains unclear – often these experiments seem comprehensible and contained only to the communities that create them. Yet the recent resurgence of alternative currencies, bartering and forms of gift exchange should not be discounted out of hand since their prospective benefits and future social impacts perhaps remain, as yet, unrealized (Gibson-Graham, 2006; Purves, 2005; Williams, 2005).

Second, we should (of course) avoid investing too much faith in the emancipatory potential of any putative digital or Internet-based democracy. As I write, culture industry corporations are lobbying hard for the tightening of copyright legislations, seeking to close down the possibilities for the unsanctioned online dissemination of their precious commodities. While Lee optimistically argues that 'disobedience to copyright authority is ripening, and all that is solid in private hands is slowly melting' (2005, p. 808), it is clear that the culture industry is not simply going to relinquish its monopoly without considerable fight. Napster was amongst the first to feel the weight of copyright legislation when it was closed down in 2002 – and then re-opened under a fee-paying, subscription-based model. Many other p2p networks have been forced to do the same. Further, organizations such as the FSF remain vulnerable to attempts by corporations to close down the digital commons through the aggressive application of digital rights management.

Finally in terms of autonomous 'home' or 'bedroom' cultural production, the majors are seeking actively to buy out or absorb these 'grassroots' cultural producers and distributors, evidenced by News Corporation's acquisition of MySpace in July 2005 and the 2006 purchase of the video-sharing network YouTube by Google (a company that was once itself the height of counter-capitalist cool). Flickr was bought by the more established Yahoo for over 30 million dollars after only a year of operation (Lanchester, 2006). Bands and bloggers that have established on the Internet quickly (and readily) get signed by record companies and publishers in order to capitalize on their commercial promise.[15] In this sense, these digital pioneers may simply be judged as the latest (Bourdieuvian) examples of the 'radical' artist – as one who is economically disinterested until the money is right – or seen simply as independent R&D organizations that build products and business models which the more hesitant majors can snap up when the commercial possibilities become apparent.[16] Thus, as Lewis warns, we must be cautious of 'the tendency of liberal and postmodernist commentators to utopianize the political potential of the technologies while neglecting or parenthesizing the significant invasion and appropriation of the cyber territory by the familiar forces of capital and commercial ideology' (Lewis, 2000, p. 114).

Yet, notwithstanding the extreme likelihood of corporate hijack, it is increasingly apparent that the autonomous and, indeed, democratic possibilities being opened up by new technology are neither pre-ordained nor easily assimilated into market culture. The theoretical utopias imagined – worlds of cultural production without corporate interest – may seem unlikely, but it is equally apparent that the slow-moving beasts of culture industry are struggling (and will continue to struggle) to fully eradicate illegal and gift-based digital economies, especially given the geographical inconsistencies in the basis and application of copyright legislation and regulation, and the ungovernable speed and trajectory of the 'lines of flight' that users are engaged. Further, the prospect of more equitable local, 'home' or 'bedroom' production systems, ones where the relationship between producer and consumer is more immediate and divested of intermediation by corporations appears a real possibility, even if – as we know – corporations will inevitably seek to monopolize the organization of any mechanisms of distribution. Once again, then, we might conclude, the full ambivalent consequences of individualized and technologically advanced modernity have perhaps yet to reveal themselves. Uricchio, while ruefully acknowledging the increasing efforts of capitalism to shackle and tame digital anarchy, does retain some faith that some fundamental sea change has occurred, one imbued with yet-to-be-realized transformative potential:

> While it is too early to consider Microsoft and its counterparts irrelevant, these large-scale, centralized and highly protective creatures seem increasingly like dinosaurs in the midst of a climatic shift...technologically enabled grassroots movements are circumventing long-dominant traditions of governmental and corporate intervention...[a]lthough they [p2p, open source, gift economies] may seem to be on the fringes of the digital scene, their impact on existing cultural practices may well turn out to be disproportionate to their apparent position; indeed their implications for how they define certain practices, including the practice of citizenship, and how we participate in cultural production are potentially transformative. (2004, pp. 85–86)

For Hardt and Negri the power of the ordinary multitude is, as yet, nebulous and unrealized, but promises to deliver a future beyond currently systematized labour and mechanized production controlled solely by the forces of 'Empire', since, as they observe:

> The new phenomenology of labour of the multitude reveals labor as the fundamental creative activity that through cooperation goes beyond any obstacle imposed on it and constantly re-creates the world. The activity of the multitude constitutes time beyond measure. (Hardt and Negri, 2000, p. 402)

As Munro (2002, p. 181) comments, for Hardt and Negri 'Empire contains within it the seeds of its own destruction, the possibility that the intense cooperation that is required in a network society will allow the means of production to be captured by the multitude.' In their work lies a 'fervent belief that contemporary capitalism, although seemingly impervious to anti-systemic challenge, is in fact vulnerable at all points to riot and rebellion' (Balakrishnan, 2000, p. 2) The faith in the power of what Ray (2004, p. 568) calls 'living labour' is duly noted, offering hope of a future beyond the universal tyranny of corporate-driven commercial exchange. Is such a world yet possible?

Conclusion

In their various ways, the diverse theoretical perspectives of critical social science have sought to account for the freedoms and constraints of cultural work. Each approach has sought to conceptualize distinctly the consequences of modern progress as it avails upon the cultural industries workplace and creative cultural workers. Let us summarize each in turn.

Critical theory approaches, derived from the Frankfurt School, posit the alienation of cultural workers (and wider populations) as industrial rationality cuts actors adrift from the possibility of authentic self-formation. More recent observers, broadly sympathetic to (if not uncritical of) Adorno's ideas, have continued to stress the power and influence exerted by organizations of the 'culture industry' as globalization underwrites the expansion and consolidation of large multinational corporations that impose both old and new relations of exploitation and control over their apparently compliant and powerless workforces. In analysing the recent corporate shift towards more 'individualized', flexible and 'soft' forms of cultural capitalism, critics such as Bourdieu, Garnham, McRobbie, Miège, Ryan and Wittel (and more recently Honneth) have variously stressed the dehumanizing and desocializing aspects of such innovation, arguing that even in the apparently decentralized and heterogeneous landscapes of 'alliance capitalism' workers remain exploited and oppressed. Additionally, while Garnham, Hesmondhalgh and Ryan have acknowledged the necessary *durability* of cultural industry 'craft' production – not only as the source of new cultural commodities but also as the arena of worker autonomy – for most critical theorists the creative and critical possibilities of this realm now appear increasingly enervated by the competitive impulses of corporations and their relentless pursuit of accumulation through generic formats.

The 'economistic' tenor of this critique appears initially to contrast with those who have adopted a more 'governmental' approach to understanding cultural work. Drawing inspiration from Foucault, it has been suggested that social control in cultural work relies less on the brutish imposition of power from 'above', and more on the ways in which power is embedded discursively and practically in everyday organizational life. Crucial here are workers *themselves* who, either through compulsion or choice, have oriented themselves to the necessary tasks of becoming self-managing, entrepreneurial and creative. However, while, ostensibly, power is understood as an enabling as well as constraining force (so suggesting the possibility of workplace 'resistance') critics have remained largely content to show how cultural workers have become de-autonomized by the power of governmentalizing discourses and practices. It has been emphasized how, through the promotion and application of complex and detailed performance rituals, rites of passage, norms, attitudes and values, cultural workers find themselves socialized into accepting the common-sense logic of the new economy, where the emphasis on being 'entrepreneurial' and being 'creative' tend to close down rather than expand opportunities for self-determination. Beyond some nascent accounts of workers' 'tactical' manoeuvrings, few, if any, writers have employed a Foucauldian perspective to highlight how the actors might utilize power in order to prioritize autonomous creative production or to progressively transform cultural work contexts through the pursuit of a more pronounced form of resistance.

It was thus surmised that – notwithstanding their differences – both critical theory and governmentality critics have tended to view cultural work as an arena of de-autonomization, exploitation and constrained possibility. Negative individualization has been the recurrent theme. Turning then to more 'optimistic', liberal–democratic theories of individualization, it was offered that the likes of Beck, Giddens, Keat and Lash and Urry have provided accounts that – while stressing the risks incumbent with modernization – have emphasized also the innovative, creative and freedom-generating possibilities of individualized modernity. Extrapolating from these theorists it was proposed that the transformative impulses of contemporary capitalism ought not to be seen as wholly (or even inherently) detrimental to autonomous cultural work. Despite its evident precarity, it was offered that individualized cultural work might furnish workers with opportunities to pilot or recover 'alternative' forms of production that prioritize aesthetically directed 'artistic', 'practice-led' or 'ethical' values alongside, or in advance of, the pursuit of profit. Thus, the ambivalent character of individualization was explored, and revealed to be not only dichotomous in the sense of offering both 'opportunity' and 'threat', but also in terms of its capacity to resuscitate as well as destroy traditional, 'premodern' (and thus arguably more meaningful) social and economic relations. The final chapter has addressed how, despite the continued scepticism of the more traditional left, cultural work remains in some sense autonomous in that it continues to require original creativity, generate internal goods, is extremely difficult to control and regulate and is performed by actors with strong utopian drives – convictions now increasingly explored through the pursuit of various nascent, esoteric and erratic 'lines of flight' that seek to deviate from the hegemonic culture industry model.

To my mind, the question of whether cultural work contains progressive or transformative potential (for both workers and society at large) remains open. A definitive understanding is perhaps obtainable, but can only emerge through further detailed investigations into the structures of cultural production – including more thorough assessment than hitherto of the motivations, practices and actions of cultural workers themselves. Yet, for others, the picture is less opaque, since – despite the best efforts of 'alternative' producers – it appears quite clear that the power of the capitalistic 'culture industry' is now absolute; but I do not wish to end on such a downbeat note. While the great majority of cultural workers are precariously positioned, under-rewarded, browbeaten and drained of political will, and the more instrumental may well seek only to establish social connections that can enhance personal gain, it is equally the case that creative cultural production remains imbued with utopian promise, and the desire to re-embed art and creativity in non-market social and political contexts is proving difficult to destroy. Over the course of a number of years studying cultural workers, despite their instrumental tendencies and inveiglement in market relations, I have often been surprised by how far divorced the motives and ambitions of so many seem to be from the rational and acquisitive modes of being adjudged to lie at the heart of entrepreneurial endeavour. Workers routinely fail to demonstrate – in words, and more importantly, *deeds* – a clear commitment to capitalist norms such as profit maximization, disinterested exchange or wealth accumulation. In fact, frequently, they are openly antagonistic to these values, and will often make strenuous efforts to sustain this (contrary to Bourdieu's analysis) over time and space. This desire may be motivated by the pure 'artistic' predilections conventionally associated with cultural workers – or may equally be driven by other aesthetically directed but also 'practice-led' or 'ethical' norms and values I have identified. In this way the 'art–commerce relation' remains core and valid, but is perhaps better qualified and understood as a constantly shifting inter-relationship between art, commerce and the *social*. Indeed, while the desire to occupy a space of aesthetic 'otherness' may remain the prime motivation for alternative cultural work, I would argue for the necessity of adopting a more open view, one that recognizes workers to be implicated in an array of economic, cultural and social forces that interrelate to the extent that they 'cannot be individually encapsulated because they are [so] mutually embedded' (Ettlinger, 2003, p. 149). This is not to discount the notion of boundaries and the possibility of identifying the specificity of the cultural or the aesthetic, or any other component realms but to recognize the characteristically fluid nature of social relations as they now circulate and intersect in multidimensional economic space. While the cultural dimension of cultural work remains distinct (if continually hard to define) it cannot be understood in isolation from the social context that significantly (if not absolutely) defines it. However, further debate over specificity is perhaps best saved for another work – for now the crucial point is that in whichever way the art–commerce relation is being reshaped and configured, the notion that cultural workers are merely the servile and alienated victims of global capital or, alternatively, self-governing agents of 'network sociality' is, to put it bluntly, a fundamentally problematic one given the diversity of business models and identity positions that now circulate within the certainly precarious – but also more open and reflexive – cultural production field.

While even previously optimistic observers such as McRobbie have resigned themselves to the triumph of neo-liberalism and accepted a world divested of creative autonomy and all artistic passion spent, I, like many others, do not wish to rule out the possibility that 'any easy projections we can now make about a corporate or state future for creative culture may be overthrown by something a little more bottom-up in construction' (Uricchio, 2004, p. 89). Indeed, returning to where we began, I would suggest that, at its heart, this faith in the future stems from the seemingly intractable paradox of the art–commerce relation. As Ryan (1992) so eloquently revealed, there is an absolute *necessity* for capitalists to ensure that art-based and creative cultural production retains some distinctive, unique or non-replicable qualities, in order that 'original' cultural commodities can continue to be created, marketed and sold. While the corporate pursuit of generic formats threatens constantly to undermine artistic autonomy and impose creative closure, it can never *fully* control and standardize cultural work since some degree of creative autonomy always remains necessary for producing new goods. It is in this institutionalized permission to rebel that we can identify the key radical potential of cultural work. The need to encourage unruliness, capriciousness and unconformity in otherwise rational organizations and firms, simply to ensure that the ongoing generation of new supplies of cultural goods, not only provides reassurance that the standardization and closure of cultural work can never be complete but also offers the further utopian promise that some rogue elements of aesthetic creativity might one day 'cut free' from corporate chains and help usher in some yet-to-be-specified progressive social transformations.

As even the arch-sceptic Harvey now argues, the contradiction of the art–commerce relation *inevitably* contains this radical promise:

> if capital is not to totally destroy the uniqueness that is the basis for the appropriation of monopoly rents ... then it must support a form of differentiation and allow of divergent and to some degree uncontrollable local cultural developments that can be antagonistic to its own smooth functioning. It can even support (though cautiously and often nervously) all manner of 'transgressive' cultural practices precisely because this is one way in which to be original, creative and authentic as well as unique. It is within such spaces that all manner of oppositional movements can form even presupposing, as is often the case, that oppositional movements are not already firmly entrenched there. (Harvey, 2001, pp. 409–410)

Of course, while corporations currently appear capable of containing *any* kind of radical impulse, this may not always be the case. Furthermore, it is notable that as more fluid social, informational and technological structures emerge to underwrite the 'democratization' of cultural production, creative and aesthetic 'unruliness' also becomes more likely to occur *outside* of the direct corporate context. It is these very 'outside' spaces that radical producers and more stringent anti-capitalists are now seeking to exploit. Their nascent, piecemeal and incomplete efforts remind us of the broader struggle that occupies the subjects of individualized late-modernity:

> What people are trying to realize in the small scale of their self-chosen lives is a cherished and internalized ideal that remains denied on the larger scale of society. They are trying to realize a more perfect democracy in miniature. They are willing to make the greatest possible efforts in order to redeem the key normative expectations of democracy – equality, justice, fairness, and the right of each individual to develop her individuality – and to accept and deal with all the consequences that necessarily flow from such efforts. (Beck in Beck and Willms 2004, p. 67)

There is only a slim possibility that the efforts of radical cultural workers to create their own 'miniature democracies' will succeed. Even less that such efforts will converge around some *collective* vision that can progressively transform the character of economic life. Yet, today, cultural work occupies an ambivalent and varied space; it is undertaken by actors that embody a multitude of moral and political impulses. This profusion of alternatives is, for now, encouraging. Whether these impulses, and the initiatives that contain them, can provide any basis for helping to contest the seemingly irresistible dominance of the 'culture industry' and the wider neo-liberal regime within which it stands, remains an intriguing and ongoing question.

Appendix 1

The original data presented in this book is drawn from a number of projects undertaken between 1998 and 2003 with colleagues at the Manchester Institute for Popular Culture and the Department of Sociology, Manchester Metropolitan University. Citations are taken from in-depth interviews conducted by myself with cultural workers during these projects:

- Cultural Industries and the City (1998–2000): a project conducted under the ESRC Cities: Competitiveness and Cohesion Research Programme (ESRC L130251048), coordinated by Justin O'Connor with Mark Banks, Andy Lovatt and Carlo Raffo. Reports and data publicly available from the ESRC and the UK Data Archive.
- SMILE (Skills for the Missing Industry's Leaders and Enterprises) (2001–2002): funded under ESF ADAPT Ufi, coordinated by Dianne Phillips with Mark Banks, David Calvey, Julia Owen and David Russell.
- Innovation and Change in the Clothing Industries (2002–2003): funded under ESF Objective 3, coordinated by Mark Banks with Mike Bull and Julia Owen.

Reports on all these projects available from the author.

Notes

1 Introducing Cultural Work

1. This is largely because, as indicated, definitions of the cultural industries vary across countries and often within regions and nations themselves. Measurement is also problematic given the somewhat outmoded systems of industrial classification that cannot adequately account for many new and hybrid cultural occupations (Pratt, 1997). In the United Kingdom, cultural industries lack their own specific 'SIC' and 'SOC' codes of industrial and occupational classification and so are often 'hidden' as they are conveniently absorbed into other categories. Further, the informal, temporary, hidden and precarious nature of much cultural industries employment makes it difficult to record reliable employment estimates.

2. The cultural workers that I am concerned with Hesmondhalgh (2002) has elsewhere referred to as 'symbol creators' – those directly involved in the composing, designing, imagining, interpreting and manipulating of symbols in order to create music, television programmes, films, art, clothing, graphic designs, images and other forms of text. While the term 'artist' is also comparable (and indeed I use it occasionally in this book), the term 'creative cultural worker' is preferred specifically in order to de-emphasise the connotations of 'individual genius' and 'higher calling' associated with the terms 'artist' and (symbol) 'creator' and, in turn, more emphatically signal that cultural work is a socially situated and purposeful process of *work*.

3. Such prejudices perhaps derive from a popular discourse that routinely identifies cultural workers as lazy, shallow and inauthentic (see Negus and Pickering, 2004). Widespread are images of self-obsessed 'trendies', 'yuppies', 'bourgeois bohemians' (Brooks, 2000) and the like, idling away the day sipping cappuccinos in cafes, surfing the net and then hitting the clubs at night. Not much 'work' appears to get done. In 2005, the UK sit-com 'Nathan Barley' provided a (very funny) (self) satirization of cultural industry occupations – based in and around the London offices of a painfully trendy style magazine. Here, the eponymous 'hero' is described as 'webmaster, guerrilla filmmaker, screenwriter, DJ' and in his own words, a 'self-facilitating media node', inhabiting a world where creatives might 'accidentally invent a new hairstyle by sleeping in paint'. Satire aside, academics themselves have not been immune to launching critical barbs at the cultural industry worker. Most notably, Bourdieu's (1984) identification of an atavistic sub-class of cultural and symbolic producers in and amongst the 'new petit bourgeoisie' is often taken to represent the archetypal form of cultural worker – that is, self-interested, restless, repressed and déclassé; always in hot pursuit of status through the latest styles, trends and 'alternative' sociality. Löfgren (2003) also offers a satirical swipe at the coterie of new informational and cultural workers now apparently underpinning what he calls the new 'catwalk economy'. In a

broader attack on Florida's (2002) theory of the 'creative class', Peck (2005, p. 746) witheringly condemns the kind of worker that new 'creative' cities are seeking to attract: 'Homo Creativus is an atomized subject, apparently, with a preference for intense but shallow and noncommittal relationships, mostly played out in the sphere of consumption and on the street.'

4. As an aside, I should state that I do not wish to downplay the necessity of undertaking research into 'non-creative' workers in cultural industries. For every musician, film director, graphic artist and fashion designer there are many more manual, clerical, administrative, technical and managerial staff making vital contributions to the production of recordings, programmes, movies, paintings, garments and the like (Pratt, 1997). These workers are subjected to various degrees of freedom and constraint, and receive differential rewards and recognition according to their real or perceived contributions to the production process – and they should not be ignored. Even in cultural industry contexts, however, it is likely that these non-creative workers are positioned within a more conventional (and well-researched) division of labour, with their work organized around a series of standardized, routinized and mundane tasks – at least compared with their more creative colleagues. Certainly, in such work, the art–commerce relation is not so pronounced. Students of the sociology of work have long since identified how principles of scientific and standardized management have become commonplace in clerical, manual and technical occupations – and a rehearsal of this work is not the aim here (see Grint, 1991; Edgell, 2006 for overviews).

2 'Culture Industry' and Cultural Work

1. The term 'critical theory' is used usually to refer to the work of critics directly or intellectually affiliated to the Institute of Social Research at the University of Frankfurt from the 1930s (most notably Adorno, Benjamin, Horkheimer and Marcuse, and later Habermas). While this is also the case here, I expand the term to specifically include writers critical of the cultural industries who, while influenced by the 'Frankfurt School', have subsequently developed their critiques in the context of a broader intellectual terrain – one that combines a Frankfurtian analysis with (for example) more empirically informed elements of Marxian political economy, as well as varied postmodern and 'cultural studies' approaches. However, despite many differences, I suggest that a common theme that unites all 'critical theory' approaches cited in this chapter is the conviction that cultural industries can only be understood through a (Marxian-influenced) critical analysis of the capitalist mode of production *and* its social and cultural impacts – a key assumption of Frankfurtian critical theory.

2. While Adorno and Horkheimer equated 'culture industry' with the more commonly utilized 'mass culture', they preferred the former term 'in order to exclude from the outset the interpretation agreeable to its advocates: that it is a matter of something like a culture that arises spontaneously from the masses themselves' (Adorno, 1991, p. 85; see also Kellner, 1989).

3. As is often commented upon, Frankfurtian concerns about media, social control and the use of propaganda were developed in the 1930s and 1940s in

critical response to the rise of European fascism and then through their own personal experiences of exile in the USA. On the one hand, opposition to the Nazi regime had underpinned their efforts to denounce the ideological manipulation and domination of mass consciousness, while, on the other, their perceptions of the USA as a new consumer-oriented, mass-mediatized and market-led society further cemented their hostility towards the incursions of industrialized, mass cultural forms (see Dant, 2003; Held, 1980; Kellner, 1989).

4. We should avoid exaggerating the correspondences between different Frankfurt School theorists on this (and any other) point – for as Held (1980) discusses at length, there are significant differences between them. While Adorno and Horkheimer were more sceptical around the notion of 'resistance' as we would know it today (but retained a belief in the critical possibilities of 'purposeless', avant-garde art) others – such as Marcuse (1979) – saw a greater possibility for actors to evade or 'negate' the effects of culture industry, while, as Held suggests, Walter Benjamin saw 'positive consequences' (1980, p. 108) in the new techniques of mechanical production and dissemination of cultural forms, not least in the possibility of providing audiences with new cultural and intellectual resources that might furnish critical thinking and, in turn, revolutionary actions.

5. For example, Scherzinger is adamant that 'the central motifs of [Adorno's] bleak and horrifying diagnosis of the culture industry ring as true today as ever' (2005, p. 23) and, as Steinert ruefully observes in Adornian fashion,

> Our understanding of culture has now been pluralized so as to include the mechanical (or rather electronic) beats and harmonies of popular music and the somewhat vulgar entertainment of soap operas and talk shows, in addition to the most exquisite and refined pieces from Europe's aristocratic heritage (Steinert, 2003, p. 171).

6. This essentially describes a co-operative model of capitalist production inherited from pre-modern guild production. Here, in a 'workshop' system, workers are allocated their role in discrete labour hierarchy, based on traditional, small-scale and skilled, handicraft production. As Ryan (1992, p. 97) develops: 'As the cooperation model develops, there are qualitative shifts in its constituent relations of production. Capitalists come to acquire ownership of the workshop, the materials and the equipment used, and employ otherwise independent craft workers as wage labour to perform the work of production'. However, elements of co-operation remain important, for, as Ryan continues,

> Retention of the craft division of labour mediates the capitalist authority relations in production; since workers retain control of the working methods and the knowledges these require, they are able to maintain a degree of control over the form and content of the labour process within the workshop.

7. For example, while firms may employ artists, writers, musicians, photographers, designers and so on within the firm on a formal basis, more often they may seek to buy in already formed cultural goods and then modify them and ready them for reproduction and distribution (for example, a record label signing a band with an already established live repertoire or set of self-developed recordings); alternatively, as is increasingly the case in a post-Fordist regime,

firms may contract in freelance labour with already established creative products, skills or credentials.

8. Since the late 1970s, the mooted transition from a 'Fordist' to a 'post-Fordist' or 'post-industrial' regime has been widely identified as a key transformation in Westernized economies (Amin, 1994; Lash and Urry, 1994; Murray, 1989). While the precise terms of transition remain the subject of debate, the central tenet of post-Fordism is argued to be 'flexibility' – counterposed to the inherent 'rigidity' (Harvey, 1989) of Fordist, industrial societies. In terms of cultural industries, this process of flexibilization has instanced some profound changes. First, as production systems became more efficient they have generated greater volumes of goods, while at the same time, their flexibility permitted the rise of new technologies and techniques that enable the production of more specialized goods, often in smaller quantities, and able to be tailored for local and niche markets (Piore and Sabel, 1984; Scott, 2000). There is a relative shift away from long-run, standardized production of a limited choice of goods, to short-term, fast turnover, more stylized, variegated and specialist forms of cultural production. Accordingly, there is a higher turnover of trends, fashions and cultural styles in this expanded and accelerated production regime. Second, given increased competitiveness, there has been a significant 'vertical disintegration', whereby large firms seek to outsource costly or specialist functions, utilize independent contractors in low-cost labour locations, and generally spread the risk of investment amongst partners and sub-contractors. The monolithic, wholly integrated cultural industry firms of the Fordist era have thus become more 'flexible', 'disorganized' and 'disintegrated'.

9. Adorno *did* appear to acknowledge the durability of craft production when he observed that in the culture industry 'individual forms of production are maintained' (2000, p. 233) amidst the standardization of the commodity, or when he offered that 'the act of producing a song-hit still remains in a handicraft stage' (1990, p. 306) though it must be reiterated that he largely failed to elaborate any detailed discussion of craft or any other form of capitalist work, largely restricting himself, as I have averred, to general comments on its mechanical and dispiriting nature.

10. Broadly put, neo-liberalism understands the world as composed of rational individuals who exercise choice in the pursuit of self-interest, with markets strongly favoured as the most effective mechanisms for enabling the satisfaction of these interests. Indeed, in neo-liberal societies the promotion of markets as the source of all virtues has become a fundamental norm. The 'opening up' of societies to 'free' trade and the adoption of market principles, even in non-economic spheres, is presented as both functionally necessary, in order that economies might grow, and socially requisite in terms of releasing individuals from the 'shackles' of dependency and tradition (Smart, 2003). It is neo-liberal values that arguably underpin the key processes that we can identify as central to transforming the nature of cultural industry organization – the post-industrial flexibilization and the attendant globalization of production.

11. As many critics have noted, outside of a privileged few, cultural workers are generally low paid, often working for free at entry level given the oversupply

of (predominantly) youthful labour attracted by the glamour of cultural work and its promise of creative freedom, and, eventually, fame and riches. Workers are often reliant on royalty payments rather than fixed salaries, or must work on an informal project-to-project basis as a freelancer with the corresponding insecurity and lack of pension and additional benefits traditionally attached to salaried and tenured employment (see Hesmondhalgh, 2007; McRobbie 2002a; Ursell, 2000, 2006).

3   Governmentality and Cultural Work

1. While power and domination are often used interchangeably, domination is better understood as merely one form of power, specifically as brute oppression against subjects' will. Other forms, such as coercion, seduction, authority, manipulation and so on may be of more importance in workplace politics than domination (see discussion in Sayer, 2004a).

2. In the United Kingdom, the turn to embrace the 'creative' rather than the 'cultural' industries can be traced to the coming to power of Tony Blair's first Labour government in 1997. While, by the mid-1980s, the idea of 'cultural industries' had started to garner support amongst left-leaning metropolitan councils' (initially and most famously the Greater London Council (GLC)), initiatives to promote cultural industries tended to be not only linked to economic development but also to cultural policy goals of inclusion and representation of popular (but marginal) cultural activities and minority groups. Cultural industries were promoted as a solution to both economic underperformance *and* social disaggregation in radically de-industrializing and depopulating 'inner cities'. Elements of the Labour Party were then, initially, enthusiastic supporters of the 'cultural industries'. However, 'New' Labour's subsequent desire to re-brand itself as the pro-business party and shed its socialist traditions, ensured, by the mid-1990s, that 'cultural industries' were now judged as an overtly political endowment bequeathed from discredited Left wing metropolitan and city councils. As Pratt confirms, one of the reasons why the term creative industries comes to the fore is because 'for New Labour, cultural industries policies were tainted with "left-leaning" old Labour values' (Pratt 2005, p. 32). O'Connor (1999, p. 2–3) similarly suggests that the use of creative industries signalled a desire to move away from the 'cultural policy baggage' that came with an 'artist centred' GLC-type approach and reflected the keenness with which the Labour government now sought to harness cultural production to the new economic agenda.

3. Advertising, architecture, art and antiques market, crafts, design, designer fashion, film and video, interactive leisure software, music, the performing arts, publishing, software and computer services, television and radio.

4. Indeed, the idea that it is individuals rather than communities or collectives who are the wellsprings of creativity is routinely evidenced in the UK Government's willingness to flag up individual success stories, promote role models and attract celebrity endorsements for its efforts in promoting cultural work. The whole of the 'Cool Britannia' period of the late-1990s was notable for the ways in which New Labour ministers tried to isolate and ally themselves with the new stars of 'Britpop' (Oasis and others) and YBA's

(Young British Artists, most notably Damien Hirst) and the like. Even today the celebration of 'talent' remains prominent on the agenda and contains within it the positive affirmation of enterprise values; James Purnell again: 'I want to scream whenever I hear a commentator saying that artists don't know how to be business like (...) People like Antony Gormley or Sam Mendes, Vivienne Westwood or Nitin Sawhney have plenty to teach those commentators about how to be entrepreneurial' (2005, no pagination)

5. Self-exploitation is widely found in other cultural industries, and indeed can lead one to further exploit others. Consider the following account from Ursell (2000, p. 814) on television production:

> ...a northern producer who, in the early 1980s, had enjoyed repeat orders and generous budgets from Channel 4, in 1999 was surviving on low-budget, mass production of travel material for a satellite station. He shot his own material and edited at home on his non-linear editing suite. The workloads, against tight deadlines, were stress-inducing. His coping strategy... was to seek free labour from students and other media wannabes.

6. In their interviews with independent UK 'retro' fashion retailers, Crewe, Gregson and Brooks found similar justifications offered for enduring tough and financially unrewarding industry conditions; here retailing work was 'seen as pleasurable, as a means of exercising control over one's life and fulfilling one's creative potential' (2003, p. 80) – workers thus saw themselves as 'free' even amidst this most precarious and poorly rewarded of sectors.

7. Smart (1999, p. 94) argues that despite Foucault's belief that relations of power are always counterable his work largely fails to demonstrate how individual subjects are able to assert their autonomy and evade governmental constriction. Smart suggests that Foucault 'leave[s] open and unanswered the respects[s] in which subjects are, or can be, recognized, as active and responsible, as opposed to being simple relays for the discharge of culturally given technologies of (self) government'. Thus, while, as Smart notes, Foucault's work sought to develop an ethics of individualism, a self-committed to the self, so to speak, there is relatively little elaboration in his work of how this self can act politically or in favour of others.

4   The Construction of Creativity

1. A view even endorsed by such an esteemed counter-cultural icon as Andy Warhol; 'Making money is art, and working is art and good business is the best art' (from *The Philosophy of Andy Warhol*, 1975 cited in Lloyd, 2006, p. 205).

2. Hence, of course, the endless stream of highly formatted and interchangeable reality shows, lifestyle magazines, TV soaps, 'make-over' shows, 'boy bands' and so on that now populate the popular cultural landscape, not to mention the formularization and standardization of various other cultural tropes, from restaurants and bars, to classical music performances, theatres, hotels, furniture and landscapes.

3. Bourdieu's analyses of 'cultural intermediaries' (taste-makers, critics, commentators, curators) also come to mind at this point:

> these new intellectuals are inventing an art of living which provides them with the gratifications and prestige of the intellectual at the least cost; in the name of the fight against 'taboos' and the liquidation of

'complexes' they adopt the most external and easily borrowed aspects of the intellectual lifestyle, liberated manners, cosmetic or sartorial outrages, emancipated poses and postures and systematically apply the cultivated disposition to the not-yet-legitimate culture (cinema, strip cartoons, the underground), to every day life (street art), the personal sphere (sexuality, cosmetics, child-rearing, leisure) and the existential (the relation, to nature, love, death) (1984, p. 370–371) (though see Chapter 6 for a more positive appraisal).

4. Though for a more positive interpretation of the ludic qualities of the contemporary workplace see Costea, Crump and Holm (2005).

5. This reminds us again that, as Foucault argued, the provision of freedom is actually prerequisite for the application of power. 'Power relations are only possible in so far as the subject is free' (Foucault 1997, p. 292 cited in Barnett 1999, p. 383). While government may offer only limited choices and work hard to ensure that preferred choices are made, the effectivity of government lies in its capacity to insinuate 'strategies that individuals in their freedom can use in dealing with each other' (Foucault 1997, p. 300; and see Barnett, 1999).

5 Choice, Reflexivity and 'Alternative' Cultural Work

1. I use this term broadly to refer to firms and entrepreneurs involved in production that pursues aesthetic, communitarian, social or moral-political ends, alongside or in opposition to economic profit.

2. A distinction is drawn between what are termed 'first' modernity and 'second' modernity. First modernity (broadly analogous with industrial society or later, Fordism) is a project that produced a clear set of institutions, social roles, life narratives and forms of regulation and reproduction. First modernity is dominated by heavy industry, stable and continuous family and kinship relations, class structures and low social mobility. While it contains individualized elements, it is for the most part integrated and routinized by tradition. In contrast, second modernity is detraditionalized, individualized 'reflexive modernity', an inchoate flow of fragmented relationships based on contingent and unstable knowledge (see also Beck, Giddens and Lash, 1994).

3. The notion that the atomized neo-liberal subject is equivalent with the 'individually institutionalized' subject has become a standard critique of the Becks' thesis. For example, Brannen and Nilsen (2005, p. 422) suggest that Beck's definition of individualization strongly resonates with New Right ideology, where the rhetoric of individual choice and sovereignty now means that 'collectivity ... has no meaning'. Beck is accused of making a virtue out of a necessity and for overemphasising individual freedoms while ignoring deep rooted inequalities and structural constraints. Yet perhaps this is to somewhat misconstrue both Beck's arguments and intentions. His work explicitly rejects the notion of the atomized, self-interested subject of neo-liberalism, operating without moral or structural constraint, in favour of a re-embedded, re-institutionalized subject, provided with freedom of choice, but also desirous of, and obligated into, new kinds of social arrangements

and collectives that arise as a consequence of institutional individualization (see Beck and Willms, 2004). Beck and Beck-Gernsheim (2002) further argue that while people may be 'sovereign' in the sense of holding enhanced choice-making capacities, these choices are not explicitly directed towards rational 'self-interest' but remain socially embedded and concerned with enhancing commitments to non-generalist forms of social commons, as is stated:

> Neo-liberal economics rests upon an image of an autarkic human self. It assumes that individuals alone can master the whole of their lives, that they derive and renew their capacity for action from within themselves. Talk of the 'self-entrepreneur' makes this clear. Yet this ideology blatantly conflicts with everyday experience in (and sociological studies of) the worlds of work, family and local community, which show that the individual is not a monad but is self-*in*sufficient and increasingly tied to others, including at the level of worldwide networks and institutions. The ideological notion of the self-sufficient individual ultimately implies the disappearance of any sense of mutual obligation – which is why neoliberalism inevitably threatens the welfare state. A sociological understanding of *Individiualisierung* is thus intimately bound up with the question of how individuals can demystify this image of autarky. It is not freedom of choice, but insight into the fundamental incompleteness of self, which is at the core of individual and political freedom in the second modernity (Beck and Beck-Gernsheim 2002, p. xxi, see also Berking, 1996).

4. This is, of course, not to underestimate the 'desocializing' impacts of individualization that emerge from forms of labour-market precarity, welfare cuts and public-spending squeezes. The tendency of neo-liberal societies to generate inequalities and thus 'reflexivity losers' (Lash and Urry, 1994) is clearly apparent. Indeed, the possibility of free and active choice is somewhat idealized in so far as not everyone is ever able to assert oneself and make choices in the way that the Becks and Giddens envisage – their analysis tends to rely upon a rather bourgeois notion of the rational, self-driven, active citizen, able to execute choice and responsibility in cognitive and clear-eyed fashion.

5. Lewis (2000, p. 112–113) underlines this distinction when he writes:

> while Marxist-derived critiques have tended to impugn the mass media as a hegemonic institution, liberal humanist analyses have been rather more ambivalent. In particular, while recognizing that information resources are unevenly distributed and commercial interests often compromise standards of ethical and public responsibility, liberal humanist analysis has nevertheless seen the mass media as pivotal to a healthy democracy, most especially through its role as public watchdog and in the *dissemination of information* (my emphasis).

6. Arguably, there are two elemental strands of reflexivity that are enhanced in 'second modernity'. First, for Beck (as for Giddens), enhanced reflexivity and choice-making are primarily understood in largely *cognitive* terms as the cool-minded ability to weigh up and evaluate ones' situation under conditions of risk – to make choices that may never be guaranteed to generate the desired outcomes but are nonetheless somehow 'calculated' to ensure that maximum opportunities to achieve what Giddens refers to as 'ontological

security' (1991, p. 114) are realized. This is the reflexivity of conscious, deliberative and active choice. Second, for Lash and Urry (1994), the transition to a post-industrial economy of information and communication structures has not only brought with it an enhanced ability amongst individuals to reflect and review their 'objective' situation but, additionally, a growth in *aesthetic* reflexivity. Here, social actors are more evidently inclined to make decisions and judgements that are not merely cognitive, rational and coupled to *need,* but are more emotional, irrational and founded on *desire.* Choices based on aspiration and a sense of style are made with reference to what Lash and Urry dub 'allegorical', 'symbolic' and 'non-linear' modes of being. This leads to an intensification and enhancement of the experiential and creative elements of selfhood – the pursuit of new 'styles of life'. As we will see, while both modes are important, aesthetic reflexivity is especially vital for underpinning artistic practice in cultural work, for it contains within it a focus on expressivity, symbolism, style and bodily performance – the creative, self-expressive elements of being.

7. As Best (2003, p. 466) comments, 'the discursive construction of flexible work as democratic, and its imbrication with other discourses of visceral democracy, impels a certain radical motion towards freedom that cannot be entirely contained'.

8. In the United Kingdom

> [t]he pool of cultural labour has increased steadily during the 1990s. At the end of 1993, 610,000 people were employed in a cultural occupation as a first or second job, or were unemployed but had previously been engaged in a cultural occupation. By 2000 this figure had risen to 760,000' (Arts Council of England, 2003, p. xii).

In the USA context, Lloyd reports that

> Counting artists is an inexact science [but] from 1900 to 1970, the number of artists, writers and performers per 100,000 of the population in the United States went from 267 to 385, an increase of 44 percent. By 1999, the proportion had jumped to 900 per 100,000, an increase of 237 percent in just three decades. In absolute terms, the number of artists, writers and performers grew from 791,000 in 1970 to almost two and a half million in 1999' (2006, p. 65).

In Australia, Throsby and Hollister (2003) estimated that between 1988 and 2001, the annual growth rate in the number of artists averaged 2–3 per cent; overall, Australia has almost doubled its number of professional artists in the past 20 years.

9. The problem here is one of establishing how far the aesthetic realm can be said to exist independent of the social conditions and constraints within which it is situated. Most sociologists (if not artists) would be loath to argue that there is some essential and universal quality that can de described as 'the aesthetic', and, indeed, many would forcefully argue that what we call the aesthetic is purely a bourgeois social construction designed to reinforce class privilege (Bourdieu, 1993), yet there is still something about the affective quality of art and aesthetic production that evades such a reductive closure. As Wolff argues, in her search for a 'sociological aesthetics', while we can accept that aesthetic value is in part socially determined, art is never a mere *expression* of ideology – in both its production and consumption it

appears to possess its own singular though often indeterminate logic and meaning; the unresolved conundrum, as Wolff puts it, is that 'the experience and evaluation of art are socially and ideologically situated and constructed, and at the same time irreducible to the social and ideological' (1993, p. 84). The aim here is not to resolve this issue but merely to identify the durability of belief in relative autonomy of the aesthetic, and then to demonstrate how this might be used to underpin more socially progressive endeavour in cultural work.

10. For example Florida (2002), who sees no contradiction between artistic and capitalistic values and whose much-vaunted 'bohemian index' attempts explicitly to identify positive linkages between economic competitiveness with artistic activity.

11. As Lloyd (2006) notes, while, traditionally, bohemians would rail against 'bourgeois' values, the 'neo-bohemian' (as he terms it) is now more likely to direct its ire towards purely 'corporate' targets – reflecting a more widespread shift towards 'anti-capitalist', 'anti-globalization' values.

12. Bourdieu (1993) describes the historical development (and continuation) of a field of 'restricted production' – a realm of autonomous creative activity, broadly homologous to contemporary forms of independent cultural production. As Johnson (1993, p. 15) comments, while the field is driven by an internalized economy of value that disavows markets the 'stakes of competition between agents are largely symbolic, involving, prestige, consecration and artistic celebrity', meaning that producers are engaged in a 'field of struggles' (Bourdieu 1993, p. 30) that revolves around the accumulation of virtues such as purity, quality, disinterestedness, innovation and the acquisition of 'symbolic profit'. Bourdieu thus describes the cultural field as an 'inversion' of the economic field, emphasizing that the pursuit of autonomy and the accumulation of symbolic capital will tend to take priority in the 'position-taking' strategies employed by its constituent members. As Bourdieu notes, the prioritization of art over commerce is, of course, precarious, for the efforts of markets to colonize and commodify art, as well as the willingness of artists to be commodified can undermine the sanctity of the autonomous realm. Art for art's sake is weakened as art markets develop and as artists lay themselves open to the seductive overtures of the 'powers that be' and their attempts to secure heteronomous, market-friendly production. Nonetheless, Bourdieu's work reminds us then that even in advanced, individualized societies, the potential for alternative and aesthetically directed forms of cultural production may prove durable and difficult to wholly diminish.

13. This is similar to Bell's (1976, p. 20) identification of 'transmitters'; those members of the 'cultural mass' whose role is to both process and disseminate 'serious cultural products' for the wider audience. Bell refers to their more downmarket variant as the 'culturati' – transmitters who more self-consciously seek to be 'trendy' and 'with it' in their tastes.

14. As we saw in Chapter 2, 'craft production' describes skilled work based on close-knit co-operative 'workshop' relations and is the standard model for cultural industries' commodity production. While more broadly and historically art and craft have been judged as separate practices – art being seen as invested with craft skills but also additionally possessing a magical, aesthetic

ingredient or intent, I judge them here as coterminous. Indeed, in cultural industries, creative cultural workers might also usefully be described as what Becker terms commercial 'artist-craftsmen', actors working in commercial organizations, using craft skills and craft relations of production but aspiring also to aesthetic and creative values:'Artist–craftsmen have higher ambitions than ordinary craftsmen. While they may share audiences, institutions and rewards with ordinary craftsmen, they also feel some kinship with fine-art institutions. They see a continuity between what they do and what fine artists do' (Becker, 1982, p. 277).

15. Indeed, the notion that work is highly 'socialized' activity has (quite naturally) long been of concern to sociology, most recently being revived in a field of inquiry known as the 'new economic sociology' (Granovetter, 1985; Granovetter and Swedberg, 1992; Swedberg, 1996). Exemplary in this respect is Granovetter's work which demonstrates, contrary to neoclassical arguments, how economic processes depend on social relations for their exercise and constraint. Indeed, in the new economic sociology a general emphasis is placed on how social 'networks' provide some potential for more 'social' and inclusive work cultures – even, as Granovetter (1985) himself notes, these may not always materialize. As we have seen, a more recent focus on the 'social', but also the 'reflexive' aspects of work has more recently been provided by Lash and Urry (1994) and Lash (1994). What is crucial here is that Lash and Urry, while identifying the social basis of economic production, have more squarely identified the radical potential of (now) post-industrialized and reflexive production – particularly in the context of the cultural industries, where the possibilities of aesthetic critique and the emergence of a more critical subjectivity have been so markedly enhanced by new mediatized flows and information–communication structures.

16. Of course, we should not forget that this can generate pathological, as well as socially constructive, attachments and forms of embedding. As Smart identifies: 'The constitution of community around commonly held feelings and emotions simultaneously brings into being excluded communities of others for whom 'we' may feel little or no responsibility, the darker consequences of which continue to cast a shadow over 'civilization' (1999, p. 182; see also Harvey, 1989, 2000).

17. It is worth elaborating on the work of Booth (1994) whose argument, subsequently developed by Keat (2000) and Sayer (1999, 2004b), is that *all* economies are intrinsically 'moral', in so far as they are reliant on norms, values and ethical presumptions for their effective exercise. However, this should not be viewed as an apologia for capital; in such work the durability of morality is not taken as evidence of the benign nature of capitalism, or as a sign that the social ills of economic progress are able to be tempered and offset by some intrinsic sense of 'good' contained within the system. Rather, a moral economy approach ensures a critical purchase on capitalism by providing an analytical framework through which to develop what Booth calls the 'normative valuation of economic regimes' (1994, p. 653) and, not least, examine the extent to which different regimes support the pursuit of non-economic, social virtues and moral 'goods'. Booth's moral economy approach is politically motivating precisely because of its core recognition that the economy is not simply self-regulating and

autonomous, but deeply structured by non-economic, socially produced, norms and values. This helps counter both the left's 'market fatalism' and the neo-liberal myth that certain 'self-governing' and 'autonomous' economic processes (e.g. 'free hand of the market') lay beyond social determination, impervious to individual or collective ethical actions. His work reminds us that if the economy is formed and operational within society and not outside it (as at least some neo-liberals appear to insist) then it becomes entirely possible for society to *change* it. This particular point is vital to this study of cultural work because it suggests – contra Bourdieu, McRobbie, Miller and others – that cultural work cannot be wholly 'desocialized' or 'depoliticized' because even in its neo-liberal form it remains embedded within societies and thus open to challenge by other, potentially more progressive, moral sanctions and normative influences. Indeed, while neo-liberalism tends to generate problems of exploitation and social corrosion, these are neither universal nor incontestable; and there are always other forms of economizing that co-existent with and often antagonistic to the dominant variant (Gibson-Graham, 2006).

18. Since 2001 the annual 'Mayday Parade' has operated as a public protest against precaritization, labour exploitation and corporate power. Its European organizers claim that over 200,000 people are now regularly involved (see http://www.euromayday.org).

19. They may also, of course, be partially or wholly profit-motivated – the significance of which we consider in the following chapter.

20. As Webb, J. (2004, p. 735) endorses:

The sense of self as a narrative project is not precluded by current restructuring, and there is evidence of people's resilience and reflexivity in the face of economic uncertainty and organizational restructuring. In this sense Giddens (1991) is correct that new organization forms do not inevitably undermine a meaningful sense of biography: people retain a capacity to resist the more oppressive aspects of their lives and to use knowledge and skills in a socially responsible way.

6 Space, Place and Cultural Work

1. The role of copyright is vital here. Ownership of the right to reproduce, translate or perform a text or cultural commodity originated in the early Modern period as the key means through which authors could prevent others benefiting financially from copying or reproducing their work. Increasingly, it is cultural industry firms that are assigned copyrights, rather than individual authors, and in doing so are able to secure revenues generated from sales and reproductions across a much larger scale (see Garnham, 1990; Towse, 2002).

2. From here on I use this term somewhat generically, not to support prevailing neo-liberal policy discourse or to endorse Porter's pro-business approach, but merely as benign shorthand to describe how various kinds of cultural production activities now appear to concentrate in relatively bounded urban milieux.

3. Consider, for example, the tremendous growth in the frequency with which Silicon Valley electronics firms now bring lawsuits against one another (or against one another's employees) for the alleged violation of intellectual-property rights. Most of the objects of the lawsuits of these big firms are the small entrepreneurial companies in the district. Granovetter explicitly offered the tendency of firms in a co-operatively competitive network to *avoid* formally suing one another as a marker of the existence of strong social embeddedness. I would agree, and therefore interpret the exponential growth in lawsuits among Silicon Valley companies in recent years as evidence of potential erosion in the social basis for the reproduction of the region *qua* industrial district (Harrison 1992, p. 478).

4. There is some comparison here with the kind of sociality that appears to underpin the recent (mooted) formation of 'creative classes' in cosmopolitan urban centres (Florida, 2002). Peck (2005, p. 740) emphatically criticizes the ways in which cities are seeking to attract what appears to be 'a mobile and finicky class of creatives' committed only to their own hedonistic pleasures and, ultimately, economic self-interest. Subjects of network sociality are also analogous with the economic subjects identified by Bauman as pioneering a new form of demoralized, individualized capitalism:

   > Around the other pole of the new social division, on the top of the power pyramid of the light capitalism, circulate those for whom space matters little if at all – those who are out of place in any place they may be physically present. They are as light and volatile as the new capitalist economy which gave them birth and endowed them with power (Bauman 2000, p. 153).

   Finally, in their apparent concern with self-performance, display and winning the approval of others, subjects of network sociality might appear to echo the kind of modern 'narcissistic' personality identified by Lasch (1980).

5. As Webb, J. (2004, p. 734) identifies, the accumulation imperative frequently abrogates the autonomy implied in reflexive production:

   > The evidence suggests that despite espoused management aspirations for 'winning hearts and minds' and 'empowering' employees to use discretion and solve problems, management practices are driven principally by the rationales of cost-cutting and market efficiency. Consequently, people experience increased responsibility without gains in authority or a stake in organizational decisions, resulting in declining trust in employment relations and low morale.

6. As Lloyd similarly argues, contradictions frequently arise 'from the need for free space in which ideas and innovations can emerge from spontaneous interactions and the relentless crush of routinization, homogenization, and rationalization that accompany the commodification of everyday life in the city' (2006, p. 112).

7. For example, see Miles (2004) on the history of urban avant-gardes, Kapur and Rajadhyaksah (2001) on Mumbai's communal riots of 1992, Becker (2001) on Moscow 1916–1930; Knabb (1981) on the Paris riots of 1968, or, more recently, Chrisafis, 2006 on Parisian 'anti-precarity' uprisings.

8. Another example, as Bourdieu (1993) would no doubt argue, of the disingenuousness of economic disinterest in the sphere of 'restricted production' (see Chapter 7).

7   Cultural Work and Moral Futures

1. A key claim here being that Microsoft are committed 'to help[ing] advance social and economic well-being and to enable people around the world to realize their full potential'. Microsoft 'Citizenship Report' 2006. http://www.microsoft.com/about/corporatecitizenship/citizenship/default.mspx

2. As Klein (2000) and Carducci (2006) describe, a form of cultural production and activist activity that primarily (but not exclusively) involves 'the practice of parodying advertisements and hijacking billboards in order to drastically alter their messages...semiotic Robin Hoodism' (Klein, 2000, p. 280); a practice designed to 'achieve transparency, that is, to mitigate asymmetrical effects of power and other distortions in the communications apparatus' (Carducci, 2006, p. 118).

3. As Heath and Potter polemicize: 'one of the biggest ironies of the antiglobalization movement in general is that for all its opposition to consumerism, it effectively reduces citizenship to consumer action' (2004, p. 330).

4. As Holmes (2004, p. 552) pessimistically comments:
    The imaginary of rebellion and liberation, the quest for individual authenticity, the ideal of self-management, the anti-hierarchical social form of the network/rhizome, all have been appropriated as rhetorical and organizational devices that respond to broad aspirations of emancipation, but deliberately channel those aspirations so as to reinstate exploitation and alienation under another guise.

5. Citing and endorsing Dewey's *Art as Experience* (1980), they argue that
    Dewey [emphasized] the importance of ordinary experience in creating and receiving artworks and cultural products. What matters aesthetically is thus not the work of art or cultural product as objects which, once reified, become commodified and fetishised. What matters is how artistic creativity and cultural production relate to experience, what an art product does with and in experience, how experience becomes aesthetically funded and so resonant with expressive meaning (Negus and Pickering, 2004, p. 42).

6. As Frith argues, aesthetics are not simply the products of ideology, patterned and determined by social structures. Though such structures are important, tastes and sensibilities are also determinants in themselves; they make as well as express identity and contain within them transformative potential – for example 'music', as Frith puts it, 'certainly puts us in our place, but it can also suggest our circumstances are not immutable' (1996, p. 276). O'Connor expresses a similar view:
    'Art as possibility' comes with the idea of transcendence, not in the Kantian sense of leaving utility and functionality behind, nor even in the Dionysian sense of madness and abandonment, but simply in the sense of changing or transfiguring life – if only for a moment. We might call it immanent utopia. In many respects contemporary talk about art is less about a particular set of objects placed apart from the real world than a particular value or quality, an impulse or aspiration to the possibility of transformation (O'Connor, 2006, p. 99).

7. Carducci adds that culture jamming is useful as a 'tactic' in that it 'serves to remedy certain 'market-failures'...namely those of the instrumental reason that touched off the expressivist turn some two-and-a-half centuries ago and

whose means–ends rationality cannot account for the bonds of civility in society, the deeper meanings of human existence, and whose myopia in this respect has led to environmental destruction and exploitation around the globe' (2006, p. 134).

8. To quote at length from the organization website:

   Art money measure 12x18 cm and is an original work of art by the artist hand. It has a purchasing power equal to 27 Euro when first introduced and increase in value by five Euro p.a. for 7 years. The increased value can be realised only when purchasing art from registered art money artists. Art money can be used to buy art or services from all the registered BIAM artists at up to 50%. Art money can be spent in registered BIAM shops and businesses up to a % set by the individual business (see www.art-money.org).

9. Given the ways in which record companies have historically taken much the lion's share of revenues from artists' sales, offering meagre payments to the majority and disproportionately rewarding only a minority of 'stars', this is a somewhat brazen claim.

10. See http://www.fsf.org/

11. In contrast to the 'free' software (FSF), Best (2003) notes how in emergent communities of 'open source' software production the principle of organization is radically different. In open source developers create or modify software not only for their own purposes but also for the good of the community of other developers and users (Linux-based systems are a prominent example). While in open source the emphasis remains on the sharing of source codes and the gift distribution of knowledge, in the FSF approach the use value and functionality of software is not the primary motivation for its continued development; instead it is the moral imperative of distributing information freely in the interest of reducing democratic deficits that is considered paramount. Put another way, it is not the quality of the goods but the fact that they are being shared around that takes precedence. In the 'open' software approach, the democratizing impulse still holds but is sublimated by a concern to ensure that the quality of the product and its benefits for users are maximized. The discursive shift from a 'free' to 'open' software approach represents, as Best notes, an important development in so far as it represents an individualization of the culture of software production, whereby involvement is now more structured by the desire to satisfy individualistic pleasure, needs and desires, and to develop a 'network' of developers that can each individually utilize the benefits of open source codes for their own personal, local – rather than collective – interests. While this appears to represent a retreat from political action, Best suggests the possibility that the emergent culture of open source might lead to some kind of reconfigured democracy, one more reflective of these now more decentred, individualized times. The notion of 'visceral' democracy is proposed as an emergent feature of individualized cultural production. The defining qualities of visceral democracy derive from its conception of the political subject as an individual body, one driven by its own sensory capabilities and desires, as the source and focus of individual freedom. In this sense there is a strong element of aesthetic reflexivity that underpins visceral democracy, the desire to invigorate the self through drawing upon and cultivating resources of style, distinction, pleasure and self-expression.

12. Other efforts to evade the stringencies of copyright and 'share the fruits' of cultural labour have become more prominent in recent years. The process of 'Creative Commons' licensing is one notable intervention. Here artists can licence their work for public use (under various conditions) rather than simply seeking licensing for commercial use (though this is not ruled out). Artists register their work (say a photograph, a recording, a film) and in effect permit themselves to give it away to other users (see www. creativecommons.org). While giving away works is not likely to provide economic sustainability for artists, some organizations have started to find ways in which to generate income for artists through creative commons – for example various music providers e.g., 'Jamendo' (www.jamendo.com/en) offer artists the opportunity to licence and make their works available for public consumption – the public can then make a direct donation to the artists if sufficiently impressed (Keller, 2006).

13 As Pareles (2006, p. 10–11) enthusiastically observes:

Low-budget recording and the internet have handed production and distribution back to artists and one-stop collections of user-generated content give audiences a chance to find their works. With gatekeepers out of the way, it's possible to realise the do-it-yourself dreams of punk and hip-hop, to circle back to the kind of homemade art that existed long before media conglomerates and mass distribution. But that art doesn't stay close to home. Online it moves breathtakingly fast and far.

14. Thus, in 2006 we find online companies such as Magnatune offering independent musicians a web-based platform through which to distribute and sell their own recorded music, their mission statement being: 'Artists keep half of every purchase. And unlike most record labels, they keep all the rights to their music. No major label connections. We are not evil'. (http://www.magnatune.com/).

15. Intriguingly, at the time of writing News Corporation were in the process of drawing up plans to enable musicians to directly sell their material through MySpace at any price they want, with MySpace taking a 45 per cent cut – replicating the more equitable 'by-pass' model of companies like Magnatune and Indiestore.com (see Johnson, 2006). Depending on ones' point of view this will either be the first step towards a more equitable form of capitalism, or the further co-option of the alternative by the 'corporate monster'.

16. Interestingly, many of these corporate take-overs are of firms that have yet to demonstrate any commercial viability or register profit (YouTube being a prime example).

Bibliography

Abbinnett, R. (2003) *Culture and Identity: Critical Theories* (London: Sage).

Adkins, L. (1999) Community and Economy: A Retraditionalization of Gender? *Theory, Culture and Society* 16(1): 119–139.

Adorno, T. (1967) *Prisms* (London: Spearman).

Adorno, T. (1990) On Popular Music, in Frith, S. and Godwin, A. (eds) *On Record* (London: Routledge) 301–314.

Adorno, T. (1991) *The Culture Industry: Selected Essays on Mass Culture* (London: Routledge).

Adorno, T. (2000) Culture Industry Reconsidered, in O'Connor, B. (ed.) *The Adorno Reader* (Oxford: Blackwell) 230–238.

Adorno, T. and Horkheimer, M (1992) *Dialectic of Enlightenment* (London: Verso).

Allen, J. (2002) Symbolic Economies: The 'Culturalization' of Economic Knowledge, in du Gay, P. and Pryke, M. (eds) *Cultural Economy* (London: Sage) 39–58.

Americans for the Arts (2005) *Creative Industries 2005: The State Report*, http://www.artsusa.org

Amin, A. (ed.) (1994) *Post-Fordism: A Reader* (Oxford: Blackwell).

Amin, A. (2000) *Organizational Learning through Communities of Practice*, paper presented at the Millennium Schumpeter Conference, University of Manchester 28 June–1 July.

Amin, A., Cameron, A. and Hudson, R. (2002) *Placing the Social Economy* (London: Routledge).

Amin, A. and Thrift, N. (1992) Neo-Marshallian Nodes in Global Networks, *International Journal of Urban and Regional Research* 16(4): 571–587.

Amin, A. and Thrift, N. (eds) (2004) *The Blackwell Cultural Economy Reader* (Oxford: Blackwell).

Arts Council England (2003) *Artists in Figures: A Statistical Portrait of Cultural Occupations*, Research Report 31 (authors: Davies, R. and Lindley, R. Institute for Employment Research and Centre for Educational Development Appraisal and Research, University of Warwick).

Ashton, D. (1972) *New York* (London: Thames and Hudson).

Atkinson, R. (2003) Domestication by Cappuccino or a Revenge on Urban Space? Control and Empowerment in the Management of Public Spaces, *Urban Studies* 40(9): 1211–1245.

Bacas, H. (1987/2006) Tapping Your Creativity, Nation's Business http://www.findarticles.com/p/articles/mi_m1154/is_v75/ai_4722533

Balakrishnan, G. (2000) Hardt and Negri's Empire, *New Left Review* 5 September–October.

Banks, M. (2000) Wearing it Out: Going Global in Small Fashion Firms, in Janssen, S., Halbertsma, M., Ijdens, T. and Ernst, K. (eds) *Trends and Strategies in the Arts and Cultural Industries* (Rotterdam: Barjesteh) 25–38.

Banks, M. (2005) Managing Creativity in the Knowledge Economy, in Rooney, D., Hearn, G. and Ninan, A. (eds) *Handbook on Knowledge Economy* (Cheltenham: Edward Elgar) 218–228.

Banks, M. (2006) Moral Economy and Cultural Work, *Sociology* 40(3): 455–472.

Banks, M., Calvey, D., Owen, J. and Russell, D. (2002) Where the Art Is: Defining and Managing Creativity in New Media SMEs, *Creativity and Innovation Management* 11(4): 255–265.

Banks, M., Lovatt, A., O'Connor, J. and Raffo, C. (2000) Risk and Trust in the Cultural Industries, *Geoforum* 31(4): 453–464.

Barnett, C. (1999) Culture, Government and Spatiality, *International Journal of Cultural Studies* 2(3): 369–397.

Barratt, E. (2004) Foucault and the Politics of Critical Management Studies, *Culture and Organization* 10(3): 191–202.

Barthes, R. (1973) *Mythologies* (London: Paladin).

Bathelt, H., Malmberg, A. and Maskell, P. (2004) Clusters and Knowledge: Local Buzz, Global Pipelines and the Process of Knowledge Creation, *Progress in Human Geography* 28(1): 31–56.

Baudrillard, J. (1981) *For a Critique of the Political Economy of the Sign* (St Louis: Telos).

Baudrillard, J. (1988) *The Ecstasy of Communication* (New York: Semiotext(e)).

Bauman, Z. (2000) *Liquid Modernity* (Cambridge: Polity Press).

Bauman, Z. (2001) *The Individualized Society* (Cambridge: Polity Press).

Beck, U. (1992) *Risk Society* (London: Sage).

Beck, U. (1994) The Reinvention of Politics: Towards a Theory of Reflexive Modernization, in Beck, U., Giddens, A. and Lash, S. (eds) *Reflexive Modernization: Politics, Tradition and Aesthetics in the Modern Social Order* (Cambridge: Polity Press) 1–55.

Beck, U. (2000) *The Brave New World of Work* (Cambridge: Polity Press).

Beck, U. and Beck-Gernsheim, E. (2002) *Individualization* (London: Sage).

Beck, U., Giddens, A. and Lash, S. (1994) *Reflexive Modernization: Politics, Tradition and Aesthetics in the Modern Social Order* (Cambridge: Polity Press).

Beck, U. and Willms, J. (2004) *Conversations with Ulrich Beck* (Cambridge: Polity Press).

Becker, H. (1982) *Art Worlds* (Berkeley: University of California Press).

Bell, D. (1976) *The Cultural Contradictions of Capitalism* (New York: Basic).

Benjamin, W. (1970) *Illuminations* (London: Jonathan Cape).

Berking, H. (1996) Solidary Individualism: The Moral Impact of Cultural Modernisation in Late Modernity, in Lash, S., Szerszynski, B. and Wynne, B. (eds) *Risk, Environment and Modernity* (London: Sage) 189–202.

Bernstein, J. (1991) Introduction, in Adorno, T.(ed.) *The Culture Industry: Selected Essays on Mass Culture* (London: Routledge).

Best, K. (2003) Beating Them at Their Own Game: The Cultural Politics of the Open Software Movement and the Gift Economy, *International Journal of Cultural Studies* 6(4): 449–470.

Bilton, C. (2006) *Management and Creativity: From Creative Industries to Creative Management* (Oxford: Blackwell).

Bilton, C. and Leary, R. (2002) What Can Managers Do For Creativity? Brokering Creativity in the Creative Industries, *International Journal of Cultural Policy* 8(1): 49–64.

Blair, H. (2003) Winning and Losing in Flexible Labour Markets: The Formation and Operation of Networks of Interdependence in the UK Film Industry, *Sociology* 37(4): 677–694.

Blazwick, I. (2001) Century City, in Blazwick, I. (ed.) *Century City: Art and Culture in the Modern Metropolis* (London: Tate Gallery Publishing) 8–15.

Bogard, W. (1996) *The Simulation of Surveillance: Hypercontrol in Telematic Societies* (Cambridge: Cambridge University Press).

Booth, W. (1994) On the Idea of Moral Economy, *The American Political Science Review* 88(3): 653–667.

Böse, M. (2005) Difference and Exclusion at Work in the Club Culture Economy, *International Journal of Cultural Studies* 8(4): 427–443.

Bourdieu, P. (1984/2003) *Distinction: A Social Critique of the Judgement of Taste* (London: Routledge).

Bourdieu, P. (1993) *The Field of Cultural Production: Essays on Art and Literature* (Cambridge: Polity Press).

Bourdieu, P. (1998) *Acts of Resistance: Against the New Myths of Our Time* (Oxford: Polity Press).

Brannen, J. and Nilsen, A. (2005) Individualisation, Choice and Structure: A Discussion of Current Trends in Sociological Analysis, *The Sociological Review* 53(3): 412–428.

Brooks, D. (2000) *Bobos in Paradise: The New Upper Class and How They Got There* (New York: Simon and Schuster).

Brower, R. (1996) Vincent Van Gogh's Early Years as an Artist, *Journal of Adult Development* 3(1): 21–32.

Brown, A., O'Connor, J. and Cohen, S. (2000) Local Music Policies Within a Global Music Industry: Cultural Quarters in Manchester and Sheffield, *Geoforum* 31(4): 437—451.

Bruchez-Hall, C. (1996) Freud's Early Metaphors and Networks of Enterprise: Insight into a Journey of Scientific Self-Discovery, *Journal of Adult Development* 3(1): 43–57.

Bustamente, E. (2004) Cultural Industries in the Digital Age: Some Provisional Conclusions, *Media, Culture and Society* 26(6): 803–820.

Buzan, T. (1995) *The Mindmap Book* (London: BBC Books).

Byrne, N., Carroll, B and Ward, M. (2006) Artists' Co-operatives and their Potential to Contribute to the Development of the Visual Arts Sector in Ireland, *International Co-operative Alliance Review* 99(1): 29–34.

Carducci, V. (2006) Culture Jamming: A Sociological Perspective, *Journal of Consumer Culture* 6(1): 116–138.

Castells, M. (1996) *The Rise of the Network Society* (Oxford: Blackwell).

Caves, R. (2000) *Creative Industries: Contracts between Art and Commerce* (Cambridge: Harvard University Press).

Chrisafis, A. (2006) 'The 1968 Crowd Had Dreams – We Are Dreaming With Reality', *The Guardian* 30 March.

Cohen, S. (1991) *Rock Culture in Liverpool: Popular Music in the Making* (Oxford: Clarendon).

Collinson, D. (2003) Identities and Insecurities: Selves at Work, *Organization* 10(3): 527–547.

Cooke, P. (2002) *Knowledge Economies: Clusters, Learning and Cooperative Advantage* (London: Routledge).

Costea, B., Crump, N. and Holm, J. (2005) Dionysus at Work? The Ethos of Play and the Ethos of Management, *Culture and Organization* 11(2): 139–151.

Crafts Council (2004) *Making it in the 21st Century: a Socio-Economic Survey of Crafts Activity in England and Wales* 2002–2003. (London: Crafts Council).

Crewe, L. (1996) Material Culture: Embedded Firms, Organisational Linkages and the Local Economic Development of a Fashion Quarter, *Regional Studies* 30(3): 257–272.

Crewe, L., Gregson, N. and Brooks, K. (2003) Alternative Retail Spaces, in Leyshon, A., Lee, R. and Williams, C. (eds) (2003) *Alternative Economic Spaces: Rethinking the Economic in Economic Geography* (London: Sage) 74–106.

Crossley, N. (2003) Even Newer Social Movements? Anti-Corporate Protests, Capitalist Crises and the Remoralization of Society, *Organization* 10(2): 287–305.

Cumbers, A. and MacKinnon, D. (2004) Introduction: Clusters in Urban and Regional Development, *Urban Studies* 41(5–6): 959–969.

Dant, T. (2003) *Critical Social Theory* (London: Sage).

Davis, H. and Scase, R. (2000) *Managing Creativity: The Dynamics of Work and Organization* (Buckingham: Open University Press).

DCITA (Department of Communications and Information Technology and the Arts (2005) *Creative Industries Cluster Study: Stage One Report* (Canberra: DCITA).

DCMS (Department of Culture, Media and Sport) (2001) *Creative Industries Mapping Document* (London: DCMS).

DCMS (Department of Culture, Media and Sport) (2005) *Creative Industries Economic Estimates Statistical Bulletin* (London: DCMS).

Dean, M. (1999) *Governmentality* (London: Sage).

Dean, D. and Jones, C. (2003) If Women Actors Were Working..., *Media Culture and Society* 25(4): 527–541.

De Bono, E. (1971) *Lateral Thinking for Management* (London: McGraw-Hill).

Debord, G. (1967) *Society of the Spectacle* (London: Rebel Press).

De Certeau, M. (1984) *The Practice of Everyday Life* (Berkeley: University of California Press).

Deleuze, G. and Guattari, F. (2002) *A Thousand Plateaus: Capitalism and Schizophrenia* (London: Continuum).

De Salvo, D. (2001) New York: 1969–1974, in Blazwick, I. (ed.) *Century City: Art and Culture in the Modern Metropolis* (London: Tate Gallery Publishing) 122–147.

Dewey, J. (1980) *Art as Experience* (New York: Putnam).

Douglas, M. (1992) *Risk and Blame* (London: Routledge).

Drake, G. (2003) 'This Place Gives me Space': Place and Creativity in the Creative Industries, *Geoforum* 34(4): 511–524. DTI (Department of Trade and Industry) (1998) *Our Competitive Future: Building the Knowledge-Driven Economy* (London: HMSO).

du Gay, P. (1996) *Consumption and Identity at Work* (London: Sage).

du Gay, P. (1997) Organizing Identity: Making Up People at Work, in du Gay, P. (ed.) *Production of Culture/Cultures of Production* (London: Sage) 285–344.

du Gay, P. and Pryke, M. (eds) (2002) *Cultural Economy* (London: Sage).

Edgell, S. (2006) *The Sociology of Work* (London: Sage).

Edwards, R. and Nicoll, K. (2004) Mobilizing Workplaces: Actors, Discipline and Governmentality, *Studies in Continuing Education* 26(2): 159–173.

Ehrenreich, B. (2002) *Nickel and Dimed: Undercover in Low-Wage USA* (London: Granta).

Elliott, A. and Lemert, C. (2006) *The New Individualism: The Emotional Costs of Globalization* (London: Routledge).

Ettlinger, N. (2003) Cultural Economic Geography and a Relational and Microspace Approach to Trusts, Rationalities, Networks and Change in Collaborative Workspaces, *Journal of Economic Geography* 3:145–171.

European Commission (2002) *Regional Clusters in Europe. Observatory of European SMEs No 3* (Brussels: European Commission).

Evans, G. (2004) Cultural Industry Quarters – From Pre-Industrial to Post-Industrial Production, in Bell, D. and Jayne, M. (eds) *City of Quarters: Urban Villages in the Contemporary City* (Aldershot: Ashgate) 71–92.

Featherstone, M. (1991) *Consumer Culture and Postmodernism* (London: Sage).

Fevre, R. (2003) *The New Sociology of Economic Behaviour* (London: Sage).

Finnegan, R. (1989) *The Hidden Musicians: Music-Making in an English Town* (Cambridge: Cambridge University Press).

Fishman, M. (1980) *Manufacturing the News* (Austin: University of Texas Press).

Florida, R. (2002) *The Rise of the Creative Class* (New York: Basic).

Flusty, S. (2000) Thrashing Downtown: Play as Resistance to the Spatial and Representational Strategies of Los Angeles, *Cities* 17(2): 149–158.

Foucault, M. (1977) *Discipline and Punish* (Harmondsworth: Penguin).

Foucault, M. (1982) Afterword: The Subject and the Power, in Dreyfus, H. and Rabinow, P. (eds) *Michel Foucault: Beyond Structuralism and Hermeneutics* (Brighton and Chicago: Harvester) 208–226.

Foucault, M. (1991) Governmentality, in Burchell, G., Gordon, C. and Miller, P. (eds) *The Foucault Effect: Studies in Governmentality* (London: Harvester Wheatsheaf) 87–104.

Foucault, M. (1997) *Ethics: Truth and Subjectivity: The Essential Works of Foucault 1954–1984* (New York: Free Press).

Fowle, K. and Larsen, L. B. (2005) Lunch Hour: Community, Administrated Space and Unproductive Activity, in Purves, T. (ed.) *What We Want Is Free: Generosity and Exchange in Recent Art* (Albany: SUNY Press) 17–26.

Frith, S. (1996) *Performing Rites* (Oxford: Oxford University Press).

Fujita, M., Krugman, P. and Venables, A. (2000) *The Spatial Economy: Cities, Regions and International Trade* (Cambridge: MIT Press).

Galton, F. (1869) *Hereditary Genius* (London: Macmillan).

Gans, H. (1979) *Deciding What's News* (New York: Vintage).

Garnham, N. (1987) Concepts of Culture: Public Policy and the Cultural Industries, *Cultural Studies* 1(1): 23–37.

Garnham, N. (1990) *Capitalism and Communication: Global Culture and the Economics of Information* (London: Sage).

Garnham, N. (2000) *Emancipation, the Media and Modernity* (Oxford: Oxford University Press).

Garnham, N. (2005) From Cultural to Creative Industries. An Analysis of the Implications of the 'Creative Industries' Approach to Arts and Media Policy Making in the United Kingdom, *International Journal of Cultural Policy* 11(1): 15–29.

Gibson, C. (2003) Cultures at Work: Why 'Culture' Matters in Research on the 'Cultural' Industries, *Social & Cultural Geography* 4(2): 201–215.

Gibson-Graham, J. K. (2006) *A Post-Capitalist Politics* (Minneapolis: University of Minnesota Press).

Giddens, A. (1991) *Modernity and Self-Identity* (Cambridge: Polity Press).

Gill, R. (2002) Cool, Creative and Egalitarian? Exploring Gender in Project-based New Media Work, *Information and Communication Studies* 5(1): 70–89.

Golding, P. and Murdock, G. (1991) Culture, Communications, and Political Economy, in Curran, J. and Gurevitch, M. (eds) *Mass Media and Society* (London: Edward Arnold) 15–32.

Gooding, D (1996) Scientific Discovery as Creative Exploration: Faraday's Experiments, *Creativity Research Journal* 9(2&3): 189–205.

Gorz, A. (1982) *Farewell to the Working Class: An Essay on Post-Industrial Socialism* (London: Pluto).

Gorz, A. (1989) *Critique of Economic Reason* (London: Verso).

Granovetter, M. (1985) Economic Action and Social Structure: The Problem of Embeddedness, *American Journal of Sociology* 91(3): 481–510.

Granovetter, M. and Swedberg, R. (eds) (1992) *The Sociology of Economic Life* (Boulder: Westview Press).

Grint, K. (1991) *The Sociology of Work: An Introduction* (Oxford: Polity Press).

Groth, J. and Corijn, E. (2005) Reclaiming Urbanity: Indeterminate Spaces, Informal Actors and Urban Agenda Setting, *Urban Studies* 42(3): 503–526.

Groth, J. and Peters, J. (1999) What Blocks Creativity? A Managerial Perspective, *Creativity and Innovation Management* 8(3): 179–187.

Grugulis, I., Dundon, T. and Wilkinson, A. (2000) Cultural Control and the 'Culture Manager': Employment Practices in a Consultancy, *Work, Employment and Society* 14(1): 97–116.

Gunster, S. (2004) *Capitalizing on Culture: Critical Theory for Cultural Studies* (Toronto: University of Toronto Press).

Habermas, J. (1989) *The Structural Transformation of the Public Sphere* (Cambridge: Polity Press).

Hale, A. and Wills, J. (eds) (2005) *Threads of Labour: Garment Industry Supply Chains from the Workers Perspective* (Oxford: Blackwell).

Hall, P. (1998) *Cities in Civilization: Culture, Innovation and Urban Order* (London: Weidenfeld and Nicolson).

Hardt, M. and Negri, A. (2000) *Empire* (Cambridge: Harvard University Press).

Hartley, J. (ed.) (2005) *Creative Industries* (Oxford: Blackwell).

Harvey, D. (1989) *The Condition of Postmodernity* (Oxford: Blackwell).

Harvey, D. (2000) *Spaces of Hope* (Edinburgh: Edinburgh University Press).

Harvey, D. (2001) *Spaces of Capital* (Edinburgh: Edinburgh University Press).

Harrison, B. (1992) Industrial Districts: Old Wine in New Bottles, *Regional Studies* 26(5): 469–483.

Heath, J. and Potter, A. (2004) *Nation of Rebels: Why Counter-Culture Became Consumer Culture* (New York: HarperBusiness).

Heelas, P. (2002) Work Ethics, Soft Capitalism and the 'Turn to Life', in du Gay, P. and Pryke, M. (eds) *Cultural Economy* (London: Sage) 78–96.

Heelas, P. and Morris, P. (1992) (eds) *The Values of the Enterprise Culture: The Moral Debate* (London: Routledge).

Held, D. (1980) *Introduction to Critical Theory* (London: Hutchinson).

Held, D., McGrew, A., Goldblatt, D. and Perraton, J. (1999) *Global Transformations* (Cambridge: Polity Press).

Hesmondhalgh, D. (1998) The British Dance Music Industry: A Case Study of Independent Cultural Production, *The British Journal of Sociology* 49(2): 234–251.

Hesmondhalgh, D. (2000) Alternative Media, Alternative Texts? Rethinking Democratization in the Cultural Industries, in Curran, J. (ed.) *Media Organizations in Society* (London: Arnold) 107–125.

Hesmondhalgh, D. (2002) *The Cultural Industries* (1st edition) (London: Sage).

Hesmondhalgh, D. (2007) *The Cultural Industries* (2nd edition) (London: Sage).

Hesmondhalgh, D. (2005) Media and Cultural Policy as Public Policy: The Case of the British Labour Government, *International Journal of Cultural Policy* 11(1): 95–109.

Hesmondhalgh, D. and Pratt, A. (2005) Cultural Industries and Cultural Policy, *International Journal of Cultural Policy* 11(1): 1–14.

Hollands, R. and Chatterton, P. (2003) Producing Nightlife in the New Urban Entertainment Economy: Corporatisation, Branding and Market Segmentation, *International Journal of Urban and Regional Research* 27(2): 361–385.

Holmes, B. (2004) Artistic Autonomy and the Communication Society, *Third Text* 18(6): 547–555.

Holzer, B. and Sorensen, M. (2003) Rethinking Subpolitics: Beyond the 'Iron Cage' of Modern Politics? *Theory, Culture & Society* 20(2): 79–102.

Honneth, A. (2004) Organized Self-Realization: Some Paradoxes of Individualization, *European Journal of Social Theory* 7(4): 463–478.

Honoré, C. (2004) *In Praise of Slow: How a Worldwide Movement is Challenging the Cult of Speed* (London: Orion).

Howkins, J. (2001) *The Creative Economy: How People Make Money from Ideas* (London: Penguin).

Hoyler, M. and Mager, C. (2005) HipHop Ist Im Haus: Cultural Policy, Community Centres and the Making of Hip-Hop Music in Germany, *Built Environment* 31(3): 237–253.

Hyde, L. (2006) *The Gift* (Edinburgh: Canongate).

Illich, I. (1978) *The Right to Useful Unemployment and its Professional Enemies* (London: Boyars).

Jackson, P. (1991) Mapping Meanings: A Cultural Critique of Locality Studies, *Environment and Planning* A 23(2): 215–228.

Jameson, F. (1984) Postmodernism, or The Cultural Logic of Late Capitalism, *New Left Review*, 146: 53–92.

Jarvis, S. (1998) *Adorno: A Critical Introduction* (Oxford: Polity Press).

Jeffcut, P. and Pratt, A. (2002) Managing Creativity in the Cultural Industries, *Creativity and Innovation Management* 11(4): 225–233.

Johnson, B. (2006) 'Threat To Music Labels as Website Offers Bands a Shortcut to Big Time', *The Guardian* 5 September.

Johnson, R. (1993) Introduction: Pierre Bourdieu on Art, Literature and Culture, in Bourdieu, P. *The Field of Cultural Production* (Cambridge: Polity Press) 1–28.

Jones, P. and Wilks-Heeg, S. (2004) Capitalising Culture: Liverpool 2008, *Local Economy* 19(4): 341–360.

Kapur, G. and Rajadhyaksha, A. (2001) Bombay/Mumbai, 1992–2001, in Blazwick, I. (ed.) *Century City: Art and Culture in the Modern Metropolis* (London: Tate Gallery Publishing) 16–42.

Katel, P. (2002) Argentina: The Post Money Economy, *Time Magazine* 5 February .

Keat, R. (2000) *Cultural Goods and the Limits of the Market* (London: Macmillan).

Keller, P. (2006) *How to Get Rich With Creative Commons*, paper presented at MyCreativity Convention on International Creative Industries Research, Institute of Network Cultures, Amsterdam 16–18 November.

Kellner, D. (1989) *Critical Theory, Marxism and Modernity* (Cambridge: Polity Press).

Kingsnorth, P. (2003) *One No, Many Yeses: A Journey to the Heart of the Global Resistance Movement* (London: The Free Press).

Kit-wai Ma, E. (2002) Translocal Spatiality, *International Journal of Cultural Studies* 5(2): 131–152.

Knabb, K. (ed.) (1981) *Situationist International Anthology* (Berkeley: Bureau of Public Secrets).

Klein, N. (2000) *No Logo* (London: Flamingo).

Knights, D. (1990) Subjectivity, Power and the Labour Process, in Knights, D. and Willmott, H. (eds) *Labour Process Theory* (Basingstoke: Macmillan) 297–335.

Knights, D. and McCabe, D. (2003) Governing through Teamwork: Reconstituting Subjectivity in a Call Centre, *Journal of Management Studies* 40(7): 1587–1619.

Knights, D. and Willmott, H. (1989) Power and Subjectivity at Work: From Degradation to Subjugation in Social Relations, *Sociology* 23(4): 535–558.

Kunda, G. (1991) *Engineering Culture: Control and Commitment in a High-Tech Corporation* (Philadelphia: Temple University Press).

Kurz, E. (1996) Marginalizing Discovery: Karl Popper's Intellectual Roots in Psychology; or How the Study of Discovery Was Banned from Science Studies, *Creativity Research Journal* 9(2–3): 173–187.

Lacey, A. (2005) Networked Communities: Social Centers and Activist Spaces in Contemporary Britain, *Space and Culture* 8(3): 286–301.

Lanchester, J. (2006) 'A Bigger Bang', *The Guardian Weekend Magazine* 4 November.

Lasch, C. (1980) *The Culture of Narcissism* (London: Sphere).

Lash, S. (1994) Reflexivity and its Doubles: Structure, Aesthetics, Community, in Beck, U., Giddens, A. and Lash, S. (eds) *Reflexive Modernization: Politics, Tradition and Aesthetics in the Modern Social Order* (Cambridge: Polity Press) 110–173.

Lash, S and Urry, J. (1994) *Economies of Signs and Space* (London: Sage).

Lazzarato, M (1996) Immaterial Labour, in Virno, P. and Hardt, M. (eds) *Radical Thought in Italy* (Minneapolis: University of Minnesota Press) 132–146.

Leadbeater, C. (1999) *Living on Thin Air: The New Economy* (Harmondsworth: Viking).

Lee, K-S.(2005) The Momentum of Control and Autonomy: A Local Scene of Peer-To-Peer Music-Sharing Technology, *Media, Culture and Society* 27(5): 799–809.

Leeming, C. (2007) Afflecks Palace Fears as Lease Row Emerges, *Manchester Evening News* 13 February.

Lefebvre, H. (1991) *The Production of Space* (Oxford: Blackwell).

Levitas, R. (2001) Against Work: A Utopian Incursion into Social Policy, *Critical Social Policy* 21(4): 449–465.

Lewis, J. (2000) Manufacturing Dissent: New Democracy and the Era of Computer Communication, *International Journal of Cultural Studies* 3(1): 103–122.

Leyshon, A., Lee, R. and Williams, C. (eds) (2003) *Alternative Economic Spaces: Rethinking the Economic in Economic Geography* (London: Sage).

Leyshon, A., Webb, P., French, S., Thrift, N. and Crewe, L. (2005) On the Reproduction of the Musical Economy after the Internet, *Media, Culture and Society* 27(2): 177–209.

Lloyd, R. (2006) *Neo-Bohemia: Art and Commerce in the Post-Industrial City* (New York: Routledge).

Löfgren, O. (2003) The New Economy: A Cultural History, *Global Networks* 3(3): 239–254.

Longhurst, B. (1991) Raymond Williams and Local Cultures, *Environment and Planning* A 23(2): 229–238.

Luetgert, S. (2006) *The Capital of Failures*, paper presented at MyCreativity Convention on International Creative Industries Research, Institute of Network Cultures, Amsterdam 16–18 November.

Lury, C. (1996) *Consumer Culture* (Oxford: Polity Press).

MacIntyre, A. (1981) *After Virtue: A Study in Moral Theory* (London: Duckworth).

Maffesoli, M. (1996) *The Time of the Tribes: The Decline of Individualism in Mass Society* (London: Sage).

Malmberg, A and Maskell, P. (1997) Towards an Explanation of Industry Agglomeration and Regional Specialization, *European Planning Studies* 5(1): 25–41.

Marcuse, H. (1955) *Reason and Revolution: Hegel and the Rise of Social Theory* (London: Routledge and Kegan Paul).

Marcuse, H. (1964/1991) *One-Dimensional Man* (London: Routledge and Kegan Paul).

Marcuse, H. (1979) *The Aesthetic Dimension* (London: Macmillan).

Markusen, A. (1996) Sticky Places in Slippery Space: Towards a Typology of Industrial Districts, *Economic Geography* 72(3): 293–313.

Marshall, A. (1890/1988) *Principles of Economics* (Basingstoke: Macmillan).

Martin, B. (1981) *A Sociology of Contemporary Cultural Change* (Oxford: Blackwell).

Martin, B. and Wajcman, J. (2004) Markets, Contingency and Preferences: Contemporary Managers Narrative Identities, *The Sociological Review* 52(2): 240–264.

Martin, R. and Sunley, P. (2003) Deconstructing Clusters: Chaotic Concept or Policy Panacea, *Journal of Economic Geography* 3: 5–55.

Marx, K. (1990) *Capital: A Critique of Political Economy Vol.1* (Harmondsworth: Penguin).

Massey, D. (1993) A Global Sense of Place, in Gray, A. and McGuigan, J. (eds) *Studying Culture* (London: Edward Arnold) 232–240.

McChesney, R. (1993) *Telecommunications, Mass Media and Democracy* (Oxford: Oxford University Press).

McChesney, R. (1998) The Political Economy of Global Communication, in McChesney, R., Meiksins Wood, E. and Bellamy Foster, J. (eds) *Capitalism and the Information Age* (New York: Monthly Review Press) 1–25.

McFadzean, E. (2000) What Can We Learn From Creative People? The Story of Brian Eno, *Management Decision* 38(1): 51–56.

McGuigan, J. (2004) *Rethinking Cultural Policy* (Buckingham: Open University Press).

McIlveen, F. (2005) Exchange – The 'Other' Social Sculpture, in Purves, T. (ed.) *What We Want Is Free: Generosity and Exchange in Recent Art* (Albany: SUNY Press) 169–182.

McRobbie, A. (1998) *British Fashion Design: Rag Trade or Image Industry?* (London: Routledge).

McRobbie, A. (1999) *In the Culture Society: Art, Fashion and Popular Music* (London: Routledge).

McRobbie, A. (2002a) Clubs to Companies: Notes on the Decline of Political Culture in Speeded Up Creative Worlds, *Cultural Studies* 16(4): 516–531.

McRobbie, A. (2002b) From Holloway to Hollywood: Happiness at Work in the New Cultural Economy, in du Gay, P. and Pryke, M. (eds) *Cultural Economy* (London: Sage) 97–114.

Meiksins, P. (1998) Work, New Technology and Capitalism, in McChesney, R., Meiksins Wood, E. and Bellamy Foster, J. (eds) *Capitalism and the Information Age* (New York: Monthly Review Press) 151–164.

Messner, M. and Sabo, D (eds) (1990) *Sport, Men and the Gender Order: Critical Feminist Perspectives* (Champaign, Il.: Human Kinetics).

Miège, B. (1979) The Cultural Commodity, *Media, Culture and Society* 1: 297–311.

Miège, B. (1987) The Logics at Work in the New Cultural Industries, *Media, Culture and Society* 9(3): 273–289.

Miège, B. (1989) *The Capitalization of Cultural Production* (New York: International General).

Miles, M. (2004) *Urban Avant-Gardes: Art, Architecture and Change* (London: Routledge).

Milestone, K. (1996) Regional Variations: Northernness and New Urban Economies of Hedonism, in O'Connor, J. and Wynne, D. (eds) *From the Margins to the Centre: Cultural Production and Consumption in the Post-Industrial City* (Aldershot: Ashgate) 91–116.

Miller, P. and Rose, N. (1990) Governing Economic Life, *Economy and Society* 19(1): 1–31.

Miller, T. (2004) A View from a Fossil: The New Economy, Creativity and Consumption – Two or Three Things I Don't Believe In, *International Journal of Cultural Studies* 7(1): 55–65.

Miller, T., Govil, N., McMurria, J. and Maxwell, R. (2003) *Global Hollywood* (London: BFI).

Miller, T. and Yúdice, G. (2002) *Cultural Policy* (London: Sage).

Mintzberg, H. (1983) *Structures in Five: Designing Effective Organizations* (New Jersey, NJ.: Prentice Hall).

Molotch, H. (2004) How Art Works: Form and Function in the Stuff of Life, in Friedland, R. and Mohr, J. (eds) *Matters of Culture: Cultural Sociology in Practice* (Cambridge: Cambridge University Press) 341–377.

Mommaas, H. (2004) Cultural Clusters and the Post-Industrial City: Towards the Remapping of Urban Cultural Policy, *Urban Studies* 41(3): 507–532.

Mosco, V. (1996) *The Political Economy of Communication: Rethinking and Renewal* (London: Sage).

Munro, I. (2002) Empire: The Coming of the Control Society, *Ephemera* 2(2): 175–185.

Murdock, G. (2003) Back to Work: Cultural Labor in Altered Times, in Beck, A. (ed.) *Cultural Work: Understanding the Cultural Industries* (London: Routledge) 15–36.

Murray, R. (1989) Fordism and Post-Fordism, in Hall, S. and Jacques, M. (eds) *New Times: The Changing Face of Politics in the 1990s* (London: Lawrence and Wishart) 38–53.

Negus, K. (1997) The Production of Culture, in du Gay, P. (ed.) *Production of Culture/Cultures of Production* (London: Sage) 67–118.

Negus, K. (2002) The Work of Cultural Intermediaries and the Enduring Distance Between Production and Consumption, *Cultural Studies* 16(4): 501–515.

Negus, K. and Pickering, M. (2004) *Creativity, Communication and Cultural Value* (London: Sage).

Nixon, S. (2003) *Advertising Cultures* (London: Sage).

Nixon, S. and Crewe, B. (2004) Pleasure at Work? Gender, Consumption and Work-Based Identities in the Creative Industries, *Consumption, Markets and Culture* 7(2): 129–147.

Oakley, K. (2004) Not So Cool Britannia: The Role of the Creative Industries in Economic Development, *International Journal of Cultural Studies* 7(1): 67–77.

O'Connor, J. (1999) The Definition of 'Cultural Industries'. Manchester Institute for Popular Culture, Manchester Metropolitan University. Reprinted (2000) in *The European Journal of Arts Education* 2(3): 15–27.

O'Connor, J. (2005) Creative Exports: Taking Cultural Industries to St Petersburg, *International Journal of Cultural Policy* 11(1): 45–59.

O'Connor, J. (2006) Art, Popular Culture and Cultural Policy: Variations on a Theme of John Carey, *Critical Quarterly* 48(4): 49–104.

O'Connor, J. and Wynne, D. (eds) (1996a) *From the Margins to the Centre: Cultural Production and Consumption in the Post-Industrial City* (Aldershot: Ashgate).

O'Connor, J. and Wynne, D. (1996b) Left Loafing: City Cultures and Post-Modern Lifestyles, in O'Connor, J. and Wynne, D. (eds) *From the Margins to the Centre: Cultural Production and Consumption in the Post-Industrial City* (Aldershot: Ashgate) 49–90.

O'Neill, J. (1998) *The Market: Ethics, Knowledge and Politics* (London: Routledge).

Osborne, T. (2003) Against 'Creativity': A Philistine Rant, *Economy and Society* 32(4): 507–525.

Papestergiadis, N. (2002) 'Everything That Surrounds': Theories of the Everyday Art and Politics, *Third Text* 57: 71–86.

Pareles, J. (2006) Express Yourself (Everyone Else is), *The Observer* 17 December.

Peck, J. (2005) Struggling With the Creative Class, *International Journal of Urban and Regional Research* 29(4): 740–770.

Peck, J. and Ward, K. (eds) (2002) *City of Revolution: Restructuring Manchester* (Manchester: Manchester University Press).

Perrons, D. (2003) The New Economy and the Work-Life Balance: A Case Study of New Media In Brighton and Hove, *Gender Work and Organisation* 10(1): 65–93.

Piore, M. and Sabel, C. (1984) *The Second Industrial Divide* (New York: Basic).

Ploeg, T. (2006) The End of the Creative Class? *The Creativity* Institute of Network Cultures and Centre for Media Research, University of Ulster, Fall Edition.

Pollard, J. S. (2004) From Industrial District to Urban Village? Manufacturing, Money and Consumption in Birmingham's Jewellery Quarter, *Urban Studies* 41(1): 173–193.

Porter, M. (1990) *The Competitive Advantage of Nations* (London and Basingstoke: Macmillan).

Porter, M. (2005) Local Clusters in a Global Economy, in Hartley, J. (ed.) *Creative Industries* (Oxford: Blackwell) 259–267.

Pratt, A. (1997) The Cultural Industries Production System: A Case Study of Employment Change in Britain 1984–91, *Environment and Planning* A 29: 1953–1974.

Pratt, A. (2000) New Media, the New Economy and New Spaces, *Geoforum* 31(4): 425–436.

Pratt, A. (2004) The Cultural Economy: A Call for Spatialized 'Production of Culture' Perspectives, *International Journal of Cultural Studies* 7(1): 117–128.

Pratt, A. (2005) Cultural Industries and Public Policy: An Oxymoron? *International Journal of Cultural Policy* 11(1): 31–44.

Prichard, C. (2002) Creative Selves? Critically Reading Creativity in Management Discourse, *Creativity and Innovation Management* 11(4): 265–276.

Pruijt, H. (2003) Is the Institutionalization of Urban Movements Inevitable? A Comparison of the Opportunities for Sustained Squatting in New York City and Amsterdam, *International Journal of Urban and Regional Research* 27(1): 133–157.

Purnell, J. (2005) *Making Britain the World's Creative Hub*. Keynote Speech to Institute of Public Policy Research, London 16 June. (London: DCMS Archive).

Purves, T. (ed.) (2005) *What We Want Is Free: Generosity and Exchange in Recent Art* (Albany: SUNY Press).

Puype, D. (2004) Art and Culture as Experimental Spaces in the City, *City* 8(2): 295–301.

Rampley, M. (1998) Creativity, *British Journal of Aesthetics* 38(3): 265–278.

Rantisi, N. (2004) The Ascendance of New York Fashion, *International Journal of Urban and Regional Research* 28(1): 86–106.

Ray, G. (2004) Another Art World is Possible: Theorising Oppositional Convergence, *Third Text* 18(6): 565–572.

Ray, L. and Sayer, A. (eds) (1999) *Culture and Economy after the Cultural Turn* (London: Sage).

Ray, M. and Myers, R. (1989) *Creativity in Business* (Jackson TN: Main Street Books).

Read, J. (2003) *The Micro-Politics of Capital: Marx and the Pre-History of the Present* (Albany: SUNY Press).

Reynolds, S. (2005) *Rip It Up and Start Again: Post-Punk 1978–84* (London: Faber and Faber).

Richards, N. and Milestone, K. (2000) What Difference Does it Make? Women's Pop Cultural Production and Consumption in Manchester, *Sociological Research Online* 5 1.

Rickards, T. (1999) *Creativity and the Management of Change* (Oxford: Blackwell Business).

Rifkin, J. (2000) *The Age of Access* (London: Penguin).

Rojek, C. (2001) *Celebrity* (London: Reaktion).

Rose, N. (1992) Governing the Enterprising Self, in Heelas, P. and Morris, P. (eds) *The Values of the Enterprise Culture: The Moral Debate* (London: Routledge) 141–164.

Rose, N. (1999) *Governing the Soul: The Shaping of the Private Self* (London: Free Association).

Rose, N. and Miller, P. (1992) Political Power beyond the State: Problematics of Government, *British Journal of Sociology* 43(2): 173–205.

Ross, A. (2003) *No-Collar: The Humane Workplace and its Hidden Costs* (New York: Basic).

Ryan, B. (1992) *Making Capital from Culture: The Corporate Form of Capitalist Cultural Production* (Berlin: Walter de Gruyter).

Savage, J. (1991) *England's Dreaming: Sex Pistols and Punk Rock* (London: Faber and Faber).

Saxenian, A. (1994) *Regional Advantage. Culture and Competition in Silicon Valley and Route 128* (Cambridge: Harvard University Press).

Sayer, A. (1999) Valuing Culture and Economy, in Ray, L. and Sayer, A. (eds) *Culture and Economy after the Cultural Turn* (London: Sage) 53–75.

Sayer, A. (2001) For a Critical Cultural Political Economy, *Antipode* 33(4): 687–708.

Sayer, A. (2004a) Seeking the Geographies of Power, *Economy and Society* 33(2): 255–270.

Sayer, A. (2004b) *Moral Economy, Department of Sociology,* Lancaster University. http://www.comp.lancs.ac.uk/sociology/papaers/sayer-moral-economy.pdf

Schiller, H. (1969) *Mass Communication and American Empire* (Boston: Beacon).

Schiller, H. (1989) *Culture Inc.* (New York and Oxford: Oxford University Press).

Scherzinger, M. (2005) Music, Corporate Power and Unending War, *Cultural Critique* 60: 23–66.

Scott, A. (2000) *The Cultural Economy of Cities* (London: Sage).

Scott, J. (1976) *The Moral Economy of the Peasant: Rebellion and Subsistence in South East Asia* (New Haven: Yale University Press).

Seabright, P. (ed.) (2000) *The Vanishing Rouble: Barter Networks and Non-Monetary Transactions in Post-Soviet Societies* (Cambridge: Cambridge University Press).

Seltzer, K. and Bentley, T. (1999) *The Creative Age* (London: Demos).

Sennett, R. (1998) *The Corrosion of Character: The Personal Consequences of Work in the New Capitalism* (New York: W. W. Norton and Co.).

Sharon, B. (1979) Artist-Run Galleries – A Contemporary Institutional Change in the Visual Arts, *Qualitative Sociology* 2(1): 3–26.

Shorthose, J. (2004) Nottingham's de facto Cultural Quarter: The Lace Market, Independents and a Convivial Ecology, in Bell, D. and Jayne, M. (eds) *City of Quarters* (Aldershot: Ashgate) 149–162.

Slater, D. (2002) Capturing Markets from the Economists, in du Gay, P. and Pryke, M. (eds) *Cultural Economy* (London: Sage) 59–77.

Smart, B. (1999) *Facing Modernity* (London: Sage).

Smart, B. (2003) *Economy, Culture and Society* (Buckingham: Open University Press).

Smith, C. (1998) *Creative Britain* (London: Faber and Faber).

Stacey, R. (1996) *Complexity and Creativity in Organizations* (San Francisco: Berrett-Koehler).

Steinert, H. (2003) *Culture Industry* (Oxford: Polity Press).

Swedberg, R. (1996) *Economic Sociology* (Cheltenham: Edward Elgar).

Swingewood, A. (1998) *Cultural Theory and the Problem of Modernity* (Basingstoke: Palgrave).

Swyngedouw, E. (2002) The Strange Respectability of the Situationist City in the Society of the Spectacle, *International Journal of Urban and Regional Research* 26(1): 153–165.

Tahir, L. (1996) The Initial Sketch and the Growth of a Creative Network of Enterprises in Early Adulthood: George Bernard Shaw, *Journal of Adult Development* 3(1): 33–41.

Taylor, I., Evans, K. and Fraser, P. (1996) *A Tale of Two Cities: Global Change, Local Feeling and Everyday Life in the North of England: A Study in Manchester and Sheffield* (London: Routledge).

Tepper, S. (2002) Creative Assets and the Changing Economy, *The Journal of Arts Management, Law and Society* 32(2): 159–168.

Tester, K. (ed.) (1994) *The Flaneur* (London: Routledge).

Thompson, P. (1990) Crawling from the Wreckage: The Labour Process and the Politics of Production, in Knights, D. and Willmott, H. (eds) *Labour Process Theory* (London: Macmillan) 95–124.

Thrift, N. (1997) The Rise of Soft Capitalism, *Cultural Values* 1(1): 29–57.

Thrift, N. (2002) Performing Cultures in the New Economy, in du Gay, P. and Pryke, M. (eds) *Cultural Economy* (London: Sage) 201–234.

Throsby, D. and Hollister, V. (2003) *Don't Give Up Your Day Job: An Economic Study of Australian Professional Artists* (Sydney: Australia Council).

Tickell, A. and Peck, J. (1996) The Return of the Manchester Men: Men's Words and Men's Deeds in the Remaking of the Local State, *Transactions of the Institute of British Geographers* 21(4): 595–616.

Time Magazine (1956/2006) *Life in Paris* http://www.time.com/ time/magazine/article/0,9171,808448,00.html

Towse, R. (ed.) (2002) *Copyright in the Cultural Industries* (Cheltenham: Edward Elgar).

Toynbee, J. (2003) Fingers to the Bone or Spaced Out on Creativity? Labor Process and Ideology in the Production of Pop, in Beck, A. (ed.) *Cultural Work: Understanding the Cultural Industries* (London: Routledge) 39–55.

Tuchman, G. (1978) *Making News* (New York: Free Press).

Tunstall, J. (1993) *Television Producers* (London: Routledge).

Turok, I. (2003) Cities, Clusters and Creative Industries: The Case of Film and Television in Scotland, *European Planning Studies* 11(5): 549–565.

Uricchio, W. (2004) Beyond the Great Divide: Collaborative Networks and the Challenge to Dominant Conceptions of Creative Industries, *International Journal of Cultural Studies* 7(1) 79–90.

Urry, J. (2000) *Sociology beyond Societies: Mobilities for the Twenty-First Century* (London: Routledge).

Ursell, G. (2000) Television Production: Issues of Exploitation, Commodification and Subjectivity in UK Television Labour Markets, *Media, Culture and Society* 22(6): 805–825.

Ursell, G. (2006) Working in the Media, in Hesmondhalgh, D. (ed.) *Media Production* (Maidenhead: Open University Press) 133–172.

Vaneigem, R. (1967/2003) *The Revolution of Everyday Life* (London: Rebel Press).

Verwijnen, J. and Lehtovouri P. (eds) *(1999) Creative Cities: Cultural Industries, Urban Development and the Information Society* (Helsinki: UIAH Publications).

Vloeberghs, E. (2006) 'Creative Re-Inventions of the Urban: About Playful, Utopian and Serious Politics in New Artistic Urban Movements', Unpublished MA Thesis POLIS Programme Manchester Metropolitan University-Free University, Brussels.

Wansborough, M. and Mageean, A. (2000) The Role of Urban Design in Cultural Regeneration, *Journal of Urban Design* 5(2): 181–197.

Ward, K. (2000) From Rentiers to Rantiers: 'Active Entrepreneurs, 'Structural Speculators' and the Politics of Marketing the City, *Urban Studies* 37(7): 1093–1107.

Wayne, M. (2003) Post-Fordism, Monopoly Capitalism, and Hollywood's Media Industrial Complex, *International Journal of Cultural Studies* 6(1): 82–103.

Webb, J. (2004) Organizations, Self-Identities and the New Economy, *Sociology* 38(4): 719–738.

Webb, P. (2004) Interrogating the Production of Sound and Place: The Bristol Phenomenon, From Lunatic Fringe to worldwide Massive, in Whiteley, S., Bennett, A. and Hawkins, S. (eds) *Music, Space and Place: Popular Music and Cultural Identity* (Aldershot: Ashgate) 66–84.

Weber, M. (1930/2001) *The Protestant Ethic and the Spirit of Capitalism* (London: Routledge).

Wenger, E. (1998) *Communities of Practice: Learning, Meaning and Identity* (Cambridge: Cambridge University Press).

Whiteley, S., Bennett, A. and Hawkins, S. (eds*) (2004) Music, Space and Place: Popular Music and Cultural Identity* (Aldershot: Ashgate).

Wilber, C. (1996) Ethics and Economics, in Whalen, C. (ed.) *Political Economy for the 21st Century* (New York: M. E. Sharpe) 45–65.

Williams, C. (2005) *A Commodified World? Mapping the Limits of Capitalism* (London: Zed).

Williams, R. (1958) *Culture and Society 1780–1950* (London: Chatto and Windus).

Williams, R. (1973) *The Country and the City* (Oxford: Oxford University Press).

Williams, R. (1977) *Marxism and Literature* (Oxford: Oxford University Press).

Williams, R. (1980) *Culture* (London: Fontana).

Willis, P. (1990) *Common Culture* (Buckingham: Open University Press).

Willis, P. (2005) Invisible Aesthetics and the Social Work of Commodity Culture, in Inglis, D. and Hughson, J. (eds) *The Sociology of Art* (Basingstoke: Palgrave) 73–86.

Willis, J. and Dex, S. (2003) Mothers Returning to Television Production in a Changing Environment, in Beck, A (ed.) *Cultural Work: Understanding the Cultural Industries* (London: Routledge) 121–141.

Willmott, H. (1990) Subjectivity and the Dialectics of Praxis: Opening up the Core of Labour Process Analysis, in Knights, D. and Willmott, H. (eds) *Labour Process Theory* (London: Macmillan) 336–378.

Wilson, E. (1999) The Bohemianization of Mass Culture, *International Journal of Cultural Studies* 2(1): 11–32.

Wilson, E. (2002) *Bohemians: The Glamorous Outcasts* (London: I B Tauris).

Witkin, R. (2000) Why Did Adorno 'Hate' Jazz? *Sociological Theory* 18(1): 145–170.

Wittel, A. (2001) Towards a Network Sociality, *Theory, Culture & Society* 18(6): 51–76.

Wolff, J. (1993) *Aesthetics and the Sociology of Art* (Basingstoke: Macmillan).

Wright, D. (2005) Mediating Production and Consumption: Cultural Capital and 'Cultural Workers', *The British Journal of Sociology* 56(1) 105–121.

Wynne, D. (1992) *The Culture Industry* (Swindon: Avebury).

Zukin, S. (1982) *Loft Living: Culture and Capital in Urban Change* (Baltimore: John Hopkins University Press).

Zukin, S. (1991) *Landscapes of Power: From Detroit to Disney World* (Berkeley: University of California Press).

Index